KOREA VOLUNTEER

An Oral History From Those Who Were There

John Gardam, OMM, CD, BA

Foreword by Desmond Morton, Ph. D., FRSC
Director McGill Institute for the Study of Canada

Published by

GENERAL STORE
PUBLISHING HOUSE

1 Main Street Burnstown, Ontario, Canada K0J 1G0
Telephone (613) 432-7697 or 1-800-465-6072

Layout design by Robert Hoselton
Cover design by Leanne Enright

Copyright © 1994
General Store Publishing House
Burnstown, Ontario, Canada

No part of this book may be reproduced, stored in a retrieval system or transmitted in any form or by any means electronic, mechanical, photocopying, recording or otherwise, except for purposes of review, without the prior permission of the publisher.

General Store Publishing House Inc. gratefully acknowledges the assistance of the Ontario Arts Council and the Canada Council.

Canadian Cataloguing in Publication Data

Gardam, John, 1931–
   Korea volunteer : an oral history from those who were there

Includes Index.
ISBN 1-896182-00-3

    1. Canada. Canadian Army—History—Korean War, 1950–1953.
2. Korean War, 1950–1953—Personal narratives, Canadian. 3. Korean War, 1950–1953—Canada. I. Title.

DS921.6.G37 1994   951.904'2   C94-900824-9

First Printing 1994

*I dedicate this book to all those veterans
who gave me their Korea stories.
May their contribution to Canada never be forgotten.*

All profits received by the author from the sale of this book will be donated to the Canadian Forces Personnel Assistance Fund to aid sailors, soldiers, air personnel, and other men and women of the Canadian Forces who are in financial distress.

By the same author:
The National War Memorial
(Veterans Affairs Canada, 1982)

Seventy Years After 1914 - 1984
(Canada Wings Inc., 1983)

The Legacy
(Department of National Defence, 1988)

Fifty Years After
(General Store Publishing House, 1990)

The Canadian Peacekeeper
(General Store Publishing House, 1992)

Ordinary Heroes
(General Store Publishing House, 1992)

The colours on the cover are from the Canadian Volunteer Service Medal Korea. Blue for the United Nations, Yellow for the Orient and Red and White for Canada.

Front Cover photographs:
Don Saxon, Jim Dextraze and Ernie Glover

Back cover photograph:
Author with Canada Remembers Contingent thanking Secretary of State (Veterans) Lawrence MacAulay. France June 1994

KOREA VOLUNTEER

CONTENTS

Korea, a poem by Pat O'Connor	v
Foreword: Desmond Morton	viii
Preface	xi
Chapter One: Why Korea?	1
Chapter Two: The Royal Canadian Navy	5
Signals from Athabaskan	6
(Gordon Edwards)	
Two Tours in Korean Waters	12
(Ed Dalton)	
Guerillas, Landing Parties and the Great Imposter	17
(Don Saxon)	
Chapter Three: The Canadian Army	23
From Whitehorse to Pusan and Beyond	29
(Charlie Hamilton)	
"Big Jim" Stone's Patricias at Kapyong	37
(Jim Stone)	
Front-Line Doctor at the Casualty Clearing Post	42
(Keith Besley)	
No Withdrawal, No Platoons Overrun, No Panic	46
(Jim Dextraze)	
Roads, Bridges and Ferries	52
(Don Rochester)	
Right of the Line. First Artillery in Korea	57
(Mac McLellan)	
Wait for the Wagon	62
(Lorne Rodenbush)	

An Oral History From Those Who Were There

From an Ordered-Around Private to the Order of Canada *(Bill McCarthy)*	67
Liaison Officer at Brigade *(Hugh Hutton)*	71
In Search of Adventure *(Lawrence Sequin)*	73
Rocky's Radio Operator Remembers *(Ken Keir)*	76
The First Armoured Squadron *(Jim Quinn)*	79
An Infantry Private Remembers *(Russ Allan)*	87
A Canadian View from Divisional Headquarters *(Ned Amy)*	92
A Tank Driver and His War *(Ron Francis)*	100
Supporting the Netherlands Battalion *(John de Hart)*	111
Wounded Six Times, Taken Prisoner *(Gordon Owen)*	117
In Tanks and Aircraft Against the Enemy *(Bill Ward)*	121
Harry Pope–The Soldier's Soldier *(Harry Pope)*	126
1 R22ᵉR "Telephone" Company *(Ramsey Withers)*	134
Canadian Provost Corps in Korea and Japan *(Jim Holland)*	140
Flip a Coin: Heads, Military College; Tails, McGill University *(Dan Loomis)*	143
Two Wars Serving the Red Cross and Humanity *(Flora Baptist)*	151
Commanding Greyhounds in the Sami-ch'on Valley *(Pat Carew)*	155
Why Men Put Their Trust in Each Other *(Herb Pitts)*	160
Books Balanced, Duty Done, Home Again *(Gordon Peacock)*	168

Medium Machine-Gun Officer with the Van Doos	171
(Bill Campbell)	
Of Soldiers Dying and KATComs Serving in 3 PPCLI	174
(Chris Snider)	
The Royal Canadian Electrical Mechanical Engineers at Parun-ni	187
(Duncan McDougall)	
The Fighting 59th	191
(Karl Snider)	
Line Crossers and Radio Intercepts	196
(Paul Mayer)	
Two Ordnance Stories from Korea	200
(Norm Crowder, Gordon MacDonald)	
The "Watch" Along the DMZ	205
(Ian Firstbrook)	
The Dragoons Arrive after the Armistice	210
(Bob Slaney)	
Guardsman on Hill 355	215
(John Hayter)	
Queen's Own – The Last to Leave	221
(John Saunders)	
Chapter Four: The Royal Canadian Air Force	226
Prisoner for Two Years	228
(Andy MacKenzie)	
Two DFCs in Four Months	238
(Ernie Glover)	
Air Photos in Korea	241
(Allan Simpson)	
Thunderbirds in the Far East	244
(George Kightley)	
Epilogue: Those Who Served in the Land of the Morning Calm	248
Acknowledgements	250
Index	252
About the Author	260

KOREA

There is blood on the hills of Korea
'Tis blood of the brave and the true
Where the 25th Brigade battled together
Under the banner of the Red White and Blue
As they marched over the fields of Korea
To the hills where the enemy lay
They remembered the Brigadier's order:
These hills must be taken today
Forward they marched into battle
With faces unsmiling and stern
They knew as they charged the hillside
There were some who would never return
Some thought of their wives and mothers
Some thought of their sweethearts so fair
And some as they plodded and stumbled
Were reverentially whispering a prayer
There is blood on the hills of Korea
It's the gift of the freedom they love
May their names live in glory forever
And their souls rest in Heaven above.

Private Pat O'Connor,
Stretcher bearer, 2 RCR
Killed in action May 1951

An Oral History From Those Who Were There

This account in *Volume Two of the RCR History* describes Pat (Paddy) O'Connor's death at the Battle of Chail-li:

> ...That evening (30 May) Second Battalion, advancing in the right brigade sector, had halted at a burned-out village just short of Kakhul-bong, a massive buttress standing against the eastern skyline. Beyond it, in the valley bottom, lay the village of Chail-li. Between the village and the great butte stood Hill 269 while on the opposite or western side of the valley a lower hummock, Hill 162, blocked the way. Major H.B. Boates planned to approach the main feature along subsidiary ridges from either side, with 11 Platoon (Lt. J. R. Woods) on the right and 12 Platoon (Lt. D.A. Stickland) on the left.

Pat O'Connor killed in action 30 May 1951.

> Midway to the crest 12 Platoon was ambushed and shot down, almost to a man. Pte. Paddy O'Connor, a gallant stretcher bearer, dashed to its assistance and was killed instantly.

In July 1994, Don Stickland wrote and gave me his account of the same event:

> About half way up to the peak, our No 12 Platoon on the west ridge approached a small plateau on the upward path. Just as the first section moved through this small grove, we were startled by a burst of machine gun fire from the edge of the path just ahead. Two or three bursts brought down most of this forward group and the move ahead was halted. All around the wounded were groaning and calling for help, while a corporal quietly died beside me.
>
> Reaction was swift as a few of the rifles and sten guns commenced firing in the general direction of the machine gun and grenades were lobbed past the tiny plateau. Sporatic machine gun bursts continued and there was much confusion as the fog of battle increased.
>
> Suddenly I looked around and was surprised to see a soldier with a

long stretcher over his shoulders come galloping up the path from below. Some of the boys in the rear sections had been calling for a "medic" and Paddy O'Connor, a company stretcher-bearer, insisted on responding, although he had apparently been advised of the continuing danger. Just as he reached the spot where I was crouching, there was another burst of fire, and Paddy stumbled over his stretcher and rolled over dead.

The above poem was found when Paddy O'Connor's belongings were gathered up to be sent to his widow in Sarnia. This soldier died helping others, a truly gallant man.

An Oral History From Those Who Were There

FOREWORD

"*The Forgotten War*", John Melady called it. Perhaps most Canadians can't remember — or never learned — that more than twenty-seven thousand Canadian soldiers, sailors and air force members served in the United Nations action to preserve the Republic of Korea from its aggressive northern neighbour or that 516 names in Canada's Book of Remembrance belong to Canadians who died in that war.

Canadians often imagine that their soldiers go abroad largely to keep the peace in distant countries. They have been reluctant to acknowledge that the United Nations Charter insists that members also join in making peace. Though Canada had endorsed the refusal of the League of Nations to stop Japan, Italy or the Third Reich in their aggressions, that had not prevented civilization's most terrible war in 1939. With that brutal experience, surely the United Nations could stop Kim Il Sung. And if the Republic of Korea was no spotless virgin, what society can ever make that claim? In Korea, as in the Gulf, Somalia and who knows where next, the UN has a charter obligation to make peace in the world as well as to preserve it.

Korea was certainly not my forgotten war. I was almost 13 in June, 1950, when Seoul, Taejon, the Pusan perimeter and a wily old politician named Syngman Rhee became part of the morning headlines and the nightly news. That summer, my father, Brigadier R.E.A. Morton, was a busy as anyone in our tiny peacetime army in trying to organize recruiting and training for the Special Force. He took me with him to Shilo, when the drafts of the 2nd Royal Canadian Horse Artillery left for Fort Lewis and ultimately, for Korea. Some of them died without leaving Canada when their obsolete wooden passsenger cars were crushed in a train collision in the Rockies.

Later, in the summer of 1952, my father was sent to head the Military Mission that represented Canada at Pershing Heights, the Tokyo headquarters of General Mark Clark, successor to General Douglas McArthur as Supreme Allied Commander. A little awkward experience had persuaded Ottawa that families were a useful adjunct in such appointments and my mother, sister and I soon found ourselves at Yokohama, contemplating life in a still-occupied Japan. That summer, thanks to Howard and Gwen Norman, the Canadian Academy, a school originally designed for missionary's children, was reborn in Kobe. Australian occupation forces relinquished the sole school building that had survived wartime bombing. Gloucester House, the former boys' dormitory, and the buildings that slowly accumulated around it, allowed me to finish two more winters of high school under the Ontario curriculum.

My summers were another matter. Well aware that idle hands produce mischief, my father arranged for me to serve, in some wholly unauthorized extension of my militia service, making myself useful first at the 2nd Canadian Administrative Unit and then at 25 Canadian Reinforcement Group at Hiro. What transient Canadian soldiers made of the fuzzy-cheeked youth passing out boots at the Quartermaster Stores, collecting rations from the Australian depot on the other side of the hill in Kure, or painfully typing leave passes in the Orderly Room, no one now will recall. For me, it was as close as I would get to the one real war of my youth.

I also learned a darker lesson. There was a price to be paid for the hurried recruiting damanded by the Minister of National Defence in the summer of 1950. All armies attract misfits and losers. By ministerial fiat, they were not screened out and, despite a common myth, few of them ever make good soldiers in the field; many ended up well behind the fighting and some had managed to nest quite comfortably in places like Hiro.

There were other memories of that war — watching HMCS Cayuga as Captain Bill Landymore brought her into Tokyo Bay, meeting the few Canadians who returned from captivity under the Chinese, watching UN soldiers, in a kaleidoscope of strange uniforms, enjoying leave in Japan. Like some of those who have shared their memories with John Gardam, my own most vivid recollection is of a cruel, needless soldier's death — at Haramura, the Commonwealth Division's battle training school in Japan. On the day I arrived, a young British sapper had been almost cut in two by an old Vickers machine gun that broke loose from its lock during a live firing exercise. In the tents that night, I heard soldiers speculate about whether he would have lived if the machine gun had been new or he had been taken to hospital by helicopter and not by army ambulance down the rutted, muddy roads that jolted him to death.

"I am afeard there are few die well who die in a battle", says a soldier in Shakespeare's Henry V [Act V sc.1]. There was no glorious death for a young Canadian who happened to be under an exploding mortar bomb or over a wood-encased land mine or who perished alone in some midnight patrol

An Oral History From Those Who Were There

action. Others, equally tragic victims of Korea, would live the rest of their lives with the pain of physical and mental injury.

Yet the memories John Gardam has collected are seldom sad and never self-pitying. Most recall their service in Korea with pride and a sense of achievement. There is pain in remembering the loss of a good friend, but there is no shame. Probably Canada has never sent better units to war than the battalions, regiments and companies in the four successive rotations of the 25th Brigade. Five years after VE Day, Canada could call on both veterans and youth and the combination produced that added fresh distinction to Canada's military reputation.

By recalling the memories of Canadians who served in the Korean war, John Gardam has put human faces back into an episode Canadians should remember with some anguish and much pride.

                                  Desmond Morton
                                  Director
                                  McGill Institute for the
                                  Study of Canada

PREFACE

The Korean war, however, was but one of several Canadian defence preoccupations during the early years of the nineteen-fifties.
    Strange Battleground, Lieutenant-Colonel Herbert F. Wood

Korea Volunteer is the book I have wanted to write since 1990. It was to follow *Fifty Years After*, but my two other books (*Ordinary Heroes* and *Canadian Peacekeeper*) came first. My time was limited as I was also working full-time as the Project Director on the Peacekeeping Monument project. When I finally retired in December 1992, the serious illness of General J.A. Dextraze made me realize that there was no time to waste. If I did not start at once I would lose his Korea story and this I wanted to avoid. As it was, I did miss out on other stories, much to my regret.

The years 1950 to 1954 are the qualifying dates for the Canadian Volunteer Service Medal Korea (CVSMK) authorized in 1992 and issued to all Canadians who served in the Far East. Therefore, I chose *Korea Volunteer* as the title for this book even though many of those who served in Korea and Japan did not volunteer, but were ordered to go.

This first United Nations military action of such magnitude was a war in the eyes of those who served there. The 516 names in the Book of Remembrance in the Peace Tower in Ottawa attest to the degree of sacrifice required to reach what was to be a cease-fire rather than a victory. Even now, in 1994, North Korea is making the world uneasy about nuclear weapons and their reluctance to have the International Atomic Energy Agency inspect a potential threat (see *Reader's Digest*, March 1994).

I have followed the same sequence and style as in my other oral history books. The people in *Korea Volunteer* are of my generation. I have served in

An Oral History From Those Who Were There

the Army with many, gone to the Canadian Army Staff College with others. The rest came into my area of interest during my forty-five years in uniform or by their well-known reputation as sailor, soldier or airman.

Sources of historical reference by Canadians about Korea are rare. The interviews I recorded on tape, snippets in official Unit histories and those wonderful "pack rat" people who saved everything all helped pull this book together. A real effort has been made to collect more than one story from each regiment or corps.

As each chronological period was examined, I felt as if I was putting together a jigsaw puzzle. I found out what was happening on "Little Gibraltar", on the flanks, in reserve and in the tanks that supported the infantry. Our artillery was indeed "ubique" — [everywhere, their motto] — they went everywhere and they acquitted themselves as professionals, as did all our Canadian military.

Care has been taken to have the contributors check their stories as I have written them. There are stories from lieutenants who became generals and a leading seaman who became a rear admiral. No matter where their careers led them after Korea, their lives were affected in ways that only fighting in a war can affect someone.

I have tried to show how ill-prepared the Canadian Army was, how the families managed on their own, with little help from the Canadian government. Most of all I have tried to reveal how many young men became seasoned veterans in a short time in a foreign land.

As I fulfil my duties as Project Director for the Department of National Defence for *Canada Remembers* — a commemoration of the war years 1944-45 — I realize the magnitude of Canada's involvement in war over the past eighty years. If I have helped to record the years of 1950-54, when Canadians became volunteers to fight in Korea, then I have achieved my aim.

Chapter One
WHY KOREA?

If the best minds in the world had set out to find us the worst possible location in the world to fight this damnable war, politically and militarily, the unanimous choice would have been Korea!
        US Secretary of State Dean Acheson

Canada's knowledge of the Korea United Nations actions in 1950 to 1954 is at best limited and at worst nonexistent. This oral history seeks to address this failing by outlining Canada's participation on the sea, on the land and in the air.

Forty years ago, under the authority of the Security Council of the United Nations, Canada committed its military men and women to a situation like no other in history. The action has been called a war, a police action, peacemaking and, in some circles, peacekeeping. *The Blue Helmets: A Review of United Nations Peace-keeping* describes it like this:

> The international force in Korea was not a United Nations peace-keeping operation in the current sense of the term since the enforcement action was not carried out by the Organization, was not based on the consent of the parties, and involved the use of force.

Given the broad range of recent United Nations – sponsored actions throughout the world, it is no wonder that confusion exists about just how to label the Korean action. In the minds of the sailors, soldiers and airmen who served there, however, it was a war, plain and simple.

James Stokesbury's *A Short History of the Korean War* spells out just how the United Nations came to take the action it did to stop North Korean aggression. Before getting into this detail however, it would be wise to answer one question: Why Korea?

An Oral History From Those Who Were There

The division of Korea had its beginning in the last weeks of the Second World War. The Potsdam Conference in July 1945 made it clear that the Americans wanted Russia to enter the war against Japan. As Stokesbury explained, "The Americans unilaterally decided that the handiest way to treat Korea would be for them to occupy the southern part of it and the Russians ... should occupy the northern portion."

This concept was confirmed in General Order No. 1 issued by the Allied Commander in the Pacific, General of the Army Douglas MacArthur on September 2, 1945. The Japanese occupation troops surrendered to the Russians in the North; in the South, Lieutenant General John Hodge, US Commander in Korea, accepted the surrender of the Japanese forces on September 9, 1945.

The ideologies of the two countries that accepted the surrenders could not have been more diverse. The Americans wanted to ensure that a democratic government was in place and then withdraw. The Russians wanted a Communist government to rule the entire country. With that dichotomy, it was inevitable that a conflict would ensue. By May 1947, the Americans had proposed free elections throughout the North and South; naturally the Russians said no. The United States handed the problem over to the United Nations in September, and on November 14 a temporary commission on Korea was authorized. The commission was to supervise free and secret elections and to oversee the withdrawal of the occupation forces. By the spring of 1950, most United States troops had gone home, the Russians had left the North, and the Koreans on both sides of the 38th parallel were left to their own devices.

With Syngman Rhee representing the South calling for war against the North and Kim Il Sung of the North fomenting trouble, it was only a matter of time before war erupted. Giving support to the two sides would be the United States, which had the atomic bomb, and Russia, which had the greatest armed force in the world. The Americans made the mistake of saying in September 1947 that "they had little strategic interest in keeping bases and troops in Korea", so the North knew that their way would be clear once they chose to attack. And that attack came early one summer morning. Here's how John Melady described it in *Korea: Canada's Forgotten War*:

> The war began in the rain. At 4 a.m., June 25, 1950, the roar of artillery shredded the silence over the ancient hills of Korea. Along the 38th parallel, from west to east, belches of flame cut the darkness ... [it was] the start of the Korean War.

The North Koreans outweighed the South Koreans in more than sheer numbers. Their eight infantry divisions of 11,000 men each were supported by the 105th Armoured Brigade of 120 Russian made T34 tanks and 6,000 men and artillery with 122 mm howitzers. This was more than a match for South Korea. Because the attack came without warning, a third of the Republic of Korea (ROK) Army was away from the front on leave, and most of the officers were attending the opening of an officers' club in Seoul. To make matters worse, the ROK was lightly armed, with no tanks and few antitank weapons; their largest artillery piece was a 105 mm howitzer. The Americans had structured the ROK Army so that it "was not good for heavy combat". Stokesbury wrote, "It was a war of 1950 fought by armies of 1945 using tactics of 1916."

In North America, it was the afternoon of June 24 when war broke out in Korea. By the morning of Sunday, June 25, the US Department of State and the US Army had begun planning for the action to be taken in Korea. The only hope seemed to rest with General MacArthur, who was still in Japan as Allied Commander in Chief, Far East. That afternoon the United Nations Security Council passed a resolution calling on "North Korea to cease its aggressive action". The United Nations also requested all member countries "to render assistance". In the end, sixteen nations provided troops of various kinds. As Stokesbury wrote, the important thing was that "it was a United Nations action, it was a joint attempt to deter aggression, and it provided an apparatus of world support for the American position [to let the United States run the war as the United Nations' agent]. ... There was to be a unified command, under a U.S. Commander [MacArthur]." All that was asked of MacArthur was that he "furnish occasional reports as necessary to the United Nations".

In Canada the news came as a total surprise. There had been no indication that North Korea would start a war of aggression. The Liberal government of Prime Minister Louis St Laurent spent that Sunday telephoning Washington and the United Nations at Lake Success, its temporary home outside New York City. When the House of Commons resumed the next day, Lester B. Pearson said that "He hoped that some action on the part of the U.N. would be successful in ending the hostilities [and] also that Canada would give full support to the United Nations in its efforts to restore the peace in Korea."

At first it seemed that there was no stopping North Korea. Just two days after war began, Seoul fell. The advance continued until all that was left by the end of July was a South Korean perimeter just inland from Pusan.

The United States moved quickly. The first decision was for MacArthur to "send arms and ammunition to the ROK; evacuate American citizens and deploy the U.S. Seventh Fleet ... under the authority of the U.N. resolution

An Oral History From Those Who Were There

passed earlier that [June 25] day." With no time to waste, MacArthur took stock of the American forces at his immediate disposal. As Stokesbury wrote, "In Japan, four understrength divisions ... a peacetime army were in for one terrible surprise. ... [For the air, there were] thirty squadrons totalling 553 aircraft in operational units. ... The U.S. navy was in better shape ... [but] throughout the entire war there was no challenge to American, or U.N. command of the sea."

The US Navy and the Royal Navy along with the US Air Force managed to destroy the small North Korea Air Force, mostly while the North Korean aircraft were still on the ground. On land there was nothing that could stand up to the T34 tanks. Knowing that the ground war was critical, MacArthur reported to Washington "that it would be necessary to commit American ground troops". *In Reminiscences,* MacArthur wrote,

> This put the bulk of the burden on the G.I. [nickname for the American soldier, from government issue]. The story of the infantry soldier is an old and honorable one. He carries his home with him–and often his grave. ... He must sleep and eat and fight and die on foot, in all weather, rain or shine, with or without shelter. He is vulnerable day and night. Death has his finger on him for twenty-four hours, in battle, going toward it, or retreating from it. It is a wonder that the morale of those uniformed gypsies never falters.

Truer words were never written, as the Canadian infantry would soon learn. Canada was to commit a total of twelve battalions and over twenty-six thousand men when all the components of the Army are included. When all components of the Army are included the infantry, as in all previous wars, was to bear the brunt of fatal casualties.

Of the 378 Canadians buried in the Pusan United Nations Memorial Cemetery, all but forty-one are from the infantry. In all, 516 Canadians are named in the Korea Book of Remembrance in the Chapel in the Peace Tower in Ottawa. These Canadians died in the name of peace for Canada and for what the United Nations was trying to achieve.

Why Korea? If a nation belongs to the world body, part of the membership fee is to provide support when needed. As Melady wrote, "Before peace was restored thousands of young Canadians, some of whom had never heard of this Asian nation, and had certainly not dreamed of visiting it, would fight on the blood soaked soil of this unfortunate land."

Chapter Two
THE ROYAL CANADIAN NAVY

It was just eleven days after the war began in Korea that the Royal Canadian Navy (RCN) set sail on July 5, 1950. This feat was possible because of Canada's state of preparedness and the fact that three ships in Esquimalt, British Columbia, were on orders to take part in a deployment that summer.

The Canadian ships that operated in Korean waters were HMCS *Cayuga*, *Athabaskan*, *Sioux* and *Crusader* from Esquimalt and HMCS *Nootka*, *Huron*, *Iroquois* and *Haida* from Halifax. The west coast ships carried the early tasking, when most of the action took place.

Korea is a peninsula bounded by the Sea of Japan and the Yellow Sea. Thus, the RCN destroyers had freedom to cover all borders of the country except in the north, where the land mass bordered Manchuria. The types of engagement were varied; train busting along the east coast; aircraft carrier escort; bombardment of shore batteries; mine destroying; and evacuating soldiers trapped in bridgeheads. The patrols were long. HMCS *Cayuga* set the record for Commonwealth ships: fifty days on patrol.

Sailors were lost at sea because of accidents or because the state of the sea just swept men overboard. On October 2, 1952, HMCS *Iroquois* received a direct hit from an east coast shore battery: three men were killed and ten others were wounded.

After the armistice was signed on July 27, 1953, the RCN remained. In *Valour Remembered*, Pat Giesler states, "the UN Naval forces remained in the theatre. ... The last Canadian destroyer [HMCS *Sioux*] left the Korea [waters] in September 1955. ... 3,621 officers and men ... served in Korea [many for more than one tour]."

Gordon Edwards with Kim Hen Gun of the South Korean Navy at Sasebo, Japan, October 1950. Kim was the Navy liaison signalman and worked with the signals crewmembers of the HMCS Athabaskan.

SIGNALS FROM ATHABASKAN

"You are to sail *Cayuga, Sioux* and *Athabaskan* from Esquimalt at 16 knots to Pearl Harbor P.M. Wednesday 5 July, 1950."

With that message to Flag Officer Pacific Coast from Naval Headquarters, Ottawa, the RCN was put into action preparing three ships for war under the command of the United Nations. Refits for the three ships were foreshortened. Sailors on leave were recalled. New recruits, some scarcely trained, were brought on board to bring the companies up to war complement.

One of the sailors affected by all this was Able Seaman Gordon Edwards, a communicator "sparker and signalman" on board HMCS *Athabaskan*. Gordon had joined the RCN in December 1948 and by the summer of 1950 was "preparing for a cruise of Europe". Recently, he described the scene on that long-ago summer morning:

> Upon returning from leave in Medicine Hat, Alberta, I was very involved for about three days in storing ship, consisting of everything from food to beer to ammunition. At the same time the dockyard was busy refitting our two 40 mm mountings on the two gun decks just below and aft of

the bridge. As far as I can recall the ship was up to strength as we seemed to have full messdecks. We were a bit out of refit, but overall in good shape. I was assigned as second signalman of the watch, along with the usual message centre, log distribution and other duties. Much of this was interesting, as when one was duty signalman there was a lot of interchange between the officers, including the commanding officer, as the log had to be brought around to all officers by hand. (As an aside, I always enjoyed taking the log to Commander Welland's cabin, as I considered him to be a dynamic and exciting destroyer captain. He always seemed calm, cool, collected and polite!)

Commander R.P. Welland, DSC, had just taken command of the *Athabaskan* three months before. The Captain of the *Sioux* changed the day before sailing, and Captain J.V. Brock, DSC, became Captain of *Cayuga* and Commander Canadian Destroyers Pacific. At 1500 hours, 5 July 1950, the three ships formed up astern of HMCS *Ontario* and sailed for Pearl Harbor, 2,000 miles away. Two days later the three destroyers refuelled from the cruiser, which then reversed course back to Vancouver Island.

To AB Edwards, "going off to action" was exciting. The young single sailors were "thrilled by it all", but the married men "were not similarly enamoured". Gordon mentioned that "the ship had no problem with twenty-four knots en route to Pearl Harbour, and the engineering crew did a superb job, under the usual trying conditions."

In Thorgrimsson and Russell's *Korean Waters*, it is explained that "*Athabaskan* had been having a busy time among the west coast islands, bombarding enemy batteries, observation posts, troop concentrations ... and supporting landings of ROKs [South Korean soldiers] on Red dominated islands."

The task of screening the carrier HMS *Triumph* was a "first" for the Canadians. Gordon recalls,

> It was terribly interesting to work with a carrier, and all the excitement that went with carrier operations. Surprisingly, there were very few accidents, partly attributable to the fact that sea conditions in the Yellow Sea were usually pretty good. I recall one barrier accident, and one Sea Fury ditched, the pilot being picked up by *Sioux*, a big disappointment for us, as we were also nearby. (*Sioux* and *Athabaskan* were deadly rivals, while *Cayuga* seemed to be more friendly, and I suspect much of this came from rivalry between the two commanding officers who were not the Squadron Commander!)

An Oral History From Those Who Were There

On several occasions *Athabaskan* supported ROK forces as they cleared the islands in the Inchon patrol area. Keeping communications with the ROK raiding parties was essential to coordinate the shelling of enemy targets. Gordon recalls going with the Korean Marines at Tok Chok To:

> My job was to act as the communications link from ship to shore, and this was accomplished with both semaphore flags, invariably too distant to be seen, and a portable aldis lamp, the latter working reasonably well. We also took an old army type radio, but it never seemed to work! As it turned out there was not much communication needed, but what was needed turned out to be vital! I think this must have been where I became rather unenamoured with war, and the lustre was wearing off quite rapidly. In the first instance, the Korean Marines had convinced us that the island was a communist stronghold, and while there were certainly some North Koreans there, I doubt it was ever a "stronghold". After *Athabaskan* bombarded for about an hour, the Korean Marines went in first, apparently shooting everything in sight.

The Marines were not too particular about who they shot, said Gordon, and the "vital service" required was to evacuate wounded civilians to the ship for medical attention.

Gordon found the bombardments far more professional:

> We were assigned targets, [then we] moved in to a predetermined position and bombarded. The targets were usually visible, and almost never seemed to be able to return fire. I recall being fired on once, a round from shore landing about 100 yards off the starboard bow while we were moving slowly. Needless to say, we pulled that good old naval manoeuvre called "Getting the hell out of there!" It was always hard to tell what we had really accomplished, but of course we always reported complete success with a message "Target destroyed!" Confidence was our motto!

With the various naval tasks and just three Canadian destroyers, the ships remained at sea unless critical repairs forced them into harbour. For the sailors, "sea time" was a way of life. Remembers Gordon,

> *Athabaskan* had an open bridge, so in the winter, which seemed like most of the time, it was absolutely mandatory to bundle up before going on watch. Our clothing was not the best, consisting of a lot of sweaters, duffle coats, and usually toques made out of our pusser scarf as they came in two sections with a blank space in the middle so they could be

rolled like a toque. Big boots, long underwear, etc., all of which often got wet either from rain or, often, salt spray, as most of our work was done in one of the side sponsons. Then all of that had to be dried before the next watch, and the messdeck was taboo for that kind of thing ... imagine already sweaty clothing, now salt encrusted, drying out! I guess we got used to it. Laundry facilities were minimal, consisting, to my recollection, of a couple of tubs somewhere near the forward funnel. Life at sea consisted of sleeping, eating, washing up and going on and off watch. Spare time consisted of reading, writing letters and, fortunately for me, learning bridge. I say this advisedly, but we shared a mess with the electricians, and overall we were just a bit different from the rest of the ship, at least in level of education, and the mess had a number of good bridge players.

For AB Edwards, two strong memories are the USS *Missouri* and a run ashore in Hong Kong. These reflections truly tell the tale:

My main memory of *Missouri* was the immense size. We went alongside at sea to deliver an injured sailor. It looked as if they could have hoisted us aboard as a seaboat. As for escorting, it was straightforward, with us moving around ahead, keeping a close watch on some mystical threat. At Sasebo [in Japan], we entered first, and later she came in and took the last and biggest anchorage. Speaking of anchorages, we were seldom alongside, and in Sasebo never!

The visit to Hong Kong was memorable because of the typhoon on the way. My roughest time ever up to that time. (Doesn't seem like much after what I was to later experience in the North Atlantic and, in particular, the North Sea, with its shallow water and very steep waves.) Hong Kong was a nice break, and although we did some painting and maintenance, we did manage a bit of play. The Brits had a club there that we could use, and of course beer was cheap in those days. There was also lots to see, and with our newly acquired Japanese cameras, we did a lot of sightseeing. It was a fascinating place, even in those days.

Did manage to get over to Kowloon, fell amongst thieves (Brit sailors) and awoke to find myself in a strange bedroom (no women involved!). Had to get back to the ship but had no money. Managed to beg for the few pennies it took to cross by ferry. Now 9 a.m., and I am "adrift", to say the least. Decided to brave it out! Picked up an official piece of paper from the jetty garbage, put on my best front, walked down the jetty, onboard, straight to mess deck, into working rig, up to upper deck and no one seemed to miss me. Miracles never cease, but crime doesn't always remain that undetected!

A major excursion into Chinnampo Harbour came in December 1950. The Chinese drive south down the Korean peninsula had trapped part of the 8th Army. Captain J.V. Brock was ordered to defend the five American ships sent to evacuate the army. The message ended with "military situation serious. Be prepared to act in fire support of Eighth Army entering Chinnampo River channel as necessary." To the young signalman on the bridge of *Athabaskan*, it was a time to remember. Gordon recalls,

> Chinnampo was interesting, dangerous and exciting. Interesting because it was at night, dangerous because we had to navigate up a narrow river apparently infested with mines, without benefit of buoys or lights, and exciting because our role was to assist in the evacuation. *Cayuga* led the force up the river, and Andy Collier as the navigator got the DSC for the event. Nevertheless our navigation was not much easier, although following in the wake of someone who has not hit anything does give a warm feeling. We arrived in the harbour around midnight and stood by for further orders. When it appeared that evacuation was imminent, we were given the task of bombarding some key installations and then departing with whoever we could take. A big highlight of that was toppling a large chimney, although I am not certain whether that had anything to do with future North Korean war effort. It toppled quite nicely. As I recall, we never did get any refugees and parted in the forenoon. On the way back we found *Sioux*, who had never made it due to catching a wire in her screw or rudder. (The usual taunts and catcalls about missing the action again, and with weaker excuses every time!) I guess one could say it was the most important mission during the conflict, because in my opinion, subsequently borne out, no USN could have done it, as they did not use the method of "parallel index", using grease pencil lines on the display to mark and run clear of obstacles, which was really the only way the river could be navigated effectively. Commonwealth navies have always been good at this sort of thing.

In a situation like Korea, ships' companies were always trying to better each other. Refuelling was one such competition. It is an activity that requires superb seamanship; the ability to maintain stations during the entire process is critical — the supplier and receiver ships must act as one. The signaller was one of the key players in this evolution. Says Gordon,

Being front and centre for all refuelling at sea, I recall vividly the time we broke the oiling record. Competition was getting rather fierce, and thus rather dangerous as well. It was probably only a matter of time. However, Bob Welland was not to be beaten, and even better we had the Master (Captain) of the Royal Fleet Auxiliary [RFA] *Wave Knight* on side. (A bottle of scotch perhaps!) Anyway, to think that today we consider it good if we can be hooked on and pumping within three to five minutes, our record was rather incredible. This was also done with the B coupling, which had to be bolted on before pumping. Anyway, on the day in question (March 10, 1951), the weather was good. Welland came so close alongside we could almost hand over the heaving line. The wire jackstay was on immediately after, and the hose was heaved in. At this stage we couldn't believe our good luck and were convinced something had to go wrong. There were six bolts on the coupling, but with three tightened, oil could be safely pumped, the rest to go on later. There was one petty officer stoker to each bolt and nut and they went on very fast, and pumping started, all in 1 minute 40 seconds. After that, Brock declared enough was enough, and declared *Athabaskan* the winner. No one could have beat it anyway!

HMCS *Athabaskan* sailed home for Canada on 2 May 1951. Commander Welland was proud of his ship's record. The first port of call was Prince Rupert to "land" a sailor who had broken an arm. "The town was wide open and a lot of booze flowed that night. It was a subdued ship that sailed the next day!"

Gordon Edwards served in HMCS Crusader *for a year, then went on to midshipman training and flying training with the Royal Canadian Air Force and Royal Navy, respectively. Over the next 15 years he was to fly Sea Furies, Banshees and, while on exchange with the US Navy, F11F Tigers and F4D Skyrays. By 1968 he was commanding HMCS* Assiniboine *and in 1971 he became the captain of Canada's only hydrofoil, HMCS* Bras d'Or. *From 1975 to 1977 he commanded HMCS* Athabaskan *(not the same hull as in Korea). A highlight for Edwards was a one-year command of the North Atlantic Treaty Organization (NATO) Standing Naval Force Atlantic in 1979. The circle was completed when, in l982 as a Rear Admiral, Gordon Edwards was Commander Maritime Command Pacific. In 1985, Rear Admiral Edwards retired after 37 years' service. He and his wife Claire reside in Ottawa.*

An Oral History From Those Who Were There

Ed Dalton just before sailing for Korea in 1950.

TWO TOURS IN KOREAN WATERS

Edward "Ed" Dalton served in Korea for two full tours. His story is like many naval stories in that he did not volunteer for either tour. In an interview with Ed held in June 1993, Ed explained:

> I was serving in the *Cedarwood* in 1950 when I learned three ships were to visit my place of birth, England. I requested a posting to one of the ships. The Commanding Officer called me in one day and said, "I've got your draft, you are going to *Athabaskan*." I was overjoyed and I reported to fill one of the sonarman billets as a "torpedo detector", as they were known as in 1950. The ship's company was looking forward to the European cruise. Three days later as we were getting ready to sail we learned Europe was off and Korea was on. What a shock! The big question on most minds was, "Where the hell is Korea?" Regardless of the disappointment to a nineteen year-old able seaman, this was part of the adventure of being a sailor.

The trip was one of blackout curtains, action stations at all times and new ports of call. Finally they arrived at Sasebo, Japan, on 30 July 1950, twenty-five days after leaving Esquimalt. Ed Dalton and the ship's company in HMCS *Athabaskan* were now part of the war at sea.

When asked how the lack of enemy submarines affected the sonarman's job, Ed replied,

> We continued to operate the sonar, every day, all day, four hour watches and all that, and this just about drove us crazy. When the Chinese entered the war [14 December 1950] we thought their submarines would appear, but I don't recall that they did. There was one favourite rock off the southwest coast of Korea and it gave off an echo like a submarine, so it was depth charged time and time again!

In late September 1950, a mine was sighted. The sighting receives mention in Thorgrimsson and Russel's book, *Canadian Naval Operations in Korean Waters*:

> On 27 September low tide was at 0900, and *Athabaskan*'s motor cutters and dinghy again set to work on the mine problem. What with the mines and the shallow water, it would have been dangerous to take the ship close enough inshore to sink the mines with the 40 mm guns, and since it proved very difficult to sink them with rifle fire the problem was not an easy one to solve.

The solution affected AB Dalton. In his own words, this is what happened:

> Part of the job of the torpedo antisubmarine department was demolitions, and I was part of the ship's demolition team. We had been doing mine detection search so when these mines were sighted we had to take action. As the tide went down we could see these "things". The enemy used to drop the mines from fishing junks at night and just leave them anchored in place. We were not sure what type they were so we had to be cautious. What we thought were horns [to explode on contact] turned out to be lifting eyes [rings for lifting the mine]. Anyway, we had to blow them.

Thorgrimsson and Russel continue:

> The solution ... was unorthodox, and it called for iron nerves, steady hands and expert boat handling — but it worked. The motor cutter went in towing the dinghy ... [then] Mr. D.W. Hurl, Commissioned Gunner, RCN, the *Athabaskan*'s demolition expert [was] rowed to the spot. ... [T]he man at the oars would bring the dinghy close alongside the mine and hold it there while Mr. Hurl ... fastened time-fused demolition charges.

An Oral History From Those Who Were There

Commissioned Officer David Hurl attaches a charge to the mine held by Ed Dalton. AB Dave Kidd is standing in the stern. Ron Soulier is at the oars, and PO Tom Shields is behind Hurl.

As Ed Dalton talked about the event in June 1993, the tension in his voice increased. His task was to "take hold of the lifting rings on the mine and hold them fast so that the dinghy did not strike the mine and Hurl could do his job." The photo with this story (*Korean Waters*, p. 19) has the caption, "Commissioned Officer David Hurl attaches charges to enemy mine while A.B. Edward Dalton holds the mine steady." Ed identified the others in the photo: "PO Tom Shields standing behind Hurl and I am in the bow. AB Ron Soulier is at the oars and in the stern and standing is AB Dave Kidd."

It is interesting to note that PO Shields was awarded a British Empire Medal and David Hurl got a Mention-in-Despatches. The three ABs also got an extra tot of rum. The history closes with the statement, "Mr. Hurl and his party were able to destroy four mines before the tide forced a suspension of operations." The mines proved to be Russian, of a type that caused considerable damage to ships that had the misfortune to hit one. Ed's work on September 27 was vitally important.

Some of Ed's vivid memories are of Typhoon Clara on November 5, 1950. It was the worst weather he saw in in all his RCN career. Winds of 90 mph and seas running 50 to 60 feet caused *Athabaskan* to roll 62°. The ship had started to recover when "we were hit again", and sea water came through the lookout sponson on the side of the bridge:

> That is when we lost OS R.E. Elvidge when he was washed overboard. ... Elvidge and Chaplain H. Todd, the ship's padre, stopped to chat on the upper deck when the storm was at its worst. This great green one came over and hit both of them. The padre was smashed up against the Carley float rack but Elvidge was swept over the side. Ron Soulier, who stuttered, was the after lookout and finally managed to shout, "Man overboard!" The Officer of the Watch was going to lower a boat, but the Captain, Commander Robert Welland, came out, saw the boat ready to be lowered and cancelled the order! He then turned the *Athabaskan* about and got Elvidge on the windward side. The waves picked up Elvidge and threw him against the side of the ship. He grabbed the bottom guardrail with both hands, a couple of sailors grabbed him by the seat of his pants and pulled him aboard — they had to pry his fingers loose from the rail. Elvidge could not swim! The Captain took this very lucky sailor to his cabin and gave him a tot of rum. The Medical Officer gave him a clean bill of health and then Robert Welland signed Elvidge's papers, "Passed swimming test."

When the news finally came that *Athabaskan* was to go home, the crew thought it was about time, for the other two ships had gone home before her. Ed Dalton went on two months' leave, got married on the 26th of June and then went to *Esquimalt* to take a long course. But the Navy had other plans for him: on 2 August he was ordered "back to Korea, again". Betty Dalton returned to International Falls, Minnesota. A year later her husband returned. Of his second tour in *Athabaskan*, under the command of Commander Dudley King, Ed comments, "I recall very little from the second tour except that it seemed less interesting." A quick glance at the index in Korean Waters indicates carrier screening; bombardment of Amgak; operations in and around Taewha; the loss of a sailor overboard; shelling from a shore battery on the south shore of the Choppeki Peninsula (which *Athabaskan* soon silenced); and, finally, the handing over of her duties to Captain Landymore in HMCS *Iroquois* on 17 June 1952.

Ed does remember the loss of the sailor overboard:

> It was a real wild night on 27 November 1951, and AB R.J. Skavberg was going on watch at midnight. He did not report to his position. Someone thought he might still be sleeping, but he wasn't. He was seen dressing

so it was assumed that when he went on watch he'd been washed overboard en route to B Gun below the bridge. The top guardrail was broken below the ladder and this seemed to be where this unfortunate sailor had gone overboard. We spent two hours looking for our shipmate but we never found him. Another case concerned a sailor who fell between two ships while they were refuelling and he was crushed.

Ed Dalton's career spanned a total of twenty-six years. He was commissioned in 1966 and one of his postings was to HMCS Griffon, *Thunder Bay, Ontario. In 1974 he retired from the Navy and completed his education at Lakehead University. He joined the Reserve Navy in 1974. In 1980 he was promoted to Commander and Commanding Officer of HMCS* Griffon *for three years. As a civilian Ed Dalton worked for fifteen years as a Probation and Parole Officer until he retired. Ed and his wife Betty live in Thunder Bay, Ontario. Ed was awarded the 3rd clasp to the CD in 1990.*

GUERILLAS, LANDING PARTIES AND THE GREAT IMPOSTER

Don Saxon had already completed a very long naval career before he served in HMCS *Cayuga* in Korean waters. He had joined as a "boy seaman" in 1937, and when the Second World War began he was serving in HMCS *Fraser* on the West Coast. When orders came to sail to Halifax there was a problem. In Don's words, "The Panama Canal Zone had been declared off limits to 'belligerent ships'. [Fortunately,] Canada did not declare war until September 10, 1939, after *Fraser* and her sister ship, HMCS *St Laurent* had passed through the canal."

During the war years Don served aboard HMCS *Fraser, Saguenay, Skeena* and *Prince David*. In 1942 he took Upper Yardman Officer Training at HMS *Collingwood* and as a Sub Lieutenant was sent aboard HMS *Newcastle* sailing out of Ceylon. He returned to England after the war to take the Torpedo Anti-Submarine [TAS] course and on graduation remained at HMS *Vernon* as an instructor. He returned home in 1950 in time for service in Korea:

> I joined HMCS *Cayuga* as the TAS officer as a Lieutenant under the command of Commander J. Plomer. We sailed from Esquimalt, British

Columbia, on June 19, 1951, doing "work ups" [preparation for operational duties] all the way to Sasebo, Japan. We stopped en route in Hawaii where we were put through our paces in target practice at sea and shore bombardment. Our ship was cleared to provide shore bombardment at the very highest level of accuracy in relation to nearby "friendly" forces.

Don's qualifications resulted in his appointment to the TAS department but, as he said, "With no enemy submarines and no large surface ships to attack with torpedoes, my job skills were not to be utilized." Instead, Lieutenant Saxon was to be appointed officer in charge of landing parties, and a whole different war was to unfold for this naval officer:

From the time we arrived in Korea, the Landing Officer was the one to go ashore in one of the ship's boats to contact the people ashore who would brief him on all the latest intelligence available. On the West Coast Islands there was an organization of intelligence gatherers. These people were called donkeys or *tognakis* (which is the Korean name for Donkey). There were 15 donkeys on as many islands from south of Pengyang-do to Tan-do, the most northerly island in the chain. This group was headed up by two majors in the US Army, one code-named "Salamander" on Chodo and the other "Leopard" on Sok-to. The ships would give passage to these people and their supporters and carry food and equipment when required. There were several other independent intelligence organizations operated by United Nations Forces with headquarters in Seoul, coordinated by a group called Joint Organization for Clandestine Operations Korea (JOCK). The Headquarters

Don Saxon being transported onto HMCS Cayuga, *Korea 1952.*

Island of Pengyang-do also had representatives of the American Armed Forces as well as a colonel in the ROK Marine Corps. They reported to Colonel Davenport of the United States Marine Corps who was the Commander West Coast Island Task Element 95.15.

In the last three months of 1952, HMCS *Cayuga* was heavily tasked in a series of operations from screening carriers to supporting South Korean actions in the Yellow Sea. The enemy increased its air strength, flying from airfields in North Korea. In their book *Korean Waters*, Thorgrimsson and Russel mention that "*Cayuga*, on the morning of 25 October, was ordered to proceed to the anchorage off Taewha to investigate reports of an enemy bombing attack on the island [in fact there were eleven casualties amongst the defenders]. The ship's Medical Assistant, Petty Officer Robert Hotchin, went ashore to treat the wounded."

This small excerpt has within it one of the more interesting stories from *Cayuga*. The ship's doctor, known as Surgeon Lieutenant J.C. Cyr, had been discovered to be a fake — the Great Imposter — so he was not allowed to treat anyone again. A Victoria *Times Colonist* clipping dated February 6, 1991, explains:

> Roy Jenkins, an information officer with the Royal Canadian Navy ... wrote the original stories about the curing exploits of the ship's so-called doctor, Joseph Cyr. Cyr's medical skills became legendary as Jenkins filed stories to the military about the doctor's successes. ... However when the real Joseph Cyr of Grand Falls, N.B., surfaced, it became apparent the man on board the *Cayuga* was a fake.

Ferdinand Waldo Demara had stolen the real Dr Cyr's papers in March 1951.

Don Saxon had seen "Dr. Cyr" perform triage on injured flyers on an earlier occasion. "He treated them, stopped the bleeding, marked their injuries down and evacuated them to a US Military Hospital." He also performed major surgery on the damaged lung of a South Korean, and the man survived.

Don's account of an operation of another type — naval — in October 1951 is the stuff of a good story:

> My landing team was to go to the mouth of a harbour on the south side of the Hwanglae promontory to evacuate friendly guerilla from the mainland. Because the water was shallow our ship could not get closer than two and a half to three miles, so our motor cutter had a long trip. As we got closer we did not meet up with the group to be evacuated but we

sent the ship the location of targets. We had to get closer and when we did the enemy guns opened up on us. We zigged and zagged to avoid being hit, but the shells landed close enough to have the shell splashes of seawater come into our cutter. Then they opened up from the other side of the bay. We accelerated to full speed and headed back to the ship. I recall three of the able seamen who were with me for most of our operations: J. Petersen, D. Campbell and D. Pierson. These same three were with me on Operation Cheerful in December along with POs G. Coghill and F. Wood.

HMCS *Cayuga* also put in some time using her 4-inch guns on junks in the Chongyang-do area. The radar-controlled gunfire accounted for a small moving target at 5,000 yards. What was about to begin was, in Don's words, *Cayuga*'s most interesting assignment. Here is how Don remembers Christmas Eve, 1951:

It involved the coordination of so many different forces. The full responsibility of control of the naval side of this operation was left to *Cayuga* — UK, Canadian and ROK vessels were involved. The Island Commanders, US Marine Corps and US Army, the Leopard and Salamander forces of ROK Marine Corps and Army and the guerilla forces were also involved. The UK cruiser *Belfast* was used in a bombardment role with their forward observation officers (from the Island of Sok-to) spotting and controlling the fall of shot from their 6-inch guns; and of course *Cayuga* very much the centre of things with Captain Frewen, Royal Navy, CTU 95.12.1 [Task Unit] on board *Cayuga* at the time. Much planning was conducted for many days before the operation. A very important vessel, JML-302 [ex-Japanese minelayer], commanded by Lieutenant Pack Cyundo, ROK Navy, carried the guerilla leader and *Cayuga*'s landing party. They were to be the on-site group providing the guerillas, who were responsible for capturing the enemy on the islands, Chongyang-do and Uri-do.

The JML-302 was in a most vulnerable position. Other considerations that added to the danger included very shallow water 100 to 150 yards off the landing beach and [the close proximity of] heavy guns on Amgak and at Wolsari. This was our second night in JML-302 so we were well acquainted with the ship's operation and had a very quick response system for keeping *Cayuga* informed as the action developed at the landing beaches. We were fortunate that there were no casualties in JML-302 and light casualties in the guerilla forces (five dead, seven missing presumed dead and twenty wounded).

I was on the bridge of JML-302 when the CO was punching the leader of the guerilla force because his people were not doing what they were told. The guerilla leader was perfectly passive and made no attempt to protect himself. I have observed this behaviour before and it seems the guerilla commander thought he deserved the beating because he had failed to train his men properly.

Every officer and man in a ship has a duty to perform in action, therefore there was no one to relieve me and even had there been someone available there was no way they could have been transported. There were no RCN casualties during Operation Cheerful.

Don was fully employed on watchkeeping duties on the trip to Kure in January 1952. From Kure, *Cayuga* moved to a new inshore patrol area known as Haeju, arriving on 8 January. The ship was fired on several times during this patrol. On 16 January *Cayuga* was relieved by HMS *Cockade* of the Royal Navy. *Cayuga* then proceeded to Sasebo in Japan where she set course for Hong Kong for two weeks of R&R.

Don's story continues:

> *Cayuga* returned to the combat area in early February 1952, at which time I was seconded to the Commander of Task Group 95.1, Rear Admiral A.K. Scott-Moncrieff, Royal Navy; I was appointed the UN Naval Liaison Officer ashore stationed on Pengyang-do. I attached myself to the United States Marine Corps Headquarters where I received a warm welcome and much assistance in conducting my duties of providing intelligence to the ships flying the United Nations flag along the west coast of Korea.

Don's biggest concern was obtaining the results of ship bombardments along the coast. "We fired thousands of rounds and did not know if we had hit anything." A system was developed whereby the carrier aircraft dropped the mail each day, giving the results of the previous day's action. On one occasion a US Marine Corps plane dropped two 500-pound bombs by mistake! The regrets contained a promise, "We'll give you whatever you need, lumber, steak, ice cream, etc."

As *Cayuga*'s time in Korean waters came to a close, Don Saxon received a medal for his unusual deployment: "For devotion to duty and disregard for personal comfort whilst acting as Naval Liaison Officer in the islands off the West Coast of Korea. For steadiness under all circumstances — The Distinguished Service Cross — DSC."

An Oral History From Those Who Were There

On return to Esquimalt, Lieutenant Commander (TAS) Don Saxon was appointed Executive Officer of HMCS Sioux. *Later he served in Key West, Florida, where he worked on the evaluation of USS* Nautilus, *the first nuclear submarine, and was promoted to the rank of Commander (TAS). In 1956 he went to the Joint Services Staff College in England, then became Executive Assistant to the Vice Chief of the Naval Staff. Don commanded HMCS* Sioux, Athabaskan *and* Nipigon. *From 1966 to 1969 Captain Don Saxon was the military attaché in Holland. He retired in 1970 and started a ten-year career as a public servant responsible for the ship branch in Energy, Mines and Resources (later Fisheries). Thirteen years later he is still busy with senior citizens housing. Don and his wife Renee live in Ottawa, Ontario.*

Chapter Three

THE CANADIAN ARMY

To conceal the mistakes and speed up the operation so that men were attested and posted within thirty-six hours of applying, Claxton intervened and ordered the recruiting officers to cut their interview from one hour to five minutes.
The Price of Command (a biography of General Simonds),
Dominick Graham

To begin this chapter on such a negative note may seem unfair but it displays the one key problem of preparing the Canadian Army for Korea. The Canadian Army could not field a Brigade for war without having to resort to actions that paralleled the four years of the First World War. In listening to the Army stories for this book, I found that the one constant factor was compromise — with personnel, weapons and ways of waging war.

There was no question that Canada would provide soldiers for Korea, but only after the United Nations made a formal request. The Canadian Army of 1950 had been reduced in strength, their major role being the defence of Canada. They had just three battalions of infantry, two regiments of armour and one regiment of field artillery. A total Canadian force of just over 25,000 personnel would not be able to sustain a brigade group in Korea. On 30 June 1950, Prime Minister St Laurent gave a speech explaining Canada's problem (quoted here from Wood's *Strange Battleground*): "... any participation by Canada in carrying out the UN resolutions ... would not be participation in war [but rather in] collective police action under the control and authority of the United Nations for the purpose of restoring peace."

My research into how Canadian Army Headquarters took the above policy and made it into a workable plan was aided by George Bell, now a retired Brigadier General but at that time a major in the Adjutant General (AG) Branch in Army Headquarters. He was part of the team that created the policies to recruit men for overseas. In a July 1993 letter, George explained that his personal circumstances were, at best, chaotic: "I had been posted to the Royal Canadian Dragoons in Petawawa, but the AG, General Macklin, held me in Ottawa from 8 July to December 1950 on temporary duty. These were sixteen- and eighteen-hour days as we worked out each problem caused by the sudden mobilization."

Having to adhere to a very tight personnel strength did not help. Just before the Korean War, in February 1950, George Bell had been told by the AG, "George, you have to stop recruiting. We are approaching our ceiling, and Treasury Board will not give us one more red cent if we exceed that number." Money controls and inflexible budgets are not compatible with sudden changes in political plans which demand increases in the military. That is like demanding sports-car response from a ten-ton truck. As quoted by George, the Minister of National Defence had expressed the defence policy in these terms:

> The fact is that by themselves our forces could never deter the Russians, nor in a general conflict could they deliver a knock-out blow. What we want are forces which can defend Canada and enable us to play such part as Parliament and the people may support in any efforts for common defence with other countries.
>
> Against this background, Canada's present defence aims and objectives are: (1) to provide the force estimated to be necessary to defend Canada against any sudden direct attack that could be or is likely to be directed against it in the near future; (2) to provide the operational and administrative staffs, equipment, training personnel and reserve organization which would be capable of expansion as rapidly as necessary to meet any need; and (3) to work out with other free nations plans for joint defence based on self-help and mutual aid as part of a combined effort to preserve peace and to restrain aggression.

As the plans progressed, obstacle after obstacle was faced and solved. For example, in one proposed French-language recruiting advertisement, the enemy was labelled "La Grande Menace Rouge" (The Red Menace). When Brooke Claxton, Minister of National Defence (MND), saw it, he exclaimed to Major George Bell, "Major, that will never do! You obviously do not understand Quebec politics. Those who oppose us will use it for political purpose and play on words, because in Quebec we Liberals are known as les rouges." Needless to say, the heading was changed to La Grande Menace Communiste.

One hindrance was lifted on 7 August 1950, when Parliament authorized the raising of the Canadian Army Special Force. Three days later, Brooke

KOREA VOLUNTEER

Claxton went to Toronto to visit Number 6 Personnel Depot in an attempt to speed up recruitment. George Bell recalls what happened when the Minister called him in Ottawa:

> In the course of the conversation, he informed me of his desire to have the [recruitment] processes shortened or eliminated, and I expressed my concern about the problems that such reduction in process would lead to. He was not pleased with my initial response and terminated the conversation. Shortly thereafter the MND made contact with the AG, expressed his views and requested changes in the process. General Macklin then called me at my office and directed me to issue orders to reduce the process sharply and eliminate both time-consuming and detailed interviews and documentation steps. As a result, most of the safeguards, learned by long experience, were eliminated. While some of the stories which resulted from this situation are apocryphal, many of them were true.
>
> The political aim was achieved quickly, the initial objective of 8,000 recruits was achieved, and the subsequent recruitment of additional twelve months of reinforcements to bring the total up to 9,979 was authorized. The problem of creating operationally trained units of an infantry brigade and a pool of trained reinforcements was begun in the camps and unit locations across Canada under a specially selected cadre of leaders with significant WWII operational experience and established reputations as battlefield leaders.

In considering this situation, it is important to note that during the planning stage the MND had been sceptical about the possibility of recruiting the numbers required yet was anxious that the objective be achieved. Consequently, when the volume of recruits who applied before personnel depot staffs could be expanded caused bottlenecks, he was concerned that the success of the project would be jeopardized. No allowance was made for the lack of warning and lack of time for preparation caused by the government's secrecy and its decision-making process.

The rail strike on 22 August 1950 was the next hurdle to be jumped, and George recalls the problems faced by the staff. (This strike would not cause problems of the same magnitude for the RCAF, which was already committed to the war, nor for the RCN, who had already left Esquimalt the previous month for Korean waters.) George Bell's story continues:

> We were directed to move the pools of recruits in the Maritimes, Quebec and Ontario into Camp Petawawa. This necessitated forming an ad hoc

25 Canadian Infantry Brigade Reception Unit to receive, quarter, kit, feed and train these personnel until they could be transferred to their future units following the rail strike. Accommodation in Petawawa was already scarce and derelict buildings had to be rapidly renovated to meet the sharply increasing need.

It is important to realize that valuable lessons from past wars were being ignored, as the following anecdote reveals. The MND had a number of ideas for recruiting men for the NATO Brigade of which Canada was to form a part. One afternoon when George Bell was in the Minister's office, the Minister picked up a letter and said, "Major, here is the source of our next 10,000 men. The next time I am going to call on the militia units across the country to provide subunits and we will form them into combined units."

> On hearing this and being somewhat brash, I suggested to the Minister that his idea, while politically astute, was fraught with difficulty and supported my argument by telling him of a WWII experience with the conversion of an infantry battalion to an Armoured regiment that had been formed in this manner. To which he replied, "Yes, I know about those difficulties; remember I was a Battery Sergeant Major in an artillery regiment in WWI which was formed from several units. But, I am still going to do it and work out the difficulties after we have the force formed."

I asked George Bell if, in retrospect, he thought the disasters caused by pre-War budget restrictions and wartime recruiting shortcuts could have been avoided. His answer was not simple, but neither was the situation:

> In the early planning phase the indication that the UN need might require a larger contribution resulted in the development of a number of alternate proposals of brigade formations with varying compositions; from a stand-alone independent brigade group to smaller, less complete brigade-type formations which were designed to fit into a composite divisional formation where many of the combat support and service support elements would be provided by another nation or other nations. As the planning developed, the Chief of General Staff [CGS] continued to press the case for the recruitment of a Special Force, so that the Mobile Strike Force would be left intact. The need to do this became more obvious late in July when the US government asked Canada to provide a brigade group for a UN Force. This indication and the knowledge that the United Kingdom, Australia and New Zealand, and India were going to

make contributions, and that others such as Pakistan and Ceylon were expected to do so, gave added stimulus to a composite division concept based on the Commonwealth.

Major (retired) Edmund "Tojo" Griffiths explained that in the General Staff Branch they had continued to plan for a Brigade Group, and thank goodness they did!

Many of the negative aspects surrounding the creation of 25 Brigade were overcome by the dedication of the soldiers fighting in Korea. In *Strange Battleground*, Herb Wood summarized the impact of Korea: "From the time the first Canadian soldier set foot in Japan [en route to Korea] until the Armistice was signed 21,940 members of the Canadian Army served in Korea and Japan [some 484 served more than one tour]. The peak Canadian Army strength in the Far East was 8,123 all ranks, reached in January 1952."

When he compares total national population to numbers serving in Korea, Wood reaches the conclusion that "Canada's contribution ... [was] significantly larger than some other more populous members of the U.N."

To me, the real significance to the Canadian Army was that large pool of volunteers who made such an impact on others who had no war experience. When a soldier had never heard a shot fired in anger, it was important that those who had could bring the others back to reality to ensure that training was effective. Tojo Griffiths, who served in Korea as a staff captain in 1952 at Brigade Group Headquarters, gave me an insight into how predictions based on a previous war were not always reliable:

> The mobilization planning for Korea was based upon attrition rates from the Second World War. These rates were used by the AG Branch to determine how many officers and men from the different corps [e.g., infantry, armour and support services] were needed. These rates were based upon a forecast of engagement which went from intense to medium to quiet operations. [Based on] this forecast, reinforcements were held in Japan ready to be moved to the war zone at short notice.
>
> In Korea the numbers of non-battle casualties were higher than those from engagement against the enemy. Living conditions were poor and rodent density was high. Conditions were ripe for many diseases and it was no wonder that many United Nations personnel succumbed to different illnesses, one of them being epidemic hemorrhagic fever. The virus is present in rodent urine, faeces and saliva and is transmitted to people through inhalation of this virus. Taken from Harrison's *Principles of Internal Medicine*: "In Korea between April 1951 and January 1953,

2,070 cases of EHF were reported among United Nations personnel. The disease usually occurs as an isolated event; hence, overall attack rates have relatively less meaning. With this reservation, attack rates in two United States Army divisions stationed in Korea varied between 1.9 and 2.9 cases per 1,000 persons per epidemic season. ... Between April 1951 and December 1976 the overall case fatality ratio in Korea was 6.6 percent. ... Of 783 surviving patients cared for at the Hemorrhagic Fever Centre in Korea between April and December 1952, only 16 were unable to return to duty within a period of 4 months. This resulted in 25 Brigade Group combat reinforcements waiting in Japan whereas support reinforcements were more in demand." This situation resulted in a US Military hospital being created for the purpose of healing these cases.

The Canadian Army achieved an enormous amount, particularly telling when one realizes that the Brigade Group was formed for service in NATO at the same time. The Second World War veterans mixed with new trainees formed an army of tremendous value. In Giesler's *Valour Remembered*, she writes, "For the first time in history an international organization had intervened effectively with a multinational force to stem aggression. The United Nations emerged from the crisis with enhanced prestige."

This chapter is much longer than the Navy and Air Force chapters because the Korean conflict involved far more Canadian ground troops than it did the other two services.

KOREA VOLUNTEER

Charlie Hamilton looks at the signpost and thinks of his family thousands of miles away in Manitoba (DND photo).

FROM WHITEHORSE TO PUSAN AND BEYOND

Charlie Hamilton was just completing a three-year tour with the Northwest Highway System (NWHS) in Whitehorse, Yukon, when the announcement was made that Canada would send troops to Korea. Charlie did not give the announcement a thought, for his one-year extension in the Yukon had just been approved by Army Headquarters. All this was to change overnight:

> Approximately a week later a wire arrived at Headquarters NWHS announcing that I had been selected as Staff Captain 25 Canadian Infantry Brigade, Canada's Special Service Force. Why me? I guess it was because I was well qualified for the job. I had Second World War experience with the Saskatoon Light Infantry (MG), and had served on the staff of 2nd Canadian Infantry Brigade and on the staff of 1st Canadian Infantry Division. In addition I was Staff trained and had four years of Staff employment. More importantly, Brigadier General Rockingham had seen me in Whitehorse during a winter exercise [Muskox] involving Regular and Militia soldiers. He was a Militia Brigadier at the time and was impressed with the job I was doing as Staff Captain, NWHS.

An Oral History From Those Who Were There

As was the usual procedure when leaving the North, Charlie applied for his annual leave plus one week's special leave. The following day another wire arrived from Rockingham in Ottawa. "I cannot concur with your leisurely program, report at once."

The responsibility for moving family and furniture rested with the soldier in those days, so Charlie made plans to pack and store his house furnishings and then drove for three days to Brandon, Manitoba, where his wife and two small sons were to reside for the length of his overseas tour. Charlie reported to Brigadier Rockingham in Ottawa just six days after getting the "cannot concur" message.

> The Brigade staff assembled at Petawawa. While there I prepared the Brigade Administrative Standing Orders and the Brigade Headquarters Standing Orders cribbing from my Staff College notes on the subject. The Brigade Major Herb Wood was very impressed and no doubt this influenced my career. [Herb Wood later wrote *Strange Battleground*.]

On 4 November 1950, Army Headquarters decided to move 25 Brigade to Fort Lewis, Washington. This gave the formation the space it needed to train and get its equipment ready for shipment. Seattle would be the port of exit and US transport would be used for the sea voyage. The pressure upon Captain Hamilton grew:

> While the units trained under General Rockingham's critical eye, I was deeply involved in personnel staff work. The scope of the work becomes clear when it is realized that almost the strength of one infantry battalion (approximately 900 men) was sent back to Canada on compassionate or disciplinary grounds. Many of the recruits had forgotten to make arrangements for their wives and families back in Canada. A file had to be completed on each soldier giving reasons for recommended release, a Personnel Selection Officer's report, a medical report and a recommendation from their Commanding Officer.
>
> There were Investigating Officer Reports and court martial proceedings to be processed. The workload was so heavy that Brigadier Rockingham put a request into Ottawa (Army Headquarters) that I be promoted to Major and appointed Deputy Assistant Adjutant General. The request was denied.

It was decided that one battalion would be sent to Korea early. As *Strange Battleground* reported, it was to be "the 2nd Battalion of Princess Patricia's Canadian Light Infantry. ... [It] was nearest to Seattle ... and had been able to start training earlier than the other units."

At last things were to improve for Captain Hamilton. Major Gosselin, the Deputy Assistant Adjutant and Quartermaster General (DAA & QMG), was appointed to Second in Command of the Royal 22nd Regiment. Charlie was told "to prepare a letter for Brigadier Rockingham's signature recommending Hamilton for promotion to major". The recommendation was approved and Charlie took over Gosselin's title.

Rockingham was anxious to get the rest of the Brigade to Korea. He told Ottawa that "in his opinion the Brigade was ready for war". Charlie says,

> During the operational exercises all Administrative wireless sets and vehicles were used by the Umpires. I summoned my courage and advised General Rockingham that until such time as Administrative Units could be exercised we were far from being ready for war. He promised me that we would have a chance to exercise Administrative Units on arrival in Korea.

The next stage was to prepare the administrative plan to move everything to Korea. There were 10,000 tons of stores and 1,200 vehicles, not to mention the soldiers. Major Hamilton completed the movement plan and then left for Tokyo, Japan, with Major George (Signals), Captain Whiticar (Senior Service Corps Officer) and Captain Finney (Welfare Officer) by US Air Force. If things can go wrong they will go wrong: when they arrived in Japan, Charlie noted that "all our medical documents had been lost and we had to have all our inoculations again". In what seemed like no time the advance party arrived in Pusan, Korea, and it was here that a special brand of diplomacy was needed. Charlie explains:

> On arrival in Pusan, Captain Whiticar and I met with the British Garrison Commander. Neither of us were impressed with his domineering attitude and decided to seek assistance from US authorities. We were offered a former prisoner-of-war camp to house the Canadian Brigade in one hundred 40-man squad tents. Whiticar and I marked out the Unit lines and then turned our attention to the problem of housing the ordnance stores and a base workshop.
>
> We spent an evening with two American Colonels sharing a bottle of Canadian Club and came away with a promise from them that pre-fab materials to build a building 90 x 220 feet would be delivered to the POW campsite three days hence.
>
> The following morning we visited the British Garrison Commander and outlined our plan to use the POW camp. The only assistance we required was the use of a wrecker truck to unload the pre-fab bundles

being delivered by the Americans.

The Garrison Commander protested that he would have to convene a sighting committee to lay out the camp. We disagreed and eventually he agreed to provide the wrecker we requested. Unfortunately, the wrecker never arrived and we were left to our own devices.

The Canadians were not to be stopped by the less than cooperative British officer. They removed the waterproof shipping materials and gassed up their own wrecker. Captain Whiticar drove and unloaded the American trucks as they arrived with the pre-fab buildings. The entire camp was ready before the rest of the Brigade arrived by sea. The 3,500 soldiers, stores and vehicles were properly looked after when they disembarked from the USNS *Marine Adder* and *General Patrick* transports on May 4, 1951. Twenty-four hours later the Infantry, 2 Royal Canadian Regiment (RCR) and 2 Royal 22nd Regiment (R22eR) were on exercises in the nearby hills.

When the Canadian Armoured Squadron left Canada their primary role had been antitank defence. The North Koreans and Chinese had few tanks, so Brigadier Rockingham decided to make an equipment and role change. The M10-17 pounder Fireflies were exchanged for Sherman tanks. Charlie explained that Rockingham "instructed me to send a message to General Simonds (CGS) in Ottawa requesting authority to purchase twenty-two British Centurion tanks." The CGS agreed, but things did not go as planned:

> When I went to arrange the takeover I was told that at the present rate of arrivals from the UK it would take a year to fill the order. I then approached the Americans informing them that until such time as we were able to equip our squadron with Sherman tanks the Brigade would be grounded in Pusan. Within 48 hours Jim Quinn [the Squadron Commander] had his tanks and work to mount the wireless sets was under way.
>
> I believe it was thirteen days from arrival in Pusan until the Brigade was committed to battle south of Seoul.
>
> The administrative units exercised their wireless net in the road movement forward [so much for the administrative exercise on arrival in Korea!].

The Canadians were accommodated and equipped, and Rockingham was "very pleased with the arrangements". The British Garrison Commander complained to the Senior British Commander in Tokyo that "the young Canadian major was not cooperating", but the Garrison Commander was soon fired for his lack of effort.

When the Canadians left for Korea they were instructed to operate as an Independent Brigade Group drawing their administrative support from the US Army. The Second Battalion Princess Patricia's Canadian Light Infantry (2 PPCLI) had been a part of the British 27th Brigade since late 1950 but they were to revert to Canadian command as soon as operationally possible. Things were to change with the formation of the British Commonwealth Division, and in one area Charlie dug in his heels:

> The British wanted us to draw British rations, but we insisted on remaining on US rations which were more in tune with Canadian tastes. Furthermore, Canada was paying the US government a per diem rate for maintaining the Canadian Brigade. Our weapons for the most part were of US design except for our Artillery which was British 25 pounders. This meant that we had to draw our supplies from both US and UK sources as well as Canadian sources. [Not unlike the situation during previous wars — untidy, but it worked!]

The problem of supply was never-ending:

> While we were still an Independent Brigade I had submitted to US Ordnance requisitions for antifreeze, tent stoves and tent floorboards about three months in advance of winter. By the time winter arrived the Commonwealth Division was formed and assumed responsibility for our needs. Repeated requests didn't produce anything. COs were complaining — Rockingham directed that I do something about it. I had 19 Coy RCASC [Royal Canadian Army Service Corps] commanded by Major Bob Laughton "down" twenty trucks and lend them to me for a day. The trucks reported to the US Ordnance Depot, loaded up with what I had previously requisitioned and delivered same to the Canadian units. The next day Lieutenant Colonel Vickers, the Div AA & QMG, paid me a visit claiming that I had drawn the entire Division allotment of winter stores. I told him to discuss his problem with General Rockingham. I had just carried out orders! [The battle didn't end there.]
>
> The next round came when General Rockingham was on leave in Japan — he told me that if any Honours and Awards came through in his absence, I was to hold them until he returned so that he could make the presentation to the recipients. A number of awards came through and Lieutenant Colonel Vickers ordered me to advise the Unit COs of the time and place for presentation by General Cassels. I informed him of my instructions from General Rockingham. After further discussion with General Cassels he insisted that I make arrangements for the presentation,

which I did. General Rockingham on his return from leave was very annoyed but understood the position he had placed me in.

Charlie hastened to be fair in his assessment of his tour in Korea, "The administrative network worked like a charm mostly because all the COs were veterans of the Second World War. To me it was like turning the clock back five years and carrying on with the job."

The key to the entire Brigade was Rockingham. He had the Field Commander's instinct and battlefield sense. Says Charlie,

> Rockingham was a soldier's soldier. He rose early each morning and after breakfast set off for the front to visit the troops. On occasion I accompanied him and noticed that he made a point of visiting the most exposed positions. He had a good sense of the battlefield and many times correctly noted sub units receiving enemy artillery fire. This would happen while having dinner in the mess tent. [His hearing was always tuned in to the war.]
>
> December 1951 brought us two very special visitors: Brooke Claxton, Minister of National Defence, and his Parliamentary Assistant, Ralph Campney. Both were old soldiers and fitted in to our field environment. I remember Campney leaving the officers' mess tent when the first artillery shell landed nearby. When the second shell landed he hit the ground without spilling a drop of his scotch and water. Later in the evening General Rockingham announced that he would be attending a special midnight church service, but the Minister and his aide, due to their heavy visiting schedule, were not expected to attend. Later still Claxton told me he would like to attend. I relayed this message to Rockingham who said, "You look after him."
>
> When Mr Claxton and I arrived at the Korean-made hut, General Rockingham made room for him in the front row. Just as the Padre was about to announce that General Rockingham would read the lesson, Mr Claxton walked to the front of the hall, took a scripture lesson from his coat pocket and very masterly presented same. General Rockingham was badly out-fumbled — and was not amused.

The DAA & QMG's job was filled with surprises as he dealt with people problems. This account tells a tale from the past:

> One incident concerns a draft of reinforcements being sent by ship from Kure, Japan, to Pusan, Korea. The draft was made up of 900 Canadian soldiers sent from Fort Lewis back to Canada for disposal and then to be

returned as reinforcements once their personal problems had been solved. They were badly needed to replace battle casualties.

The hold of the ship was filled with beer. Some soldiers from the draft were assigned as guards. The guards decided to share the beer with the rest of the Canadians. By the time the ship's Captain and crew caught on the soldiers were in no mood to give up the cache. The crew resorted to fire hoses against the Canadians, and before the rumble ended all the fire equipment had been thrown overboard by the soldiers.

I received a very lengthy Investigation Officer's report to be used as a basis for laying charges. The reinforcements were despatched to Brigade units at once — the report was filed. I really didn't know how we could handle in excess of 150 court martials, plus we needed the soldiers in the front lines.

Rotation time came and things were under way. Detailed handovers were carried out over a week or more. Just as things had not been smooth on Charlie Hamilton's arrival, the departure went badly:

I had turned over my duties as DAA & QMG to Major Jeff Baker. Don George, the Brigade Major, had turned over his duties to Major Jim Allan. Brigadier General Bogert, Brigadier Rockingham's replacement, came down with the mumps and was confined to bed for three weeks. Major George and I went to Brigadier General Rockingham and told him we had turned over our duties and were ready to leave Korea. Rockingham's response was "You will stay in Korea until I am relieved by Brigadier General Bogert." It was a long three weeks with two DAA & QMGs and two Brigade Majors.

We left with Brigadier General Rockingham. Every unit had set up a bar at the side of the road to see us on our way. We saw the last of Korea in a most jovial mood.

Charlie Hamilton was recommended by Brigadier Rockingham for an award for his work in Korea. The citation for the Member of the Order of the British Empire (MBE) award reads, in part,

Major Hamilton ... was responsible for the loading and unloading of equipment and stores necessary to move the Brigade overseas. ... The fact that the Brigade left Pusan ready to fight thirteen days after arrival by ship in Pusan indicates the efficiency with which this task was carried out. [He] spared no effort nor sought any rest during the period. ... The supply of the Brigade has been most complicated with supplies originating from

Canada, United States and United Kingdom sources. ... [T]here has never been a shortage of any supplies and the troops have been promptly supplied with their requirements. ... This officer's untiring efforts, his devotion to duty and his quick clear thinking have been a major factor in the successful operation of the Brigade.

When Charlie came home he was posted to the United States Staff and Command College in Kansas. On graduation he went to Washington, DC. He commanded 2 PPCLI and served on the Directing Staff of the Canadian Army Staff College. Later he was a student at the Imperial Defence College in London, England. During the Nigerian Civil War he was Canada's senior military representative on the International Observer Team as a Brigadier. In the late 1960s, two command appointments followed in Gagetown, New Brunswick, and Calgary, Alberta. In 1972, he was loaned to the Great West Life Assurance Company under the Executive Interchange Program. Charlie took early retirement in 1973 and worked for Great West Life for the next ten years. He retired to Chaffey's Locks, Ontario, where he and his wife Anna now reside.

KOREA VOLUNTEER

Jim Stone just after returning to the Canadian Army to command 2 PPCLI.

"BIG JIM" STONE'S PATRICIAS AT KAPYONG

Mention the Korean War to a Canadian and the one name that comes to mind is Kapyong. The Second Battalion Princess Patricia's Canadian Light Infantry (2 PPCLI) brought fame to the Canadian Army and Canada with their collective action on 24-25 April 1951.

The Commanding Officer of 2 PPCLI was James Riley Stone. "Big Jim" was a natural nickname for such a tall, dynamic man. Jim had joined the Loyal Edmonton Regiment in 1939 as a private and rose through the ranks to Company Sergeant Major. By 1942 he had been commissioned as a Lieutenant. In Italy he rose to the rank of Lieutenant Colonel and won a Military Cross and a Distinguished Service Order and Bar. In 1946 he left the Army, but in the Reserve Army he commanded the Rocky Mountain Rangers. In a March 1993 letter to me, Jim wrote,

> John Rockingham was the Brigade Commander. He persuaded me to join with him in the force being recruited for Korea.
>
> Korea was not a war of heroics. It was for the most part uncomfortable, fatiguing and boring. The troops attacked when ordered and

An Oral History From Those Who Were There

defended with courage and tenacity. The war was a stupid one, but the soldiers were superb. The survivors of my battalion still think of themselves as Big Jim Stone's Patricias, and I am proud of them.

In August 1950, 2 PPCLI started recruiting for the Special Force. Jim's "Memoir: Kapyong" in the Autumn 1992 issue of *Infantry Journal* states, "Many recruits were re-treads from World War Two [not all were fit to be soldiers] and broke down under the rigorous training program and were got rid of prior to going into action." (Author's note: When I joined the Army in January 1951 I met one member of 2 PPCLI who evaded the "unfit for battle" category. He had been in action when he was caught not firing his weapon. It was soon discovered that he had a glass eye. He had made it through the enlistment medical by holding first his left then his right hand over his glass eye to read the eye chart.)

When General Foulkes decided to send just a battalion to Korea, 2 PPCLI was training in Wainwright, Alberta. As the closest to the embarkation port of Seattle, Washington, 2 PPCLI was chosen to be that battalion. The rest of the Brigade would concentrate and train in Fort Lewis, Washington. Jim Stone's unit was to spend "less than four days" in Fort Lewis, one day being devoted to an inspection and march past for the Minister of National Defence, Brooke Claxton. On 25 November 1950, 927 all ranks sailed on the USNS *Private Joe P. Martinez*.

To the soldiers on board ship, it appeared as if the war would be over by the time they arrived. As Wood writes in *Strange Battleground*,

> The Chinese ... may have decided to intervene in North Korea in early October ... when US troops had crossed the 38th parallel [the border between North and South Korea]. By the end of October six Chinese Armies, each of three divisions of 10,000 men, had crossed the Yalu River. ... Within weeks two more Armies, the 50th and 66th, had entered the battle zone.

It was no surprise that the United Nations Forces under US Command were quick to press 2 PPCLI into action as soon as they arrived in Pusan. Jim Stone's article tells the story:

> The G3 of the 8th Army [US] informed me that I was to be "married up" with my stores and vehicles and was to proceed within three days to Suwon and join the British 29th Brigade. [Jim objected and asked to see the Commander 8th Army.] I flew to Seoul to see General Walker [who said] that my troops were trained as well as the U.S. reinforcements, and

the situation was desperate. [Jim had an "out"] ... a piece of paper which gave him the authority for the decision committing his battalion [to battle]. The British 29th Brigade was seriously mauled in the ensuing week. I can imagine what would have happened to us.

After six more weeks of intensive training, 2 PPCLI's Commanding Officer said they were ready for action. Shortly afterward Jim came down with smallpox. Major Pat Tighe, the Second in Command, took over until April 22, when Jim returned. It was just two days before what was to be called the Battle of Kapyong.

The Kapyong conflict saw 2 PPCLI left forward with the First Middlesex Regiment [British] centre and rear and The Third Royal Australian Regiment right and forward. As Jim wrote in "Memoir: Kapyong",

> One feature, Hill 677, was much larger and, I must confess, much more difficult to attack. If you ever have to take up a defensive position on a mountain of that size with a battalion of infantry, make sure, first, that you listen carefully to orders and know your objectives, and, second, that you search your memory for everything you have been taught about the selection of vital ground from which to conduct a defence.

The very next day Jim Stone took his reconnaissance party of company commanders, support weapons officers and his artillery representative [a New Zealander] to the enemy side [which was still free of Chinese], "which gave us a good idea of probable attack approaches". Once everything had been considered, Jim issued his orders and the battalion moved in. Jim appreciated that his "platoons were in individual defended localities within the Company area." Every weapon was sited so that mutual support was organized to bring maximum fire to protect each slit trench. Where the battalion weapons could not reach, artillery targets had been included. Superimposed along the entire 2 PPCLI front were the battalion mortars and Vickers machine-guns. The New Zealand Field Regiment of 25 pounders supported the whole battalion position. All that remained was for the Chinese to attack and for the Canadians to hold while the 6th ROK (South Korean) Division withdrew.

The Australians were the first to be hit at 0800 hours on 23 April. They held until midday on 24 April, when they were overrun and ordered to withdraw. *Strange Battleground* states, "2 PPCLI were deployed on the north face of Hill 677 with 'A' Company on the right, 'C' Company in the centre and 'D' Company on the left. 'B' Company occupied a salient in front of 'D' Company."

The first sign of the enemy came at 0700 hours on 24 April when a small group of Chinese were detected by B Company. Jim Stone had ordered

B Company to move to counter the threat when the Australilans withdrew. Imagine the feelings as the soldiers left the trenches they had been preparing in readiness for the anticipated attack by the Chinese! It was a good move: B Company could now "observe enemy movement across the wide valley" of the Kapyong River.

Before noon the Chinese attack began on the newly located B Company. The Company's forward platoon, Number 6, was hit by an estimated 200 enemy. The Chinese started to infiltrate the companies and threatened Battalion Headquarters. An eyewitness report states, "The battalion 81 mm mortars firing at their shortest range 200 yards together with their .50-calibre machine-guns" forced the Chinese back. Individuals, small groups and the combined use of all weapons in the battalion plus the New Zealand gunners saved the day. As night came the attack became more intense. "Memoir: Kapyong" tells the tale:

> D Company received special attention [from the Chinese]. The Company Commander, Wally Mills, reported to me [Stone] over the telephone ... that his position was overrun and that the enemy had infiltrated everywhere. ... He asked for an artillery concentration [of high explosive shells] right on top of his position. I obliged. [Wally received the Military Cross for his part in the battle.]

The Patricias had held their hill, but, as explained in *Strange Battleground*, "The battalion was, however, cut off from the rest of the brigade–the supply route to the rear was held by the enemy — and the ammunition reserves and emergency rations had been depleted."

In a letter to me in March 1993, Jim gives his Intelligence Officer, Lieutenant Mackenzie, credit for "suggesting we request an air drop from Japan". Six hours later, four 119 Flying Boxcars dropped all but four of their parachuted supplies on the battalion position. This final summary from *Strange Battleground* gives the conclusion of Kapyong 1951:

> It [2 PPCLI] had maintained its positions intact, and these positions covered the ground vital to the defence of the brigade area. In addition, its relatively light casualties of 10 killed and 23 wounded testified to the skill with which the position had been organized and defended. Lieutenant-Colonel Stone's outstanding leadership during this action led to the award of a second bar to his Distinguished Service Order. [In the March 1993 letter, Jim wrote that the second bar was for his "service generally in Korea".]

A first happened at Kapyong when 2 PPCLI was awarded the Distinguished Unit Citation by US General Order 47. This blue ribbon is proudly carried on the Regimental Colour of the unit. No other Canadian Unit has been so honoured.

In "Memoir: Kapyong", Jim Stone wrote,

> Kapyong was not a great battle, as battles go. It was a good battle, well planned and well fought. ... The Chinese soldier is tough and brave. All he lacked at the time of Kapyong was communications and supply. Perhaps death was preferable to the life he was compelled to lead, for he certainly was not afraid to die.

Jim gives six reasons why 2 PPCLI was successful:

- 2 PPCLI had high morale. The men believed in one another. No one panicked when they were surrounded.
- Subordinate commanders had ample time for reconnaissance in daylight.
- A good eye for ground was essential, for ground was vital to defence.
- B Company's move saved the right flank and alerted battalion headquarters to the infiltration of the enemy.
- Evacuation of the wounded by US helicopters gave a great boost to morale (and cut down on fatal casualties).
- The airdrop saved the day.

I would add the superb support from the New Zealand Artillery. Nonetheless, Jim's is a most stirring story of the unit that was first in Korea and who upheld the traditions of regiment and Canada at Kapyong.

Jim Stone became the Chief Instructor at the School of Infantry in Camp Borden and later became the Provost Marshal of the Canadian Army until his retirement. In 1959 Colonel Stone was seconded to the Department of Justice. In 1960 he was appointed Senior Deputy Commissioner of Penitentiaries, a post from which he retired in 1973. Jim is the Honorary Patron of the Military Police Fund for Blind Children, a fund which he founded and which has collected and dispersed over $2 million to aid visually handicapped children. Colonel Stone is now retired and lives alone in Victoria, British Columbia. His wife Esther died four years ago.

Captain Keith Besley in a pensive mood, Korea, December 1951.

FRONT-LINE DOCTOR AT THE CASUALTY CLEARING POST

Doctor Keith Besley of Ottawa had been a fighter pilot in the Second World War, but in Korea he served as a doctor. In an April 1994 interview he spoke about his time in the RCAF:

> I joined the RCAF in September and was posted overseas in 1942. I flew the Hurricane aircraft in North Africa at the Battle of El Alamein where our job was ground strafing. The dust conditions were very bad. After that I served in Àbādān, Iran, Cos Island in the Aegean Sea and off the coast of Italy as an aircraft identifier aboard a Royal Navy destroyer for four weeks. I was injured during a crash in the Persian Mountains and was sent back as a casualty to Canada by mid-1944. I was released from RCAF Station Uplands when the war ended.

Keith had been an apprentice in pharmacy before the war, but in the fall of 1945 he began working toward his medical degree at the University of Toronto. In 1949 he joined the Royal Canadian Army Medical Corps (RCAMC).

KOREA VOLUNTEER

After graduating in 1950 he began his internship at St Michael's Hospital in Toronto. In December 1950, just five months into his internship, he was warned he was to go to Korea. Keith said, "I had not joined the RCAMC with the idea of going back to war, but Korea changed all that."

Keith was posted to Fort Lewis, Washington, DC, where he and other doctors (MOs) underwent extensive field training. Keith remembers, "One day a young Van Doo [a soldier from R22ᵉR, that is, a "Vingt-Deux"] soldier came to see me about pains in his chest. I examined him and told there was nothing wrong and to keep on with his training." Keith was in Fort Lewis just weeks when he was sent to the Canadian Reinforcement Group (CRG) in Japan. "I was surprised when the same young soldier came to see me with the chest pains. Again I told him there was nothing wrong with him, so he went to Korea." After three months working at the CRG, Captain Besley was posted to 25 Field Ambulance in Korea. He was ordered to set up a Casualty Clearing Post (CCP) just to the rear of the front lines. "Once again that same soldier came to see me about his chest pains and for the third time I again pronounced him fit for service and sent him back to the front."

Keith explained the role of the CCP:

> The casualty clearing system worked from the front lines to the rear areas. A wounded soldier would be taken on a stretcher or if possible would walk from the place of wounding to the Regimental Aid Post. He would be seen by the Regimental Medical Officer and then placed in a jeep ambulance and driven to the CCP. At the CCP I would examine the patient, stabilize him and then have him placed in the Army Service Corps box ambulance and send him to the Advanced Dressing Station or, in our area, to the Norwegian Mobile Army Surgical Hospital (MASH), or to a United States military hospital in Korea. The most serious were flown to Japan. On many occasions the more seriously wounded came direct to the CCP because I could have them evacuated by helicopter.

The whole subject of casualties always gets into the area of statistics and the mortality rate. In the Second World War the rate was 66 per 1,000 wounded soldiers. In Korea the rate dropped to 34 per 1,000. Keith explained, "This was no doubt due to faster transportation by air of casualties, the advent of better drugs and antibiotics and quick access to surgical and medical treatment."

One night at midnight, after intense shelling, an ambulance was readied for the trip to 25 Field Ambulance with casualties.

> One casualty was an R22eR officer I knew. I spoke to him just before the ambulance left. I felt a tap on my back. I looked into the lower stretcher

The first Chinese soldier to surrender (at right) to the Royal Canadian Army Medical Corps outside Keith Besley's CCP.

and there was the little fellow with the chest pains! He said, "You can't send me back now, Sir." He had a big sucking chest wound. Thank goodness he made it! He was pleased to have been wounded!

That night the R22ᵉR had many fatal casualties who never went further back than the CCP.

Keith described the CCP: "I had twenty-six men with me. There was an RCAMC Sergeant to supervise the medical team and an RCASC Sergeant to organize the eleven drivers and their ambulances. One very young stretcher bearer was Les Pike [in 1994, the President of the Korean Veterans Association, Ottawa Chapter]."

One morning at the CCP, Keith was shaving when he "sensed something". He turned, and there was a Chinese soldier, complete with weapon. The soldier said something in Chinese, threw down his weapon and put up his hands. Keith called for help and one of the orderlies came and took the prisoner away. Said Keith, "That was the first prisoner-of-war captured by the RCAMC!"

Captain Keith Besley was awarded a Mentioned in Despatches for his service in Korea. The Eastern nation was a valuable training ground for this front-line doctor, who had had just six months' training after passing his exams at the University of Toronto. It was the place to make a difference between life and death. Friendships forged with JADex (General Jacques Dextraze), for instance, continued until just hours before the General died in the National Defence Medical Centre in 1993.

When Keith returned to Canada he went back to Toronto and St Michael's Hospital to complete his residency. Postings in Canada and in Europe saw his rank increase to Colonel and his responsibility grow and change. For twenty of his service years, he was also a clinical teacher in surgery at Ottawa University. In 1981 he became Chief Medical Officer for the Order of St John. Keith completed twenty-five years of military service as Chief of Urology at the National Defence Military Hospital, a position he held until his retirement in December 1985. He was knighted in 1985. Keith Besley is now retired. He and his wife Shirley live in Ottawa.

Lieutenant Colonel Jacques Dextraze in the front lines of Korea watching over his men.

NO WITHDRAWAL, NO PLATOONS OVERRUN, NO PANIC

When the Second World War ended, Jim Dextraze (JADex) left the Army and returned to be the Woodlands Manager for Singer Manufacturing Company. (For his World War Two story, see *Ordinary Heroes*.) Selecting the wood to be used in Singer sewing machines was a far cry from commanding men in battle, but it was a job with a real future: a move to Brazil to take over the South American operation was in the offing. But as JADex explained to me during an interview on February 8, 1993, all this changed when the Korean War erupted:

> In the summer of 1950, Canada had committed itself to send troops to Korea at the request of the United Nations. I don't know why the government and DND [Department of National Defence] decided to man the force for Korea the way they did, but one day I found out that it was going to affect me. I was in the woods when I was given a message by

radio from my wife that an important phone call had come in from Ottawa. I had not planned to come out of the bush for two or three days, but I came out that night. My wife Frances had her ideas of what it was all about. Frances said, "You have to talk to Guy about the Korean operation." Next morning I contacted Guy Gauvreau [wartime CO and Brigade Commander]. Frances said nothing — but she is a "soldier's wife" always ready for sudden changes. Guy and I met at the golf club at LaChute. I told him, "They must be crazy in Ottawa to want me after the way I was treated in 1946." [At the end of the Second World War, JADex was offered a captaincy, junior to all Permanent Force captains in the Infantry; at that time he was a Lieutenant Colonel with two DSOs.] I was not good enough at the end of the war, and now they wanted me to raise a French Canadian battalion for Korea. Two days later Paul Sauvé, a minister in the Quebec government [also a wartime CO] called me and said, "Jim, you have got to go, for we have so few French Canadians in the service and you are the one I put all my trust in. You are the one who will do the right job and we'll do our share and keep our reputation." Frances hated them all! We had three childre and a nice home and we were happy where we were.

I decided to go to Ottawa to see Brooke Claxton, the Minister of National Defence. I arrived by company plane, straight from the bush, and at the meeting was Lieutenant General Simonds, the Chief of the General Staff, and Major General W.H.S. Macklin, the Adjutant General. The Minister explained what he wanted of me and we discussed my treatment in 1946 — he knew it all. Macklin explained that the selection of officers would be done in a certain way by Army Headquarters. Simonds, whom I admired in every way, was amused when I told Macklin, "We'll discuss this outside the Minister's office." Simonds had a glint in his eye, for he knew me and knew the conversation would be stormy. I made sure everyone knew how pleased I was with my Singer Company job, but Brooke Claxton said that they had been in touch with Singer and Singer knew why the government wanted me. Singer was mad as old hell, for they had invested in me for five years and entrusted me with 1,500 men in their woods operation.

Once the decision had been made for JADex to raise the battalion of the Royal 22nd Regiment (R22ᵉR), he made it clear to everyone at Army Headquarters that he was interested in just his unit, not the rest of the Brigade. He also insisted that he and he alone would select the officers — his way: "All majors would be selected from captains who had wartime experience. Captains would be selected from senior lieutenants with wartime experience, and the subalterns (lieutenants) could be green as grass. I would then train my officers *my* way."

Macklin was not amused: "Here you are just coming back in and already you are laying down the law."

JADex stood up. "I have had my word and obviously you don't need a guy like me." There was a lot of noise from the General, but JADex was firm. "In the end," he said in our interview, "I got what I wanted." JADex immediately began forming his battalion. One officer who had served with JADex in the Second World War, Gilles Lamothe, was serving in the office of the Minister of National Defence. JADex promptly promoted him to major and made him a company commander.

The family disruption began with Frances moving from her grand home to a two-bedroom apartment in Montreal, but "she never complained". In Valcartier, JADex was working against the clock, selecting and training his officers. Lieutenant Colonel L.F. Trudeau of 1 R22ᵉR was given the essential task of training all the other ranks. Luckily, most of the older men had wartime experience, some with JADex in the Fusiliers Mont-Royal. As he explained, "I could not train the men in the short time I'd been given, so I decided to train the officers. I did not have to reject any once I had selected them. The lieutenants were direct from the Infantry School; they wanted to join with me. They were so keen."

Once the training was over the 2 R22ᵉR left by train "on 11 November, 1950, with 14 officers and 267 other ranks". The remainder would soon follow, and then it was time for sub unit training. As JADex explained, "We had time for platoon and some company training but no time for battalion exercises." JADex continued, "Brigadier General Rockingham was a tough Brigade Commander, but he was good. He was demanding but he knew what he wanted."

2 R22ᵉR travelled to Korea by ship. After only a few days for the men to become fit "running up and down mountains", 25 May saw JADex's unit join with 2 RCR (Royal Canadian Regiment) on Operation Initiate. JADex's 2 R22eR "made contact during the day with a small force ... north of Hill 329". Two days into action saw the Canadians on line "Kansas", but the advance did not stop there; by the end of the month the Canadians had reached their objectives.

The first casualty lists showed six killed and fifty-four wounded from the entire brigade (2 PPCLI rejoined the Brigade on 27 May 1951). When speaking of casualties, JADex recalled a young officer (Carrier) who was killed [20 July 1951] while just doing his job. "I carry his picture with me in my mind. I got attached to them all, you know."

After a few weeks in action JADex realized that the weeks of training in Canada and Fort Lewis, Washington, were paying off. Strong personalities like Charlie Forbes were like a rock (JADex used him a lot to train the young officers). Luckily, the unit was broken into the routine gradually, for there was no chance to learn from anyone about fighting in Korea. Once General Rockingham made his plan and had given his orders, it was up to the units to get on with the battle.

JADex recalled the assistance he received from Jim Quinn's Armoured squadron:

> On one operation we were moving up a steep hill, clearing out the Chinese. I said to Jim, "Tank guns are so accurate that I want them to fire into the enemy dugouts just ahead of my advancing infantry." He agreed, and the advance moved forward. Lieutenant J.P.A. Therrien was commanding the left forward platoon. The tanks were getting their orders from Jim Quinn and the tank gunfire was just forty to fifty yards ahead of the infantry.

Herbert Wood wrote of Therrien in *Strange Battleground*: "[He] led his men up the hill with such vigour that the enemy fled their defences, leaving sixteen dead behind them." A Military Cross was awarded to this young R22^{e}R Lieutenant. JADex's closing remark on the incident was, "Those tankers were good. They could hit a dime with their tank guns."

During the Second World War, JADex had been saved time and time again by timely, accurate artillery fire. Korea was no different. Artillery targets had to be engaged promptly and with such force that the Chinese would be stopped. JADex watched every action and injected his wishes by radio at the appropriate time: "One thing you have to understand is that I am a meddler." He influenced the battle by using supporting fire, shifting his own support weapons' fire as the battle developed. Of Tony Bailey, the Commanding Officer of the Artillery, JADex said, "He was a first-class gunner, one of the best I've ever known. What he wanted he got; what I needed I got."

When asked if any one person deserved praise but was never recognized, JADex's answer was prompt — "Yes. Lieutenant MacDuff":

> He was a very brave young officer. On one occasion when D Company was in a left forward position, MacDuff had the left platoon. The Chinese overran the platoon and one of our sections left their position. MacDuff rallied several soldiers from the in-depth section and led them forward and drove the Chinese back. The odds were too great, but this powerful, brave officer performed so well in battle.

An Oral History From Those Who Were There

Another officer who got in behind the enemy lines was Phil Plouffe. He was so close to the Chinese that JADex could hear the enemy talking nearby when Plouffe said over the radio, "I cannot talk any longer." Although highly recommended, neither of these two brave men received awards.

When comparing the Chinese to the Germans, JADex had one simple statement, "You cannot compare them. The Germans were masters of war, whereas the Chinese used sheer numbers to overwhelm us."

On November 22, 1951, 2 R22ᵉR was in a position on Hill 210 between the Second Battalion of the 7th US Infantry Regiment on their right and 1 PPCLI (who had arrived only two weeks before) on their left. This battle was to be one of constant action. The UN forces repulsed wave after wave of attacks. Many courageous acts were attributed to numerous fine officers and men. When asked how he wanted his unit to perform, JADex answered, "In a typical Van Doos manner — no withdrawal, no platoons overrun, and no panic." He was confident in his unit's ability to perform that way:

> My rules in the defence were simple. At night no one moved out of his trench. There were 12 grenades and 3 bandoliers of ammunition in every trench and all weapons were fully manned from last light [darkness] to first light [dawn]. Anything that walked above the ground was a Chinese or Korean enemy. When we were under attack and the enemy was on top of our positions, we used every weapon to defeat them. We lived! We could bring down our own artillery on top of our own trenches, have machine-guns fire along the top of our trenches but we lived to fight another day.

Despite the intervening years, JADex's memories of Korea were crystalline. He recalled one patrol vividly:

> I sent [Lieutenant J.J. Paradis] on patrol and, as I said earlier, I'm a meddler, so I started to direct the patrol by radio. I knew that the return trip wasn't going to be easy. I told J.J., "You are going to follow what I'm going to tell you to do. We shall box you in with artillery concentrations to protect your patrol." I knew every inch of the ground, and I knew where the shells had to land. It took a couple of hours. The report lines on the map were Jackie, Bobbie and Dickie [JJ reported by radio each time he crossed the lines]. These were my sons' names.

When asked about coming home to Canada in December 1951, JADex smiled and said, "Mike Brennan, Senior Appointments in Ottawa, had come to Korea and we had discussed my future. Staff College was a must, and the course started in January 1952 and was a year in length." Frances moved with him to Kingston, and from that day on she retained control of the family finances plus everything else, for JADex knew that there would be many separations in the future. Said JADex, "The sacrifices my wife made for us! Many times I think of what an outstanding woman she is — sticking by the old man all those years in the Army."

The interview closed with a serious reflection of Canada's knowledge of its military: "Too often the understanding of Canadians in war has come from TV programmes where the Germans looked like the victors and we looked like damn fools [he was referring to "The Valour and the Horror"]. The important thing to remember is that the enemy was good but so were we, and we did win the war."

JADex commanded the School of Infantry and was the United Nations Chief of Staff in the Congo [he was made a Commander of the Order of the British Empire with an added Oak Leaf Cluster for gallantry]. He commanded the Brigade in Petawawa and was Chief of Personnel in Ottawa. In 1972, Prime Minister Pierre Trudeau promoted JADex to General and appointed him as Chief of the Defence Staff. When JADex left the Army he became Chairman of Canadian National Railways. In *We Stand on Guard*, John Marteinson states, "JADex has a well-deserved place among Canada's soldiers. ... A soldier's soldier, he readily inspired confidence in those who served under him". No truer words have ever been written.

General Jacques Dextraze died on May 9, 1993, at age 73 after a long battle with cancer. His widow, Frances, lives in Ottawa.

Don Rochester as a Colonel, Base Commander of Canadian Forces Chilliwack, British Columbia, 1966 – 67.

ROADS, BRIDGES AND FERRIES

Don Rochester was the Chief Instructor at the Royal Canadian School of Military Engineering, Chilliwack, British Columbia, when the news of Canadian participation in Korea was first made known. At once he volunteered, but was told the Active Force would not be going. Rather, the new Special Force would be sent.

Some weeks later, Don was called into the School Commandant's office to meet Brigadier John Rockingham, who told Don that he was to be the Engineer CO and to "pack a bag and fly back to Ottawa to plan for the Engineer Field Squadron". Don had Second World War experience in both Kiska and Northwest Europe (see *Fifty Years After*) and he had a good idea about what would be needed in the hills of Korea:

> This was a golden opportunity to organize the squadron as I felt it should be, particularly from the equipment point of view. I was sure that road building would be one of our prime tasks. Canadian squadrons, at that time, were designed for service in Europe and contained very little road-building equipment. The squadron was designed with three troops and a

KOREA VOLUNTEER

field park troop which would possess the heavy equipment that was necessary.

Don requested that all the vehicles for hauling be dump trucks. Most importantly, he insisted on having a crane with a backhoe to enable it to be used for loading road materials into the trucks. All the earth-moving equipment had tracks instead of wheels, making it easier to use on the Korean terrain. The unit had the option of acquiring British, Canadian or US equipment. Don chose explosive equipment from the U.S., but the water-supply equipment was standard Canadian Army issue. There was no bridging equipment, but the Squadron trained on U.S. equipment in Fort Lewis before going overseas.

With the wheels in motion for the procurement of equipment, Don returned to Chilliwack to recruit and train the men. That is when an event occurred that "came to plague the planner". As explained in *Strange Battleground*: "The non-operating employees of ... the Canadian National and the Canadian Pacific went on strike [on 22 August 1950]. ... The railway strike interrupted the process of sending recruits to Active Force Army camps across Canada."

In the case of Don Rochester's unit, only those engineers recruited in the West were able to go Chilliwack. The situation was so grave that, as stated in *Strange Battleground*,

> On 29 August, Parliament was recalled. After a very brief speech from the Throne the strikers were ordered back to work and less than two weeks later the Canadian Forces Act was passed. ... Cabinet now had the authority to place 15,000 of the regular forces on active service. ... Some 45 percent of the volunteers had seen service of some sort during the Second World War. ... As for specialists [like engineers], 20 percent of the new men had trades useful in the Army.

Don explained that the bulk of his rank and file (sappers) were new to the Army, but "a few tradesmen came from the Regular [Active] Force as did some NCOs and 50 per cent of the officers." To train his officers and men for the task that lay ahead, Don instituted a regime that included every night and weekend; there was no respite. He did a constant weeding out of the unsuitable, and by the time the squadron left for Fort Lewis, Washington, the unit was coming up to the standard Don knew they required. Said Don, "All these young men needed was a challenge and something to give them excitement. In Korea they got that and they applied themselves."

In Korea the Canadians would use U.S. equipment for bridging. It was decided that the training would be done in Fort Lewis, not that far from

53

An Oral History From Those Who Were There

Chilliwack. The first unit to go to the United States was 57 Independent Field Squadron (October 1950), followed later by the rest of 25 Brigade. The time spent in Fort Lewis brought the squadron up to full efficiency and it sailed for Korea, where it arrived in a time of frantic activity. Don recalled,

> We got our equipment and moved by road to the Seoul area. Unit commanders were flown ahead to the front to arrange for a takeover. My unit was not to be deployed in an engineering role but rather to replace a US infantry battalion in a defensive position a few miles to the east of Seoul. Before my squadron arrived by road the plan was changed, and we were deployed as a close bridge garrison at a railway bridge over the Han River. This meant we were to establish trenches and find positions for our weapons. We had a company of US anti-aircraft artillery and a US Marine Corps platoon with amphibious vehicles which would patrol the river. To provide them with security, the Canadian Mobile Laundry and Bath Unit was located at the bridge inside the defensive perimeter.

It was a busy time for Don. His first crisis was the accidental shooting of a US Marine by a Canadian sapper. It "took a while to smooth that out". The next event was a Chinese or North Korean raft coming down the river. It was loaded with explosives, which were to be set off under the bridge. The raft was captured by the Mobile Laundry and Bath Unit.

When the task at the bridge ended, Don's squadron headed north in support of the Brigade with an engineer troop in support of Bob Keane's 2 RCR and Jim Dextraze's Royal 22nd. The advance moved quickly until resistance caused the Brigade to consolidate. It was here that the road network ended and the Squadron was "required to build roads, mostly lateral ones to link up infantry locations". Don recalls, "There were two problems with roads. The terrain was mountainous and required a lot of cutting and levelling. Then there were the rice paddies, almost bottomless bogs which required tons of fill. Rock quarries were set up and all equipment was in full use." The use of light aircraft in the forward areas also required that landing strips be developed.

One major project was a bridge: "It was the Mr.5 John Labatt Anniversary bridge in recognition of the free beer sent to Korea by Labatt's in Canada. Labatt's altered their beer bottle label by printing a picture of the bridge on the inside of the label. The 50 on the label was also the tactical sign of the squadron.

Ferrying the Imjin River was the next task. The river was "quiet so it was no problem". The Chinese would "cut the ferry cable at night on their side of the river bank". Then the monsoons came with a twenty- to thirty-foot rise in the river level overnight. The river width went from 300 feet to over a mile wide. Don recalls, "We were caught with a 2 R22ᵉR patrol on the far side [enemy area]. The ferry was washed out and we could not extract them. The river was in full flood and filled with fast-moving debris. The Chinese would launch rafts loaded with rock to knock out the ferry. The R22ᵉR were stuck for several days."

57 Independent Field Squadron then moved to another part of the front on the Imjin River to do a "major task of road building". This event resulted in Don Rochester becoming the only Canadian Army major awarded the Officer of the Order of the British Empire (OBE) in Korea. The citation read, in part,

> A particular achievement was his organization of work for the construction of roads to the bridge site on the River Imjin, at the worst of the rainy season, over extremely difficult terrain, which had hitherto been considered impassable. This involved personal supervision, often in drenching rain, while his plant operations and men worked in shifts. [This] laid the foundations for the successful crossing of the Imjin River in the first week of September [1951].

Don remembers well the daily operations of the squadron: "We could move freely by day, but the nights belonged to the North Koreans and Chinese." One day on a road reconnaissance by scout car, Don's second sense made him stop below the crest of a hill. On foot he walked forward quietly. "A couple of hundred yards ahead was a Chinese infantry battalion." Luckily, the enemy was being engaged by Canadian infantry. Don "tiptoed back, got into the scout car and went back."

Don remarked that once the Commonwealth Division had been organized in July 1951, his unit became part of the Divisional Engineer Regiment. For the most part the system worked well. The excellent cooperation with the US Corps of Engineers continued, so the Canadians received superb support. Being part of 25 Brigade was a real bonus. In Don's words, "One of the delights of being under command of General Rockingham was that he was always available 24 hours a day. All I had to say over the radio was 'fetch Sunray', and he would pipe up. 'Sunray speaking.' I could get a decision on the spot [see also Ken Keir's story]."

Don also discussed the subjects of mines and booby traps. He described one event that will live forever in his memory. The event took place on 9 July 1951:

> I was going forward in my scout car to check on a demolition job. A sapper stopped me and said, "Come on this way. It's a short cut!" Major

J.P.L. "Goose" Gosselin of 2 R22ᵉR was behind me, and he remained on the road. His vehicle ran over a large parcel of explosives which was detonated by his scout car. Gosselin and two of his men were killed; two others were wounded. If I had not turned off the road I would have been killed. The night before the Chinese must have mined the road while we were inside our defensive perimeters.

Don Rochester left Korea in October 1951 and was posted to the Canadian Army Staff College in Kingston, Ontario. He served in many command and staff positions before retiring on the 8th of April, 1970. He commanded Canadian Base Unit Middle East at Rafah for two years and was the first commanding officer of the Canadian Airborne Regiment in Edmonton. Don Rochester is now living in Vedder Crossing (next door to CFB Chilliwack), where he is the minister responsible for the Anglican Church at Rosedale and, part-time, for the Cultus Lake Community Church.

Mac McLellan at age twenty-two at the gun position.

RIGHT OF THE LINE, FIRST ARTILLERY IN KOREA

Harold A. (Mac) McLellan's service in Korea was from 4 May, 1950, to mid June, 1951. He was twenty-two on arrival in Pusan with the 2nd Field Regiment Royal Canadian Horse Artillery (later designated 2 RCHA). They were the first Canadian Artillery in Korea. During his time in Korea he served as a gun position officer, spending occasional short periods as relief for the observation post officer or as liaison officer to supporting US Army Artillery units. Mac's story begins in Camp Shilo, Manitoba, when he was an officer cadet on a Command Contingent training course to qualify Canadian Army Reserve Force officers:

> I had been in the Reserves (31st Field Regiment RCA), Sarnia, Ontario, for the two years and was sent to Shilo on a course that was scheduled to end late November, 1950. One day in October on morning parade, our troop commander stated that the 2nd Field Regiment, which was then formed and in training in Shilo for service in Korea, was short of lieutenants. We were asked if we were interested in volunteering for service with the unit. Most volunteered. Shortly after we were interviewed by the CO of the 2nd Field Regiment, Lieutenant Colonel

An Oral History From Those Who Were There

A.J.B. Bailey, as a group and accepted. The course was immediately condensed, we were commissioned as lieutenants, were taken on strength of the unit, and were off on our embarkation leave within a matter of days. I was assigned to E Battery commanded by Captain S.M. [Sam] Pinkerton.

Before its arrival in Korea, the artillery suffered a tragic loss. In his book RCHA — *Right of the Line*, Major G.D. Mitchell wrote about the Canoe River train wreck:

> Late on the 19th [October], 2 RCHA departed on two trains bound for Fort Lewis. ... The trip on the first train was uneventful, but at 10:35 on the 21st the second train was met head on, just east of Canoe River, B.C., by a Vancouver/Montreal passenger train. In this tragedy the engines and coaches of both trains were derailed without casualties to the eastbound passengers.

In an interview in June 1944, Mac gave this eyewitness account of what he remembers of that fateful day:

> I had just visited E Battery Headquarters, which was in the first passenger car of the train, and was walking through the cars on my way to the officers' car, which was the last car. The collision happened just after I started down the aisle of the fourth car. I found myself on my back at the other end of the car. It felt and sounded like a very heavy "shunt" such as trains did in those days. I got to my feet and saw that one of the upper bunks had dropped due to the forces of the crash and struck one of the men on the side of the head. He was bleeding quite heavily but it did not appear to be serious. Then I heard someone shout in a loud voice, "Jesus Christ"! The train was on a curve skirting a mountain, so I could see ahead from a window. It was absolute chaos. Steam was rising from the tangled mess ahead, and I could see one of the cars resting crosswise on the car ahead of the one I was in. There was a mass of our men running forward, so I decided to organize some sort of first aid station in the car. I began instructing the gunners to make up bunks and collect more blankets and that sort of thing, in order to be ready for casualties, which would undoubtable soon begin arriving. About four hours later a rescue train with doctors and nurses from the Red Cross hooked into our train. We went first to Jasper, where we left the more seriously injured. We went to Edmonton with the remainder of the injured and finally to Camp Wainwright for reorganization. When we arrived at the railhead in Wainwright we marched to the quarters in the

bitter cold. Many of the troops were in shirtsleeves or without gloves, having lost their kit in the wreck. When we left Wainwright for Fort Lewis later in November the officers' car was behind the engine. No doubt that made the troops feel a little better.

In *Right of the Line*, Major G.D. Mitchell mentioned other details of the wreck:

> Seventeen fatalities and 42 injured... were treated by a doctor from Edson, Alberta. ... One coach was used for the injured and another as a morgue. One casualty was nearly sent to the wrong car. A young subaltern, seeing a stone-grey stretcher case going to the casualty car, bellowed out, "Take him to the morgue car, he's dead." The casualty suddenly sat bolt upright and screamed back, "Dead? Like hell I'm dead!"

The list of the Canoe River casualties (all gunners) is as follows: A. Atchison; W. Barkhouse; N. Carroll; F. Conway; R. Craig; A. George; U. Levesque; R. Manley; B. McKeown; A. Orr; D. Owens; L. Snow; A. Stroud; J. Thistle; J. Wenkert; J. White and W. Wright.

Mac's story continues:

> Most of the officers, almost all the non-commissioned officers and about half the other ranks had Second World War experience, although not necessarily artillery experience. After we had been in Korea for over three months, the Commonwealth Division was formed and we were then employed as divisional artillery. With us were the Royal Artillery and Royal New Zealand Artillery regiments. 2 RCHA was able to prove that it was 'second to none', when it came to speed and accuracy in getting rounds on the ground.

The equipment used by 2 RCHA was the tried and proven 25 pounder, which was towed by US-made 2-ton trucks instead of the Canadian gun tractor. The ammunition almost exclusively used was high-explosive point-detonating, however other fuses such as time and variable time proximity were also available, as was smoke and coloured smoke, which was often used to mark targets for close air support by aircraft. As Mac recalls, ammunition became a problem at times.

> Two of the regiment's guns were destroyed by rounds exploding in the breech, and now and then, but seldom, rounds exploded prematurely, that is, before they should have, such as just outside the muzzle. Rumour had it that some of the ammo delivered to us was dredged up from Hong

The 25-pounder that exploded. Sgt. V.K. Cornish at right was killed.

Kong harbour after being dumped there to avoid capture by the Japanese during the war.

Several months after the regiment's arrival in Korea, an E Battery gun was destroyed, killing Sergeant Vic Cornish and Gunner J. Wilson. It was believed that the explosion was not caused by faulty ammunition but by an equipment failure in the barrel of the gun. Days and weeks in action were long and hard but morale remained high despite the conditions. The troops realized that all the hard training in Shilo, Fort Lewis and Yakima had been worth it. On occasion Mac was sent out as liaison officer to US Army batteries whose personnel were not too familiar with Commonwealth terminology and procedures. One of these was the Persuaders as they called themselves. The battery was US Regular Army and was very efficient. As part of the Commonwealth Division, Mac remembered that the Americans proudly wore the Commonwealth Division UN blue shield with the crown and the word COMMONWEALTH embroidered on it.

Judging a unit from its time in action goes by many standards, but this quotation from Mitchell's book puts it all in perspective: "2 RCHA could indeed be proud of their record, over the year the unit had fired close to 300,000 rounds."

As this quote from Colonel G.W.L. Nicholson's *The Gunners of Canada* points out, the artillery paid a high price for its successes: "Of the 1,543 battle casualties in Korea the artillery lost one officer and eight men killed or died of wounds, two officers and twenty-five men wounded."

Mac's career took him to Germany, Palestine, Yemen and Indo China after his service in Korea. In 1983 Major McLellan retired from the Canadian Forces and was then employed as a civilian for four years with National Defence. He and his wife Monica live in Ottawa.

Sergeant Lorne Rodenbush, Korea, summer 1951.

WAIT FOR THE WAGON

Lorne Rodenbush's Army career began in August 1950 when he was the fifty-second person to enlist in the Special Service Force in Regina, Saskatchewan. "Although qualified to take officer training I decided to enlist as a private, for that was the quickest way to get to Korea. After basic training at Camp Borden I was slated to go for clerical training, but the clerk's course did not happen." This did not stop Private Rodenbush from fast advancement to the rank of Sergeant.

Arnold Warren described the formation of 54 Canadian Transport Company (CTC) in his book *Wait for the Wagon*:

> Authority was granted on August 5, 1950, to form the unit, the Army Service Corps component of the 25th Canadian Infantry Brigade Group. ... On August 11 the strength of the Company was two other ranks; [eleven days later] there were 319. ... Major R.C.D. "Bob" Laughton ... became the officer commanding. ... By October the unit had eleven officers and 378 other ranks. ... seventy percent of them were veterans[; some] came off civvy street.

Lorne was one of the civilians. In November the unit left for Fort Lewis, Washington, and Lorne's rise in rank began:

> I became the C platoon clerk under a Lieutenant Roger Flynn and became a Lance Corporal. I was transferred to the Supply and Transport office under Captain Doug Johnson. Some 75 days later I was promoted to Corporal and eight days later I was promoted to Sergeant and moved to the senior NCO [non-commissioned officer] club. Needless to say the Company Sergeant Major Tug Wilson was not impressed with this wet-behind-the-ears 90-day wonder.

Bob Laughton had his unit go through its paces in Fort Lewis. The Company War Diary tells the tale:

> They could
> a) move a platoon from a main road into a platoon area in 2 min.,
> b) move all platoon vehicles into sections in 5 min.,
> c) camouflage all vehicles in 10 min., and
> d) have slit trenches dug, weapon pits manned, guards posted, orders issued, alarms tested and defence plan submitted to Company Headquarters in 35 min.

54 CTC was a no-nonsense unit, ready to fulfil its role in Korea. It is just as well, for when the USNS *Marine Adder* arrived in Pusan at 0830 hours on May 4, 1951, the men of the Royal Canadian Army Service Corps (RCASC), expecting to disembark last, were surprised to hear a call over the ship's loudspeaker: "Will the officer commanding 54 Transport Company report to the ship's office." Bob Laughton received his first Korean assignment: transport the men and equipment of 25 Canadian Infantry Brigade from the port to the concentration area (see Charlie Hamilton's story). So within just minutes of setting foot in Korea, 54 CTC was at work. By late that night, they had moved the 2,000 men of the Brigade and their equipment into their respective unit areas.

The problems encountered by 54 CTC were numerous. Lorne mentions one:

> The availability of both USA and British supply lines was a double-edged sword. ... We had to draw ammunition from both systems to meet the demand. During Company moves, which were rather frequent in the early days, the additional holdings of ammunition gave rise to double handling and turnaround of vehicles, all of which added substantially to my duties as NCO responsible for tasking.

Another difficulty is described in *Wait for the Wagon*:

> The job presented a number of unique problems. One of these was the fantastic diversity of ammunition natures ... something like 312 of them, including explosives, mines and pyrotechnics, a mixed bag of United States and United Kingdom natures — and it was not sufficient for 54 Transport Company merely to carry it. It was also essential that the men should know what they were carrying. This involved a program of education.
>
> Major Laughton arranged for a big tent to be erected at the Company location. The men called it Loblaw's, and in it was placed every ammunition nature in its container. A master recognition chart was prepared, and for days the men spent their spare time going through in groups, identifying the natures, getting accustomed to the pack, and learning to recognize them by feel, as at night. They organized identification names and competitions, and worked at it until they reached a high degree of proficiency.

The lessons learned in the Second World War about the use of 25-pounder artillery ammunition had to be relearned in Korea. Warren's *Wait for the Wagon* explains:

> Perhaps the main difference was the rapidity with which the enemy could mount a "ganging" attack. One moment the front would be perfectly quiet. The next moment all hell would break loose. The United Nations forces learned very quickly that the best way to break up these ganging attacks was with lots of artillery, sometimes as much as 200 rounds per gun. In World War II, this rate of expenditure would have been preceded by an ammunition dumping program. In Korea, 200 rounds per gun might be ordered at any moment.

This unpredictability meant that ammunition had to be kept in trucks well forward to enable the artillery simply to order trucks to come forward as needed.

When it was time for a relief in the line, the new Infantry units were trucked forward by the RCASC. These movements in the forward area used to cause attacks, and fast reaction, from both Chinese artillery and mortars. Lorne explained, "We did not stay in one place for long as we came under fire." In *Wait for the Wagon*, Arnold Warren goes into detail of how this was done:

> Usually the Chinese could be counted on to attack when our infantry troops were in the process of being relieved or shortly after the arrival of

replacement units. Apparently they counted on a certain amount of mild confusion existing at such times, and it seemed obvious that the presence of 54 Transport Company troop carriers in the forward area gave them the tip-off. So, during periods when the enemy displayed a reluctance to make contact, the Brigade Commander adopted an ingenious plan to draw him into the open. This involved the employment, among other things, of two transport platoons in a highly organized troop lift, without troops. It was known as Operation "Big Switch."

Whenever orders were received to carry out Operation "Big Switch" all available unit drivers manned the vehicles and an assortment of Korean porters, interpreters, pot wallopers, and house boys played the role of passengers, like so many extras in a Hollywood production. The convoy would proceed in the general direction of Seoul, pick up mythical replacements, and then move directly to the forward location of the particular battalion selected to participate in the deception. On arrival, engines were raced, vehicle tail gates dropped with abandon, doors slammed, and much loud talk and laughter encouraged.

After a reasonable interval, the convoy moved to a prearranged assembly area in the rear. On the down route, drivers might lead their Korean passengers in a ragged chorus or two of "Hail, Hail the Gang's All Here," and "Road to the Isles," in order to convince enemy observers along the main supply route that Canadian troops were being relieved. Usually the Chinese were unable to resist the opportunity of catching the incoming replacements off balance. They would launch a spirited attack, only to be met and repelled by seasoned troops from well established positions.

As the war in Korea progressed, there came to be a demand for more and more officers, not just for the infantry but for all corps. Lorne explains how he was selected for officer training:

> The notion to apply for officer training came from Captain Doug Johnson, my boss. Because scholastic records were not readily available, those applying — over 250 if I recall correctly — had to write a series of exams. COs then recommended, and some fifty went before a board consisting of Major Whiticar, Charlie Hamilton, Jim Stone, I think JDex and Major Jim Quinn. Later Quinn just about ended my chance to become an officer. The five of us returning for officer training hitched a ride by air to Japan rather than take the train to Pusan and boat to Japan as our orders dictated. Major Quinn, by this time serving in Japan, was not amused by our actions. Back to the selection process! The board recommended 18.

Then came a one-on-one interview with Brigadier Rockingham. I recall his asking me why I wanted to become an officer. I'm not sure how I answered except I know I didn't say to get home, which probably was a major reason for applying. I think the Brigadier recommended about a dozen, and Army Headquarters reduced the number to six. Five entered the Officer Candidate School in Camp Borden.

Lorne had served in Korea from May 8 to early September 1951. When asked whether Korea was the highlight of his career, he pondered a challenging and interesting thirty-plus years: a dozen ranks, serving royalty and prime ministers, doing arms control and protocol in Vietnam, Rome, Vienna and Brussels. He finally answered,

> Although it was Korea that launched my military career it was not the war that was the most memorable involvement. The most noteworthy experience is not public knowledge. In fact, those involved would deny even more than thirty years after the event that it took place. It was a United States Army expedition. It happened in early May 1960. A pilot by the name of Gary Powers had the misfortune of being shot down in a U2 reconnaissance plane over Soviet territory the very day the exercise that I was involved in, Exercise Pole Hop, landed the first single-engine airplane on the North Pole. With Soviet scientists conducting experiments on an ice flow in the vicinity of the Pole, it was an easy decision for President Eisenhower to remove a day from the lives of the Pole Hop explorers rather than add to his problems with Khrushchev.

After Korea, Lorne Rodenbush took officer training and was commissioned in the RCASC. He became a pilot of both fixed wing aircraft and helicopters and commanded 450 Helicopter Squadron for almost four years. In 1980 he retired and went into business. He is currently the Honorary Colonel of 450 Squadron. Lorne and his wife Vivian live in Perth, Ontario.

Father "Bill", Order of Canada, CD. Chaplain at Ste Anne de Bellevue Veterans Affairs Hospital, 1994.

FROM AN ORDERED-AROUND PRIVATE TO THE ORDER OF CANADA

Bill McCarthy of Montreal enlisted in the Special Force on August 16, 1950. He had served in the Royal Montreal Regiment for two years, so when he was posted to Camp Petawawa he was made the A Company clerk. Bill recalls some of those early days:

> Very few beat the system. Everyone had to take general military training and by the time we left for Korea everyone was well qualified, slackers were not accepted. Thirty per cent of the regiment were Second World War soldiers. I was very proud to have made the big team in Second Battalion, The Royal Canadian Regiment [2 RCR].
>
> We had one very bad accident in Petawawa. Defective mortar ammunition exploded, and we lost men killed and wounded. I gave blood at the Pembroke hospital for some of the wounded.

The situation in Korea was not clear. For a while it looked as if the RCR and R22ᵉR battalions in Fort Lewis might not go to Korea, but that all changed:

An Oral History From Those Who Were There

"One morning on parade we were told we were going, and everyone cheered and cheered." Under the command of Lieutenant Colonel R.A. Keane, 2 RCR served in Korea from 15 April 1951 to 25 April 1952. Just twenty days after arrival, 25 Brigade was ready to go into action. In *Strange Battleground*, Herb Wood reports,

> The Brigade moved off at 9:30 a.m. on 25. ... No opposition was encountered until mid afternoon, when the leading elements ... were fired on by a small party of enemy on Hill 407. ... The advance was to resume on the 30th with the 2nd RCR replacing 2nd R22eR on the right. Since Kakhul-bong dominated the RCR axis of advance, a plan was made to put in a battalion attack on this feature, and the village of Chail-li that lay beyond it. ... Major R.D. Medland's A Company was to push rapidly ... and capture Chail-li.

Private Bill McCarthy was Major Medland's runner at Company Headquarters. Bill remembers the Chail-li event very well:

> We learned we were to attack in the morning. We got ready; rations and ammunition were issued and put into our small packs and the pouches on our web belts. We moved out in a driving rainstorm. We got to Chail-li easily but it was tough slogging. We saw our first enemy, prisoners moving toward the rear. I was the Company runner, and one of my jobs was to keep an eye on our Korean translator in case he was needed. The experience of this action was tremendous as I ran from Company HQ to the platoons. I ran like a deer that day. There was confusion with the location of the enemy. I went forward to tell the exposed members of A Company to take cover. One said, "They can't shoot me." I screamed at him, and he jumped into a trench as a hail of bullets hit where he had been standing. We were about to throw grenades when Skinny said, "Stop! Hold your fire!" Out came one old fellow plus women and children. Skinny said, "My God, I would have regretted that for the rest of my life." I was so proud of my pals that day.

Company Sergeant Major (CSM) Fuller came forward to replenish the platoon's ammunition. The requirements were made known to the runner, who gave the CSM the information. Now A Company was to withdraw. Bill says, "It was then that Private J.A. Sargent distinguished himself by the skill and courage which he displayed handling the Bren gun while covering the Company withdrawal." (Sargent was awarded the Military Medal.)

Bill remembers the tanks from C Squadron of the Strathconas: "We saw the enemy mortars all around them. While there is no doubt the tanks saved us that day they did draw fire, and that terrified us. When we got to a safe area we got close to the tanks and the exhaust from their engines dried us out. The tank crew gave us chocolate bars to eat."

That night the soldiers of A Company were on an exposed hillside south of Chail-li. Those who managed to sleep dreamt of Chinese soldiers seeking them out in a counterattack. Herb Wood's *Strange Battleground* describes the situation:

> The RCR attack was failing; A Company was in a fair way to being surrounded, D Company was pinned on the rocky slopes of Kakhul-bong, while C Company, between A and D, had found its fire could not reach the enemy moving against the other two companies. ... 2RCR lost six NCOs and men killed, 2 officers and 23 men wounded.

Bill's final thoughts on Chail-li are these: "In retrospect, the air support we needed never came, and the US Artillery support we depended on never came where and when we needed it. We were relying upon our battalion support weapons and they did not have the range."

Bill McCarthy was chosen to go to Uijongbu for the Junior NCO course. These are his words about it:

> It was a good respite from the war, the place to learn leadership skills. We learned all about leading infantrymen in battle. We not only upgraded our skills, but passing the course gave us an upgrade in pay. Being a Royal meant that upkeep of kit, dress and deportment had to be the best. The course was a good morale booster. At the section level friends became closer than brothers; we had pride and respect for each other. In the unit, Pete Taylor was our platoon commander; we were his and he was ours!

It is interesting to hear a former soldier's view on the fighting soldier of Korea. The Special Force got the odd "black eye" in the history of the Korean war but, Bill said, "We were melded and moulded together; 25 CIB was a truly effective fighting machine. One former Commander said, 'The men, they were magnificent!'"

Personally, I hope that this book explodes some myths and corrects some imbalances about Special Force achievements despite the odds.

An Oral History From Those Who Were There

Bill McCarthy returned from Korea in May 1952 and took his release, returning to Canadian National Railways as a brakeman. In 1956, Bill entered the Montreal Diocesan Theological College. Four years later he was ordained. Bill spent three years as a parish priest in Roxboro, Quebec. He then spent the next thirty years as the Director of the Old Brewery Mission in Montreal, during which time he was the padre of the Leclerc Penitentiary for three years. He also served as the padre of the Royal Canadian Hussars. Today, Bill is the priest for Ste Anne de Bellevue Veterans Affairs Hospital. This former runner for 2 RCR has lost both his legs to complications of diabetes. He closes his story by saying, "42 years after Korea, my buddy Moe Mulholland, who lived in the same trenches with me, twice a week picks me up at the hospital and drives me to my home." A remarkable man and humanitarian, Bill McCarthy received a justly deserved Order of Canada in 1984.

Hugh Hutton, Liaison Officer at 25 Brigade Headquarters.

LIAISON OFFICER AT BRIGADE

Hugh Hutton was a lance corporal with the Queen's Own Cameron Highlanders at the battle of Dieppe during the Second World War. As a sergeant, he was chosen for officer training in Brockville, Ontario. After the training at Brockville and a stint as an instructor, he rejoined his regiment in Holland in 1945 as the war came to an end.

Hugh took his release in 1946 in Hamilton, Ontario, but four years later he volunteered to go to Korea. Lieutenant Hutton was posted to the Second Battalion The Royal Canadian Regiment (2 RCR) and, in due course, was chosen by Lieutenant Colonel Bob Keane to be a Brigade Liaison Officer in Fort Lewis, Washington. For his wife Dorothy and young daughter to be able to join him that winter, "We had to sell the family car to pay for the train ticket." Dorothy and their daughter returned to Hamilton when the news came that the Brigade was to leave for Korea.

On the final march past before leaving for Korea, a memorable mistake was made by the US military band:

> As the R22ᵉR under the command of Lieutenant Colonel J.A. Dextraze approached the saluting base, the band started to play "Wait for the

Wagon", the Royal Canadian Army Service Corps march, instead of the Royal Twenty-Second Regiment march. Lieutenant Colonel J.A. Dextraze just marched his men off the square in disgust!

One of Hugh's first memories of the Brigade's arrival in Korea was Brigadier John Rockingham's decision to toughen up his soldiers by having them run and walk up the sides of mountains. On 30 May 1951, Hugh Hutton moved out with 2 RCR to keep the Brigadier informed of the Unit's progress in battle using the wireless in the Liaison Officer's jeep:

> The first battle was at a place called Chail-li. I was at Lieutenant Colonel Keane's headquarters. The unit performed well in battle and, from where I was, I felt the CO was doing a fine job. One day the CO, Major Jim Quinn, the Armoured Squadron CO and I were sitting at the edge of a rice paddy–the Chinese shells were getting closer and closer. Jim Quinn said, "Just like the big war, isn't it?" With people like that — cool in battle — we could do no wrong, and we didn't.

On another occasion Hugh was sent to a site on a river where a Chinese floating explosive charge had taken out a small bridge. The engineers were putting the bridge back into shape after dark. One sapper carrying a full sandbag called out, "Hey, Corporal! Where do you want me to put the sandbags?" In the dark there was a loud whisper, "Don't call me Corporal! Don't you know these Chinese are looking for us leaders?"

Another incident occurred when a group of politicians from Ottawa was visiting the Brigade Headquarters officers' mess. The Chinese started to shell close by, and Hugh found himself on the floor behind the mess piano along with a newspaper man, Bill Boss. When the Brigade Signals Officer left the mess tent to go back to his own tent he discovered it had taken a direct hit from a Chinese mortar shell. His kit was strewn everywhere and there was a crater where his tent had been.

Captain Hugh Hutton took over as Camp Commandant at Brigade Headquarters, where he was responsible for siting the tents and vehicles at the headquarters. He did this until he returned home to Canada. Of Brigadier General John Rockingham, he says, "He was a good commander who instilled confidence in everyone."

Hugh spent the remainder of his days in the Army working with Army Cadets in Central Command, Oakville, Ontario. When he retired, he went to work for the Hamilton Board of Education for over thirteen years. Hugh and his wife Dorothy spend their winters in Florida and their summers in Canada.

Lou Seguin at age twenty-three in Fort Lewis, Washington.

IN SEARCH OF ADVENTURE

Laurent (Lawrence) Seguin was twenty-three years old in 1950 and living in Valleyfield, Quebec, when he decided to join the Special Force for eighteen months to go and fight in Korea. Why? "For adventure and to see that part of the world."

He had been in the Merchant Navy, working for Imperial Oil in 1946 and in 1948 sailing from New York City to Aruba, West Indies. His subsequent job in carpentry did not give him the kind of challenge that Lawrence was looking for, and that is when he joined the Royal 22nd Regiment in Valleyfield. He was to begin a totally new life of regimentation, following orders and learning new skills.

The First Battalion was training the other ranks for the Second Battalion (see J.A. Dextraze's story) in Valcartier, Quebec, where Lawrence began his training in September 1950. After Christmas the battalion was moved to Fort Lewis, Washington, and Private Seguin was assigned to D Company as a rifleman in a platoon. It was here that the reasons for weapon training and field craft should have started to make sense, but to Private Seguin it seemed that the rush to get overseas was the top priority. The sergeant and corporals

An Oral History From Those Who Were There

thought there would be time to sort things out once they were in Korea.

The move of the Battalion to Japan and on to Korea was through some very rough weather. Lawrence's Merchant Navy experience stood him in good stead, for he was one of the few soldiers who was not seasick on the journey.

At this stage of his training Lawrence was proficient with the .303 Lee Enfield rifle, the Bren light machine-gun and grenades. He also knew how to dig field defences, string barbed wire and go on day and night patrols. Frequent personnel changes in the Company meant that Lawrence made no close friends, but he still remembers

> going out to the observation posts or listening posts at night. There would be three of us and we had to remain out of sight, wide awake, and never take our eyes away from the enemy positions to our front. It was very scary. Our time on duty was four to five hours at a time but seemed at least twice as long. We saw and heard all kinds of things that were not there — there is always the fear of the unknown. The imagination plays tricks on you.

These young soldiers had every reason to be scared, for the enemy infantry soldiers were masters of infiltrating the United Nations lines to snatch or kill unwary soldiers who let their vigilance drop even for a second.

The 2nd Battalion's first encounter with the enemy came three weeks after their arrival on May 4, 1951. Herb Wood's *Strange Battleground* records that on May 25th, "The Royal 22^e also made contact during the day with a small force immediately north of Hill 329. At last light both battalions [2 RCR was the other] occupied tight defensive positions north of Changgo-ri."

Private Seguin had found out what adventure was in that part of the world! He comments, "I weighed just 115 pounds and was carrying that weight upon my back, up and down hills, hour after hour." He remembers an attack when a hill was taken and then "coming back down again because of the enemy counterattack." He also remembers the enemy attacks at night and early morning when their shells filled in the trenches and the "ground just shook when the shells and mortar rounds landed".

Events in early summer would see Private Seguin out of the front lines for ever. He explains: "My hearing got very bad from the shelling and was made worse by sleeping on the wet ground. At the hospital in Korea the doctors said I had to go to Japan to see a specialist. Once there my problems [deafness in one ear] could not be repaired and I was flown to Vancouver by the RCAF in a North Star." By this time, Lawrence was happy to be leaving Korea, "for I wondered why I was there. Much of what I was doing did not make a lot of sense." His adventures in a far-off land were not what he had expected, perhaps because he had never had a chance to make that critical bond with his fellow riflemen.

When Lawrence returned to Montreal, "We were interviewed six at a time in the Personnel Depot, and when I said no to being a paratrooper I was placed on general duty. In March 1952 I was released from the Canadian Army." The release medical assigned Lawrence was an H4 or H5 — a loss-of-hearing category.

Lawrence Seguin moved to Ajax, Ontario, six months after he left the Canadian Army. He worked for MacMillan Bathurst corrugated paper mill for 33 years, retiring in 1992. He and his wife Kathe are now retired and living in Ajax, Ontario.

An Oral History From Those Who Were There

Ken Keir just prior to leaving for eighteen months in Korea.

ROCKY'S RADIO OPERATOR REMEMBERS

Ken Keir joined the Royal Canadian Signals in September 1949 after an unsuccessful attempt to join the RCAF as a pilot. He passed his basic training and trades course in Kingston, Ontario. After being posted to Active Force Brigade (Airborne Signals) and passing his Group (2) course, he volunteered for the Special Force and Korea. The Active Force was not keen to lose its tradesmen to the Special Force, but Ken and others were nevertheless sent to Fort Lewis, Washington, to join 25 Brigade Headquarters. Ken says, "We were equipped with the 19 and 52 radio sets, and we soon established a good communications set-up." March and April 1951 saw parades for Lieutenant General Simonds followed by one for Field Marshal Viscount Alexander of Tunis, Governor General, Prime Minister Louis St Laurent and Brooke Claxton, the Minister of National Defence.

On 19 April, Ken sailed on the USNS *Marine Adder* for Pusan, Korea. On arrival it took just two days for all the vehicles and stores to be landed. Ken was a lance corporal operating the Brigade frequency to the battalions. After six months, Ken replaced the Brigadier's radio operator. Ken was now to work very closely with John "Rocky" Rockingham, the Brigade Commander, riding in the back of his jeep operating the 19 set or the 52 set in the "M8". Ken carried out most of the radio procedures, but occasionally Rocky himself used the set. When Rocky, using his code name, said, "This is Sunray speaking," the receiving radio operator had better answer quickly.

Besides Ken and a driver, the General also used a Liaison Officer (LO), who rode in the back with Ken. Ken recalls, "He was hard on LOs but he treated me very well, and I had now reached the dizzy rank of Corporal." The General was a stickler for punctuality, so Ken made sure "we were always there for him ten minutes ahead of time." Brigadier Rockingham had a "nose for public relations. He could smell a press camera at fifty miles." He made sure that the Canadian Brigade always got the best press possible.

On one occasion Ken was alone in the jeep with an LO, who was driving. The LO had stopped on a bridge to talk to another officer when "a Chinese mortar shell landed just beyond us, then another just behind. We'd been bracketed! I told the LO in no uncertain terms it was time to get our ass off the road, and he did, just in time." Later the same day, they passed some Strathcona tanks stuck in a rice paddy off the road, mud up to the turrets. The crew had neutralized the guns and abandoned the tanks. As Ken and the LO passed close by, the Chinese started to shell the area. Ken and the LO jumped out and climbed under their vehicle till it was safe to emerge.

Ken remembers many of the Brigade staff officers. The Brigade Major, L.V. Perry, is remembered because he was "an excellent officer who got along well with the men and was easy to please and good to work with." One Unit CO whom Ken recalls with pleasure was Teddy McNaughton of the Artillery: "a real gentleman who even gave me a parting gift–which we drank before I left Korea."

An event that almost ended in disaster came when Ken and Jack Schlapback, a driver, were sent with a radio-equipped half-track to join an American Army Armoured column on a raid north of the 38th parallel. No one thought to put on aircraft recognition panels, so a Mustang strafed the column with machine-gun fire. Fortunately, he had dropped his napalm before he found the column. On the return trip Jack threw a track, and the Americans left them behind in never-never land. Jack and Ken got their vehicle mobile, but they still had to get back through the Royal 22nd lines. Their radio was not working, so they could not tell the infantry that it was a friendly tracked vehicle approaching. Fortunately, they made it through unscathed.

One day when Ken was using his radio in a cave under a Korean hill he read a letter from his father. In the envelope he father had tucked a second letter, this one from the RCAF. They were recruiting pilots, and his 1949 application had finally been accepted. Ken reflected that their timing was poor, to say the least.

After Brigadier Rockingham was rotated out, Ken was asked if he would stay on for six months as Brigadier Pat Bogert's radio operator. He agreed, and therefore spent 18 months overseas.

Ken showed me two of his favourite souvenirs from Korea. One was a Safe Conduct Pass from the Chinese People's Volunteers' Headquarters, offering safe conduct to anyone who wanted to defect. The pass offered

1. Security of life.
2. Retention of all personal belongings.
3. Freedom from maltreatment or abuse.
4. Medical care for the wounded.

The offer, which concluded, "lay down your weapon and come over to us", was written in perfect English script. The second piece of rice paper was a statement about officers captured in April 1951. Ken found both these notes in mailboxes in no-man's land.

Back home in Vancouver after his tour of duty, Ken was given seventy days' leave. Remembering his father's letter, he went to the RCAF recruiting office, where they rushed him through medical and exams before he said he was still in the Army. An Army officer at Work Point Barracks in Victoria released him on 12 September 1952, and Ken was free to join the RCAF.

As a pilot in the RCAF, Ken flew Dakotas, Harvards, Mitchells and Expeditors. He had one tour on Lancasters and two tours flying the Neptune. He flew with the Royal Australian Air Force on exchange and then flew the Argus, Tutor and the T33. In May 1980, after over 8,500 flying hours, Ken retired to Mill Bay, British Columbia, where he and his wife Billie lived for fourteen years. Ken was very active in the Malahat Branch of the Royal Canadian Legion in Cobble Hill; he was Zone Commander for Cowichan Mid-Island when he died of cancer in February 1994. His widow now lives in the British Columbia Interior.

Colonel Bob Purvis, Director of Armour, presents a scroll to Major Jim Quinn, Commanding Officer 1/2 Armoured Squadron, Camp Borden, Ontario.

THE FIRST ARMOURED SQUADRON

During a long interview on 16 November 1993, Jim Quinn, who was the first squadron commander in 25 Brigade, told me how the 1/2 Royal Canadian Armoured Corps Squadron was raised in Camp Borden, Ontario. This is the first time the full story has been published; therefore, for historical purposes, more detail is included in this account than in others in this book.

The designation 1/2 Royal Canadian Armoured Corps Squadron was given to recognize The Royal Canadian Dragoons and The Lord Strathcona's Horse. These two regiments, would provide the majority of squadron members for the Squadron and were designated as the First and Second Regiments respectively in the Canadian Armoured Corp Regular Force Order of Battle. Hence, "1/2".

The summer of 1950 saw Major Jim Quinn teaching tactics at Meaford, Ontario, when he was informed that he had been selected to raise a Squadron of armour for service in Korea:

> I had a free hand in my choice of officers, Squadron Sergeant Major [SSM] and Squadron Quartermaster Sergeant Major [SQMS]. I chose Captain Vic

Jewkes [wartime Royal Canadian Dragoons and 1st Hussars], Captain Ken Kennedy [former Indian Army Major, Central Indian Horse] and Lieutenants Glendinning, Corbiere, Wyant, Neelin, Macdonald and Debert [RCEME]. Finally there was SSM Jake Kennedy [former IVth Princess Louise Dragon Guards officer who had reverted in rank at the end of the Second World War]. Lots of people wanted to go to Korea but the ones selected were senior NCOs in the various teaching wings at the Armoured Corps School and officers who were at the School or who had just left for regimental duty. For equipment we were told we were to get the M10 an antitank gun with a limited-traverse 17-pounder, mounted on a tracked chassis with an open turret. This bit of news, together with our unit designation, quickly made us the brunt of many jokes when we were referred to as "The Half [½] Armoured Squadron". It should be understood that from the outset the Director of Armour and others set out to have the M10 replaced, as it was a Second World War artillery weapon system totally unsuitable to be used as a tank. The Minister of National Defence, Brooke Claxton — an old gunner — could not see the difference or that it mattered.

The Squadron came together quickly with many Second War veterans (regular and militia) plus some new soldiers who had just completed their trades training (gunnery, wireless and tracked vehicle driver). The SQMS was Staff Sergeant Doug Eveleigh. In Jim Quinn's words, it "was the nucleus of a first-class Squadron".

As soon as the Squadron had been formed and personal kitting completed, orders were received for the Squadron to concentrate with the Brigade at Fort Lewis, Washington. Tactical training and familiarization between units began under the Brigade staff. The advance party left immediately under Ken Kennedy, followed a few days later by the remainder of the Squadron. They shipped out by train from the Bog Road Station in Camp Borden. The M10 was issued in Fort Lewis and crew familiarization began immediately. Then followed tactical training with the battalions. The culmination was a series of Brigade exercises, and live firing was carried out at the Yakama Range.

The Squadron quickly learned that their commanding officer Jim Quinn was a no-nonsense soldier who ruled with an iron hand. His requirements for professional competence and strict discipline soon became well known. Those who failed to reach his standards could expect twenty-eight days' detention, with no time off for good behaviour. The twenty-eight day detention earned him the nickname of "February Quinn" from the soldiers. Jim has an interesting anecdote about the possible side effects of these forced periods of adjustment:

One of my soldiers, a tremendously hard-working individual, who was the armoured recovery vehicle driver, was an alumnus of the military prison in Korea. He served two periods of detention, twenty-eight days each time. When not working he could get into more trouble in an hour than any soldier I had ever seen. He would always find something to drink, and this was his downfall. About six years after our Korea experience I received a letter from this former soldier. He was now working for Euclid heavy equipment sales in the United States. He apparently had become a born-again Christian and had been agonizing for some time over all the trouble he had caused me in Korea. He just wanted to write to tell me and ask for my forgiveness.

In Fort Lewis the Armoured troops were to meet the other units and the Brigade Commander, John Rockingham. Jim says that "they were a mixed bag", as some units were still weeding out the men who should not go into action for a variety of reasons. It was in Fort Lewis that a friendship developed between Quinn and Jim Dextraze of 2 R22ᵉR. In Jim's words, JADex "was really a tough officer who was working his unit hard" (see the J.A. Dextraze story).

Along with commanding and training units, Jim Quinn and several other officers were studying for the Staff College entrance exams. As it turned out later, this extra effort to study while simultaneously preparing a unit for war was not required. Subsequently, all commanding officers in 25 Brigade who had not been staff trained were waived into the Staff College without writing entrance examinations.

In Fort Lewis, the Squadron trained in the field with the infantry using the M10. To say the crews were unhappy with the antitank vehicle would be an understatement. It was not a tank, and stories from Korea about mass assaults in which the enemy got through to tank positions and climbed onto the M10s created concern among the Canadians. Jim recalls one of his own efforts to get a different vehicle:

> The last major event before embarking was a parade for General Guy Simonds, Chief of the General Staff [CGS]. Afterwards the CGS spoke to each CO and I asked him for three things: a tank, a regimental affiliation for the Squadron, and the location and speeding up of the delivery of Squadron war establishment stores, binoculars and personal weapons known as the G1098.
>
> The CGS asked me what I recommended with respect to unit designation. Vic, Ken and I were all RCD [Royal Canadian Dragoons] but, on balance, we had as many Strathconas as RCDs. [Besides,] it would be easier

An Oral History From Those Who Were There

for us in Fort Lewis to liaise with [the Strathconas in] Calgary. This I recommended to the CGS, and that is how we became C Squadron, Lord Strathcona's Horse (Royal Canadians) [LdSH (RC)].

As soon as the CGS returned to Ottawa he had the requests for the unit title and the G1098 put into action. Soon, two complete sets of war establishment stores arrived. Major Quinn was authorized to proceed to Calgary to visit Lieutenant Colonel Gerry Chubb, CO of the Strathconas, and to pick up unit cap badges.

The business of the tank was resolved after the Squadron arrived in Korea. Active consideration was given to the Centurion and Patton tanks being used by the British and the Americans. The British Centurion tank was still under War Office control, meaning that its tactical deployment had to be restricted so that the Chinese could not capture them and gain information about the new fire control equipment. To make matters worse, the main Centurion tank repair depot was in Japan.

> The matter was resolved after discussion with the US Marine Corps, who spoke so highly of their Sherman tanks [M4A3] in Korea. We decided to wait no longer but to recommend they be purchased, the authority to buy thirty tanks having been received from Canada. The conversion was no problem, and our only concern was the radios, which we wanted changed to the Canadian 19 set.

The British tank regiment, 8th Hussars, wanted the Canadians to become a fourth Armoured squadron under their control. Quinn gave an adamant "No go", and despite repeated efforts Brigadier Rockingham blocked any further attempts. The Squadron was all set to go into action but still had no tanks. In a newsletter written by Ken Kennedy, this synopsis explains the situation in Korea on 11 May 1951:

> There was still no word about the delivery of the tanks. On the 14th word was received that the Brigade would go North without us but that the M4A3s would be ready for collection in 48 hours. On 16 May the Squadron was informed the tank trains were ready and on one hour's notice the Squadron would go to the US Ordnance workshop and take delivery of 16 M4A3 tanks. By mid day 17 May the Squadron was fully equipped, tank combat storage completed, the old M10s turned in, and on 19 May the two tank trains left for Suwon, south of Seoul. The next day the tank train arrived and the rest of the wheeled vehicles arrived by road, some 250 miles.

C Squadron was finally ready for action, and it was not long in coming. At 0730 hours on 25 May a general advance was ordered in the western sector. The newsletter outlines what happened:

> With the R22ᵉR were 2 Troop [Neelin], 4 Troop [Corbiere] and Major Quinn at battalion HQ. 3 Troop [Glendinning] was under command 2RCR. Captain Kennedy and Lieutenant MacDonald were in charge of the resupply echelons and Captain Jewkes and 1 Troop [Wyant] were in Squadron reserve. Contact was made in just two days. Almost at once the Squadron had its first casualty — Corbiere's tank ran over a mine!

The Squadron had done well. With the first-day jitters behind them, Jim Quinn led an Armoured patrol 15,000 yards across the 38 parallel into North Korea, looking for the Chinese. Four Chinese were captured and brought back on the back deck of the tanks; there was no sign of a large Chinese force.

As the days progressed each of the four troops went into action along with the infantry of the R22ᵉR and RCR. Two Russian T34 tanks were seen across from the Americans, so the Canadians were aware of an armoured threat. The newsletter sums up the Squadron's actions to the end of August:

> There has been over 100 miles of hard driving by the tanks. We like the M4A3 very much. It has plenty of power with the 500 horse power V8 Ford engine and the 76 mm gun is excellent for what we need it for. The climbing ability of the tank is superb, often enabling it to get into positions impassable to any other vehicle. Getting out of the position and coming back down the hills was the most hazardous.

In June 1951 there was much talk of an offensive by the Chinese. The Canadians were poised for it along the main approaches to Seoul. Kennedy's newsletter records a more immediate problem: "the urgent need for tank spare parts". While in reserve all the tank tracks had been changed, but "the installation kits for the Canadian 19 [radio] set were still not in the supply system".

Half of the Squadron under Captain Vic Jewkes went to "support 2 PPCLI who were still serving in 28 Commonwealth Brigade". A week later, real confusion began as patrolling increased. The newsletter states,

> Other units of the Commonwealth Brigade had been crossing the river and a high degree of confusion [existed] as the different units crossed paths with a minimum of liaison. Greeks, ROKs (South Koreans), British, American and Australian patrols began to infiltrate the hills in front of the R22ᵉR despite the fact that boundaries had been allotted to keep them out. ... There was physical contact on the ground [sometimes shooting at

each other by mistake]. Further confusion was caused to the R22ᵉR by them receiving orders from both 25 and 28 Brigade HQs.

Little did the Canadian soldiers realize that United Nations duty would see this multinational, multilanguage problem surface time and again. Indeed, it still exists today in 1994.

Jim Quinn concluded that the situation was "pretty quiet with lots of boring days". The main problems facing C Squadron were mines, target identification and the accuracy of tank gunfire. The latter was solved by the Tank Observation Officer (TOO). Jim says that the TOO solved the problem by

> sending an Armoured officer or NCO forward with the infantry with a portable radio and a coloured identification panel, which was positioned so that the Squadron tanks that could not get forward could see it but the Chinese could not. The target was described to the crew commander, for example, "reference panel, right 2 o'clock, 50 yards, MG, high explosive, fire when ready." The tank crew commander would advise firing and the TOO would correct the fall of shot until the target was destroyed. Targets as close as 15 yards were often engaged with spectacular results.

C Squadron became got very good at the TOO procedure, and the British 8th Hussars copied the Canadians. The newsletter says, "Sergeants Murray and Barr and Lieutenants Corbiere and Wyant had all done this chore." The summary at the end of June was "500 miles on each tank so far and four tanks damaged by mines".

Jim Quinn departed from Korea earlier than planned. He explains:

> The Staff College list came out [concerning who was to report to Staff College in the autumn as a result of the exams written earlier in Fort Lewis], and my name was on it along with Major Dubé of the R22ᵉR and others. Major Dubé was killed when a Korean batman [officer's servant] accidentally discharged a pistol he was cleaning. Major Dubé died instantly and this caused an immediate problem. He had been slated to fill a position for two months as a pre-Staff College trainer in Kure, Japan, at the Canadian reinforcement camp. I was asked if I would like to fill the vacant post. I said I would and that is how I left the Squadron. I knew I had to give up command in a few months as a posting to the Canadian Army Staff College in Kingston was imminent. I felt the training in Kure would provide me with good experience in an area in which I had no prior training or exposure. The Squadron was well trained and a good successor existed with the Unit in the form of Vic Jewkes.

Captain Vic Jewkes took over as Commanding Officer and Captain Ken Kennedy took over as second-in-command. The SSM position was taken over by SSM "Smokey" Shaw. Jim has a story about Smokey:

> The tanks were on the move through a burned-out Korean village. There at the corner stood the SSM, all decked out with a clean uniform and his pace stick under his arm patiently waiting to get his hands on the scruffy tank crews. As the tanks rounded the corner, Smokey took a step back and vanished in the charcoal rubble into a hidden Korean toilet [latrine pit]. He crawled out and, covered in you-know-what and soot, marched smartly into the Imjin River, removed the majority of his clothing and then marched out again. All of this was to the unconcealed glee of the soldiers.

Another story concerned Jim's SQMS, Doug Eveleigh. One of the SQMS's jobs was to collect the Squadron rum ration. The first time Doug drew the ration he said, "Don't forget the tank delivery troop that's with us." The troop was a figment of Doug's imagination, but the ruse remained undiscovered until the next Squadron asked, "What tank delivery troop?" Thus ended a free rum issue that had lasted for a year.

Under Vic Jewkes' leadership the fame of the Canadian Armoured soldiers grew and grew. The close cooperation with R22ᵉR under Lieutenant Colonel Jim Dextraze on 13 September against Chinese bunkers caused seventy-five Chinese killed, still at their machine-gun positions. Kennedy's newsletter states, "The bursts of the tank High Explosive shells could be seen on the inner walls of the bunker slits. It had been a costly and fruitless defence." The Divisional Commander, Major General Cassels, said that "he had never seen more intimate and effective tank/infantry co-operation in his life." Action against the Chinese grew more hectic as tank troops supported the Canadian infantry both in the defence and out on patrols. As the battle moved backward and forward, the tank crews began living among the forward platoons. The newsletter records the procedure: "This system, although foreign to all Armoured handbooks, is a practical one and accounts in part for 138 Chinese dead counted after a battalion attack failed to dislodge two companies of Patricias." The fact that so few tanks were out of action for long was credited to "Lt. James and the Armoured Recovery Vehicle crew and the work of 191 Workshop (RCEME)."

In October a large raid used tanks in firing positions beside which ammunition had been stockpiled. The tank crews and Korean porters carried in the ammunition under the cover of darkness. TOOs were sent forward to the battalions and the 8th Hussars loaned a troop of four Centurions to thicken the firepower. Three-quarters of the objective — Hill 166 — was quickly taken, and Brigadier Rockingham called off the attack. Once again the key to the combined tank and infantry battle was good communication. In the evening Lieutenant Colonel Jim Stone telephoned to say that 2 PPCL1 "could not have taken its objective without the support of the tanks". The Chinese reacted to the raid with shelling, local attacks and the employment of self-propelled guns. Tank troops fired against advancing Chinese to the point where emergency resupply of ammunition by the Armoured recovery vehicles became essential. Sergeant Thwaites' tank caught a Chinese Company in the open and fired with bow gun, coaxial machine-gun, main tank gun and 50 Browning, fired by Thwaites himself from the turret mount. "Only one Chinese soldier got away."

As Christmas neared, the newsletter included a note about the support from home: "Christmas parcels have been sent to ex-members of the Royal Canadian Dragoons serving with the Squadron. The Ladies Auxiliary of the RCD have been very kind. ... The men are glad to be remembered."

The superb tank support to the infantry in Korea has been acknowledged from all quarters. This excellence was achieved by accepting right from the beginning that there was no such thing as impossible tank country. When soldiers have the will to get to the place of action to meet obligations to the tank and infantry team, then get to the place of action they will, by whatever means necessary.

Jim Quinn went on to command the 8th Canadian Hussars, the Brigade in Petawawa and Canadian Forces Europe. He retired from the Canadian Forces as the Associate Deputy Minister (Personnel). He later filled the appointment of Colonel Commandant, Royal Canadian Army Cadets from 1979 to 1989. Jim Quinn and his wife Edna live in Ottawa and at their summer home in Chaffey's Locks, Ontario.

Russ Allan centre, at nineteen on graduation from basic training 1951.

AN INFANTRY PRIVATE REMEMBERS

Finding an infantry private who would talk about his Korean service proved to be a struggle. Russ Allan ended that struggle when he granted me an interview in April 1994. His story begins with his enlistment:

> In January 1951, I enlisted in the Infantry at Wallis House in Ottawa. I did not join for any particular reason. I'd left school, there was a war on in Korea, and I was at loose ends. Three days later I was at the Royal Canadian School ofInfantry at Camp Borden. In early April the basic training course was over and I chose to go to the PPCLI, for I had never been out West. As a nineteen-year-old, this whole scenario was a big adventure.

In Calgary, the emphasis was on conditioning and sub unit training in the Sarcee training area. Says Russ, "We did a lot of digging, route marches and in general getting ready for a more static war than the Second World War veterans had been used to. Almost everything was done in daylight, and yet we found out later in Korea that all the fighting was done at night." Private Allan took a side trip to Rivers, Manitoba, to take the Jump Course, Serial 95. After graduation in late July, Russ was sent to Wainwright, Alberta, for more training. It was here that the CO, Lieutenant Colonel Wilson-Smith, informed all ranks that they were going to Korea to replace 2 PPCLI.

A couple of days before embarkation, Russ and two others came down with food poisoning, and their battalion draft left without them. When their health improved the three began their long journey to Korea — first the train ride to Seattle and then the long voyage in the USNS *Marine Adder* to Japan. Russ had been moved to D Company under the command of Major George; Bill Stirling became Russ's platoon commander. On October 30th, after a short stopover in Yokahama, Japan, the *Marine Adder* took them to Inchon. Inchon was in ruins, but the Canadians were marched to the railway from where "the small rail cars took us to the next stop". The final ride to the battalion B Echelon (administrative area) was in blacked-out trucks.

After two or three days the soldiers began the long march to join the rest of the battalion. It was the night of 3–4 November 1951 before Russ's D Company of 1 PPCLI replaced a Company of 2 PPCLI. Russ recalls, "We moved into their slit trenches and bunkers. Those first few days consisted of improving the field defence. The odd enemy round came in, mainly mortars. On 5 November the Chinese put in a major attack on Hill 355."

Herb Wood's book *Strange Battleground* describes the attack on D Company of 5 November:

> D Company ... [had] one platoon forward and two back. [Russ was in a rear platoon.] Mortar fire had started to fall on the company area at 2:20 p.m., becoming heavy at four o'clock. By half-past four, shells as well as mortar bombs were falling on D Company. ... At six o'clock enemy flat-trajectory guns and howitzers joined in the bombardment, and ten minutes later Chinese infantry were seen forming up across the valley. ... The attack developed at 6:15.

The NCOs, mostly Second World War veterans, realized early that this was the real thing; one likened it to the German attacks he had gone through in Italy. It was the first time Russ had seen shots fired in anger. He said, "We did a lot of shooting even though we didn't know who we were shooting at. In the morning, everyone felt great because they had survived." In fact, 1 PPCLI had three killed in that battle and fifteen wounded.

Another first for Russ that night was seeing a wounded Chinese soldier up close while he was being carried back for medical care. "There was no animosity toward him, no hatred."

Images that have stayed with Russ through the years are of comrades dying: "I remember Private E.J. Handspiker, who was killed on 23 November

1951." He had hit a wooden mine with his foot; his foot was blown off and he died. "There was another soldier, Private Ray Enos, we had shared a trench. He was killed by a random shell on 25 November 1951." The front-line soldier's thought — "maybe I'll be next" — often went through Russ's mind. "It bothered you, you were not frightened but concerned."

Russ's recollections of early mornings in Korea epitomize "the land of the morning calm":

> The mornings were calm, no wind. When the sun came up it was quite beautiful when you looked out at the hills as the suns ray's hit them. If you could just take yourself from the war. Things like the sound of a machine-gun firing away off in the distance or the odd shell landing with a "Crump!" really reverberated through the countless valleys and peaks. I remember seeing the smoke from small cooking fires as the Chinese cooked their breakfast. We would be doing the same thing. There seemed to be an unwritten rule not to fire at each other at breakfast. We left them alone; they left us alone. It was unusual.

Part of every morning was the soldier's relief that he had made it through the night, for it was at night that patrols of both sides probed into enemy territory. Night-time meant artificial moonlight catching a patrol in no-man's land or, worse still, parachute flares dropped by an aircraft that could not be seen; it meant an ambush either set by "our side" or being sprung by the enemy; it meant bursts of automatic weapon fire, grenades bursting their deadly slivers of steel into the bodies of fellow soldiers; it meant rapid messages passed on the radio; the cries of the wounded; the rush of adrenalin making the mouth dry and the heart pound.

The soldier knew that the dark of night not only hid him from sight but destroyed his own chances of seeing the enemy. The patrols returned drained as much from the emotional strain as the physical effort needed to walk, run, crawl or fall. Each soldier followed the lead of the person out in front. It is no small wonder that leadership at the infantry platoon or section level was paramount in the eyes of the soldiers who were part of the team. Russ still feels admiration for his platoon commander:

> Bill Stirling was a good soldier. There was something about him that made him different and unorthodox, but I cannot remember what it was. I rather liked him, for he had great empathy with his soldiers. [He died before his time, as a Major. He choked to death in a restaurant — a great loss.] We all looked up to him in Korea. We were all young; 19 was the average age except for the Sergeant and Corporal who were vets.

An Oral History From Those Who Were There

Russ sums it up by saying, "I was just a private soldier. I didn't know what was going on. The significance of the war didn't phase me. ... I was just trying to stay alive."

On 10 December 1951 Russ found that events happened over which one had no control. He recalls,

> I had been sick for a couple of days and the reason was my appendix. It was acute and I was evacuated. It was embarrassing! First came the Field Hospital and then it was back to the US Army, 8055 MASH. My appendix was taken out under a local. I remember the operation. Three days later I had pneumonia; I was really sick. Beside me were soldiers who had been wounded and I was here because of my appendix. I then became acquainted with the "evacuation chain". I went from the 8055 MASH by ambulance to the hospital at Yon Dong Po [see Flora Baptist's story]. After a few days the padres came to see me — that worried me! I ended up being flown back to the Commonwealth hospital in Japan after I had passed through two more American hospitals. Wounds did not heal quickly so it was some time before I was released to the Battle School at Haramura.

In February 1952, after a few weeks of light training, Russ went back to Korea as a reinforcement. This time Russ joined C Company, whose Company Sergeant Major was WOII Buxton, remembered as "a good soldier, tough but fair". C Company was on The Hook, a feature never forgotten by anyone who served on it. Russ recalls a few assaults by the Chinese, but more than that he remembers the same problem of not being able to see much as a soldier in the trenches.

Russ remembers the night that "one of our soldiers was hit. He was too close to a Chinese grenade and he got a lot of the blast and steel slivers in the back." This was Russ's last action, for in Russ's words, "I became sick again and was evacuated to Japan. This time I was lucky as I remained in an administrative job." In all, Russ Allan served eighteen months in the Far East.

On leaving Japan, Russ looked back at Korea — the patrols, the trenches, the shellings, the Japanese Asahi beer which came in quarts and, above all, the medical care — and thought about leaving the Army. Back home in Canada, however, he was convinced to remain. He transferred to the Royal Canadian Army Service Corps (RCASC) as a clerk and a vehicle driver. In 1954 he was selected for the first Officer Candidate Program. Over the next thirty-two years Russ served as Commanding Officer of 4 Service Battalion, Germany; as Base Commander in London, Ontario; and in the Sinai Desert and Suez Canal zone in United Nations Emergency Forces I and II. He retired in July 1986 with the rank of Brigadier General. After retirement, Russ worked for ADGA Group (Consulting Engineers) for five years. He now has his own company. Russ and his wife Liz live in Ottawa, Ontario.

Ned Amy, left, and Major General West, Korea 4 Feb 1953.

A CANADIAN VIEW FROM DIVISIONAL HEADQUARTERS

Ned Amy had already fought in one very hectic war by 1945. He was a Lieutenant Colonel serving in Edmonton when he learned he was to go to war again:

> In 1952 I was General Staff Officer (GSO1) Western Command in Edmonton and I had to visit HQ British Columbia Area, Camp Chilliwack, Vernon Cadet Camp and the garrison in Victoria. Jean and I had not had a holiday since our posting the previous summer, and this trip appeared to be ideal to combine business with pleasure. We hired a housekeeper to look after the boys and drove to the coast.
>
> On July 16th, just before noon, I arrived in Chilliwack, only to be told to telephone Brigadier Megill immediately at his HQ in Vancouver. My first thought was that something had happened to one of the boys. While relieved on that count, I had another problem. The Brigadier told me to report immediately to the Medical Inspection Room for shots, including

one for yellow fever. Impressing me with the urgency, he explained that I was posted to the Commonwealth Division as GSO1 to replace Norm Wilson-Smith. I was to leave next Thursday, July 31st, from Vancouver for Tokyo.

Short notice of a foreign posting was a common way of doing things as Army Headquarters in Ottawa wrestled with the problem of replacing people in Korea. To make matters worse, there was the urgent requirement to form a Brigade for NATO in Germany, plus a general overall increase in the size of the Canadian Army.

Ned's story continues:

> Understandably we were concerned as we headed home that afternoon through the Rockies with zero notice and a two-day drive ahead of us. Where would Jean and the boys go? Since officers on a foreign posting had to vacate Married Quarters, only one option seemed open, and that was for Jean to put our belongings in storage and stay with my parents until she could make other arrangements. This would involve driving to Nova Scotia with the boys (aged six years and nine months) and Prince, our six-week-old Chesapeake dog. It was not a happy trip back [to Edmonton] but it was a fast one. Fortunately, when General Vokes heard of [our concern], he said, "Of course the family can remain in quarters."

The trip to Korea was by air all the way. After a day's briefing in Tokyo, the final leg on August 5th was by a single-engine Auster aircraft between Seoul and the 1st (Commonwealth) Division airstrip on the south bank of the Imjin River. Ned was to serve at the GSO1 from 5 August 1952 to 3 August 1953:

> The original G [Operations] Staff of the Division had been put together by Lieutenant Colonel Dick Danby with the blessing of the General Officer Commanding [GOC], Major General Jim Cassels. Dick was a very experienced staff officer with WWII staff experience. This obviously was the reason he had been selected for the appointment. When Norm Wilson-Smith took over from him, he made no changes. Since Norm had been commanding his unit [PPCLI] in Korea for ten months and had been my Directing Staff [instructor] at the Staff College, I couldn't visualize any change I might suggest that would improve anything, much less influence the GOC to agree to any changes.
>
> Major Bob Thomas [Royal West Kents] was the original GS Ops who had worked with Dick Danby from the beginning in organizing the HQ.

> He coordinated the work of the G Staff, ran the Ops Room and coordinated the daily staff briefing for the GOC, which took place each morning and covered the details of patrol activity across the Division front during the night. In the afternoon he and I had a session when I passed on anything the GOC wished done, signed any papers requiring my signature and briefed him on any visits I made during the day to the Brigades or Units and any follow-up required. When I arrived General Cassels was in the final stages of his tour, and when he was absent from Divisional Headquarters he wished me to remain there.

The ease with which the Commonwealth Division worked might seem unusual today in 1994, but in the early 1950s it was normal. All the officers had served in the Second World War and Korea was, by comparison, far less hectic. Once routines had been established it was a case of serving one's time and not causing waves in the system.

The old hands often took any chance to make a joke at the expense of the "new boy", and Ned was given no exception:

> The GOC's briefing on the Jamestown Line, a couple of days after I arrived had an amusing aspect. Norm and I were to meet the GOC at a prearranged rendezvous halfway up one of the mountains on the south side of the Imjin River. I drove out with Norm, and as soon as the jeep stopped he took off up the hill like a mountain goat. He had been doing this for a year and was very fit. The fastest and farthest I had had to move for the past year was a few hundred yards over flat prairie to get into a duck blind before the evening flight began. When I reached the rendezvous, the GOC immediately started to direct my attention, using binoculars, to a specific hill nestled amongst the multitude of small mountains and large hills spread out in front of us. He used the normal system of going from one identifiable reference to the other, all of which were mountain peaks and most of which looked alike. After he had gone through about half a dozen references, he asked me if I had identified the hill. I was still puffing from the climb and the hills were going up and down in my binoculars like a moving picture. When I asked, "Where was that first reference again, Sir?", I realized that he and Norm had set me up and I reacted as they had expected or at least hoped I would. It was my indoctrination.

Because General Cassels enjoyed Western novels, Ned was expected to bring back a supply each time he visited the Canadian Brigade. Once a week there was a movie in the General's mess, and the General made the decision of which film was to be shown — if a Western movie was on the list of available films, that was it. When the lights went on while the operator changed reels, the General would stand up in front of the screen and practise a few make-believe fast draws with "Bang! Bang!" sound effects. This sometimes startled an unsuspecting guest.

In September Major General Michael Aston-Roberts West (Mike West) took over from General Cassels. Ned was now the Korea veteran; the GOC, the newcomer. General West operated differently from Cassels, as Ned soon found out:

> When I asked if he wished me to remain at the HQ when he was absent, he replied, "That would be a frightful waste of time. Coordinate your visits with mine and be on the air!" He encouraged both the other senior staff officer (AQ) and me to visit brigades and units as much as possible. I was also encouraged to visit the staff at I Corps and to develop friendly working relations with the Chief of Staff and the G2 and G3 sections. This task was pleasant, as we had Major John Clancy (RCR) there as our Division Liaison officer and he was always able to get me in to see the right people, who without exception were courteous and helpful to any requests which we in the Commonwealth Division made. John was usually able to tip us off on unexpected casual visits from the Corps Commander or other senior visitors.

In Korea, the front was small and by 1952 static. As a result, common ways of referring to locations could be meaningless bafflegab to newcomers. Ned describes a couple of examples:

> Three figure map references (spot heights) were used to a large extent, e.g., "I'll meet you at 159 shortly after 1200." It was frustrating to a newcomer but before long one was using these references with ease.
>
> [Also,] the old-timers referred to places that were a mystery to the newcomer, e.g., "We'll RV where the Van Doos B Echelon was last March when they had their big party." This was meaningless to one who hadn't been there in March or who hadn't been at the party. It was recognizable to most, however, because the Division moved from its Jamestown positions only once to my knowledge, and then for only two or three weeks in 1953 when the 3rd American Infantry Division relieved us so the Division could come out of the line for a short breather and to run some training exercises for the Brigades.

Keeping track of the Chinese and trying to determine their intentions was a full-time job. Ned explains that during his year in Korea,

> we relied a great deal on air photos for our intelligence on changes in the enemy defences. The USAF flew the coverage and invariably it was of excellent quality. We were able to get routine coverage across our front frequently and emergency coverage of specific positions on demand depending on air force commitments. This involved reading a great number of photos on each update. We had a British Captain, heading up our photo interpreters section, with a remarkable ability to examine very quickly the latest coverage and spot changes immediately. If the Chinese extended a trench system by a few feet or dug a new gun pit he would catch it right away. This information was vital to battalion commanders when such changes were noted across the Samichon River opposite their positions. To have it right away was important, since it often had a bearing on their own patrol plans or alerted them to possible enemy actions or intentions.

The situation in the air in Korea was one of almost total advantage for the UN forces.

> Close air support somewhat similar to WWII cab rank [aircraft flying over friendly forces on call to put in an attack on the enemy] was used frequently in an attempt to take out pinpoint positions in the enemy defences. In spite of the static nature of operations, it was not entirely successful. The British pilots flying from carriers were in my view the most effective because the pilots would take time to visit a battalion with a target on its front, identify it beyond any doubt and then return and fly the mission. On the other hand, American pilots were trained primarily for operations in Europe and they adhered to the system necessary for that theatre. Unfortunately the nature of the terrain made it very difficult to talk a pilot on to a pinpoint target while he was piloting a plane doing something short of the speed of sound. I asked a South African pilot who had flown these missions if he had difficultly being directed onto a target by either the ground controller or an airborne controller flying in a slower plane. He said, "Hell, flying at our speed with nothing but hills below us, most of which looked alike, particularly if you were trying to pick it out over your shoulder, we were lucky if we identified the right hill, let alone identify a small target on the hill." In my view, the American system unfortunately could not be slowed down to accommodate the nature of this type of an operation in Korea. We discussed this matter with some visiting senior British and US air force officers. When I compared the two systems, the senior US officer was a mite unhappy

when I explained that if the pilot couldn't identify the target he might just as well not fly the mission. If the bomb did not go in the gun pit nothing was achieved. The only reasonable chance of a direct hit was with the British system.

The Korean front may have been static, but that did not mean that nothing happened. It was essential that the UN forces be active, controlling the area in front of their positions and harassing the enemy in every way possible. Our Commonwealth Division activities centred around

> an active patrol policy established by the GOC and directed by the Brigades and an occasional raiding foray in an attempt to capture a prisoner for identification. As an example of the latter, an Australian Battalion carried out one such raid at company strength. The detailed planning and several rehearsals for the raid were very thorough, and although no prisoner was taken, enemy casualties were assessed to exceed our own and wireless intercepts revealed that the Chinamen were concerned.

The matter of estimating enemy casualties proved to be an interesting exercise, bearing in mind that the Commonwealth Division was part of an American Corps. Ned explains:

> The Daily Situation Report [SITREP] which each Division submitted to Corps was an example. There was nothing unusual about it since it covered what activity occurred on the Division front, patrols, prisoners taken, casualties, etc. However, it did include an estimate of enemy casualties. The Americans used some formula based on the number of artillery rounds fired from which they estimated how many enemy had been killed and how many wounded. Our GOC insisted that we not report any enemy casualties in our SITREPS unless we had a dead or wounded body to prove it. During the year I was with the Division we claimed perhaps a handful of enemy killed. Consequently our SITREP had a noticeable "nil" in this column for weeks on end whereas every other Division in the I Corps were killing Chinamen every day and in large numbers. The Corps Commander understood the GOC's views on this, but I was suspicious that some of his staff and perhaps the other Divisions in the Corps wondered why we never seemed to kill anybody.

As the GSO1 at Division, Ned Amy had an excellent opportunity to compare the different nationalities from the Commonwealth. In an April 1993 letter to me, he made a special point of saying:

You will appreciate that pride and competition were front and centre twenty-four hours a day between the various national elements making up the Commonwealth Division. While this was par for the course within the Division, pride in being part of the Commonwealth Division was evident when its members were involved with outsiders. From my neutral position I was impressed with the calibre of all nationalities and I would hesitate to compare one with the other in a book written by someone other than myself. Each country had every reason to be proud of its soldiers who served in Korea during my time. Each national group attempted to accentuate the positive. If you were talking to an Australian he wanted to talk about world-class cricket and would challenge all comers to try to down a pint of ale faster than him. [For the Brits it was] rugger; and the Canadians, hockey. The New Zealanders seemed to have a bias for the Australian point of view, while the members of the Indian Field Ambulance were always correct and very polite and taught our cooks and others how to prepare a curry dinner, still a favourite in many Canadian units.

How big was the First Commonwealth Division? Here are figures for 30 June 1953:

United Kingdom	10,739
Canada	6,080
Australia	2,079
New Zealand	1,304
India	71
Total	20,273
Korean (KATCom)	882

In August 1953, Ned was replaced by another Canadian Armoured officer, Lieutenant Colonel Mike Dare. Ned Amy was awarded the Order of the British Empire and the United States Bronze Star Medal for his frequent visits to front-line positions–often under very heavy enemy fire — which assisted immeasurably in the overall mission of the Commonwealth Division.

Ned returned to Canada to command the Royal Canadian Dragoons. In the years that followed he served on the staff at SHAPE (Supreme Headquarters Allied Powers Europe) and the Standing Group Representatives Office in Paris. He was the Armoured Corps Director and Commander of the first Canadian Contingent to Cyprus in 1964. He commanded brigades in both Calgary and Germany. When Ned retired as a Brigadier in 1971, he founded E.A.C. Amy & Sons Ltd, Management Support Services. He served as Colonel of The Royal Canadian Dragoons from 1970-75 and Colonel Commandant The Royal Canadian Armoured Corps from 1977-81. He and his wife Jean live in Mahone Bay, Nova Scotia.

An Oral History From Those Who Were There

Ron Francis (right). That is snow on the Sherman tank as the crew get ready for a day's maintenance. February 1952. (DND photo)

A TANK DRIVER AND HIS WAR

Ron Francis's story covers an interesting period in the history of the Royal Canadian Armoured Corps. I have therefore included pre-Korea events in some detail. His story begins with why he joined the Army:

> In 1945, while attending Scarborough Collegiate Institute, I was compelled, as were all other male students of that era, to join the Cadet Corps (Queen's York Rangers). Two years later, having left high school, I joined the Governor General's Horse Guards [GGHG], which solidified my allegiance to the Armoured Corps. When the opportunity came in May of 1951 to enter the Active Force with the GGHG by means of a newly formed 27th Brigade, it had little to do with patriotism at that time; more than anything else, it represented an exciting opportunity for adventure.

Twenty-seventh Brigade was formed to meet Canada's commitment to Europe and NATO, in competition with the needs of 25th Brigade fighting in Korea. The method used to raise the NATO Brigade was to take subunits from the Reserve Army (see George Bell's comments in Chapter Three) — the plan was given the code name Panda Force. The major problem was one of accommodation for the newly created Brigade. Ron's story bears this out:

> I reported to the University Armouries in Toronto for transport by bus to Borden with a capacity busload of regimental [GGHG] comrades, led by none other than the illustrious Captain Tony Hawkins. During the initial part of the journey, conversations were both loud and jovial. As we got closer to the unknown, however, the conversations diminished and the atmosphere became much quieter. On arrival, a corporal wearing a strange cap badge entered the bus and, with the personality and growl of a pit bull, led us to our quarters, which he described as being far too lavish for such a motley group of misfits. This was hardly borne out; we found our supposedly lavish new home to be nothing more than a recently vacated vehicle hangar, complete with 400 bunk beds, cold water ablution facilities (outdoor) surrounded with hessian. There was some coconut matting on the floor to cover the grease and oil left by vehicles some 24 hours earlier.

The GGHG sub unit could be sent to join the Royal Canadian Dragoons in Camp Petawawa or Lord Strathcona's Horse (Royal Canadians) in Alberta. As Ron said, "It was the West, and soon we were Alberta bound." The large training camp in Wainwright, Alberta, near Edmonton was now home. In Ron's words,

> Reveille that first morning in Wainwright came at 0500 hours. Confusion reigned supreme, with troops running about in total disarray trying to find a spot to wash and shave, determine where one was to go for breakfast and, finally, figure out where and with whom one was to fall in for morning parade. This three-ring circus did not escape the keen-eyed surveillance of our new SSM, WOII "Squint" Armer. It didn't take Squint too long to eloquently enlighten everyone about the routine that had been designed for our enjoyment. Within a week, tents had been properly "dressed" from the right, as well as from front to rear, as had all the tent pegs. Whitewashed stones adorned roadways, pathways and entrances to tents and we all had become accustomed to performing magnificent drill movements on a parade square of loose sand. Everything was done on the double, and the new phrase of the day was "If it doesn't move, paint it". The Army's supply of paint and brushes was endless.

Even though most of the Reservists had been qualified on their basic training, the standard was not what the Strathconas would accept. Trooper Francis found that our total occupation for the next twelve weeks was on-again — off-again, basic training — which was forever being enhanced for parade rehearsals in honour of a variety of general officers and politicians — sports meets, and the dreaded needles parades. At the end of August, however, I finally graduated from basic training and was immediately despatched to a training area called Brummelville, where I was selected from a cast of many to attend a driver mechanic track course. This selection process was obviously the result of an exhaustive and careful study of character and physical profiles, as I, with a body mass weighing all of 115 pounds, spent the next five weeks breaking track, dropping belly plates and lifting engine doors. My good friend and protector, Robby Robinson, at six feet and weighing in at 235 pounds, became a wireless operator, lifting nothing heavier than the canvas cover protecting the front of a state-of-the-art [Second World War] wireless set known as the 19 set.

By October, Ron was a tank driver. Winter had set in, and the GGHG group was to join the rest of Panda Force in Calgary, the home of the Strathconas. It was to be a big improvement:

Calgary was indeed a paradise. Living in open barracks (H-huts, complete with three pot bellied stoves per side) was luxury at its best, compared to the past five months of living in a marquee in Wainwright. This excitement was soon to diminish and turn somewhat to boredom, as each day became a routine of mindless job opportunities, ranging from hut orderly to kitchen fatigues.

Panda Force was now offered a choice: join either of the Regular tank regiments and be rebadged, or hope to be chosen for service in the NATO Brigade in Germany. Trooper Francis made a decision:

Pastures started to appear much greener with those who wore the badge of the Strathcona's, and I had not become entirely thrilled with the organization and the training received from this strange lot called Panda Force. We had never been accepted as Regular soldiers; we were considered to be much less. All of this, combined with the lack of any positive information or direction concerning our greatly anticipated move to Europe, prompted me to parade myself to the hallowed Orderly Room and to seek a transfer to the Strathcona's.

After a short course in fire-fighting, Ron soon learned he was on the move overseas, but not in the direction he had expected. In Ron's words,

[The squadron commander explained,] "Trooper Francis, you will start your clearance immediately, after which you will be sent home via train to enjoy 72 hours of embarkation leave with your family, following which you will proceed to Jericho Barracks, Vancouver, for final overseas processing."

I was totally unprepared for this rapid turn of events, but even in my state I could not imagine why the sudden urgency for someone of my rather limited capabilities to be whisked off to Europe so quickly. And why would my final processing take place in Vancouver? Even my geography was better than that! When asked if I had any further questions, I asked rather hesitantly where in hell I was going. When he replied, "Korea," I was too shell-shocked to do anything but accept his congratulations, shake his hand, pick up a clearance form and start my clearance. By evening, I was adorned with a 25 CIBG patch on my upper right sleeve and a 1 Commonwealth Division patch on my upper left sleeve. Needless to say, I was the envy of every member of the Panda Force. It was my intent not to tell my parents that I was going overseas, however, with a rifle on my shoulder and burdened down with marching order complete with bedroom (two grey blankets), I chose to tell them that I was being posted to Japan. Seventy-two hours later, I was back on the train and heading west to Vancouver. In Vancouver, I met with seven other Strathcona's, who were also a part of this first reinforcement draft to Korea. We learned that our initial destination would be the Canadian 25th Brigade Reinforcement Depot in Hiro, Japan. We were to fly from Sea Island Airport, Vancouver, to Anchorage, Alaska, on to Shemya Island in the Aleutians group and from there to Tokyo, Japan. This was all pretty heady stuff for a nineteen-year-old who had never been away from home before joining the forces only eight months previously. On the 17th of December, 1951, we took off from Sea Island aboard an RCAF North Star transport.

As the other stories in this book attest, the wait in Japan could be days, weeks or even months. Ron's story continues:

We were soon in an American landing craft for our journey to Pusan, Korea. At Pusan, we embarked on one of the oldest looking trains I had ever seen for our trip northward to the railhead in the Brigade rear area. From this administration point, it was on to the back of a truck and a long, cold drive forward to C Squadron, B Echelon. [After I had] jumped to the ground with all my kit, the truck immediately drove off into the dark evening, leaving me very much alone to ponder my existence. At this point in time someone started beating on a final drive sprocket ring with a track pin, which was obviously recognized by all as being the local, improvised fire alarm. From a myriad of small holes in the ground came dozens of troopers in a variety of dress, all running to the tank park. I wandered over to this area of activity, only to see a Sherman [tank] fully ablaze, with all the internal ammunition stowage lighting up the sky like the 24th of May. I was later told that a young trooper by the name of Clifford Brown had previously fuelled the vehicle and had moved it up on to the hill beside the bunkers. Apparently, while [he was] moving the vehicle, fuel had spilled on to the exhaust system, and the rest was history. Brown did, however, redeem himself by jumping into the burning vehicle and releasing the tiller bars [steering brakes], allowing it to roll harmlessly down the hill and away from the bunkers before the ammo started exploding. An hour later, I finally found a van with an Orderly officer inside. After taking my name and a few other rather significant details, the young officer led me to one of the holes in the ground, pulled back the poncho covering the entrance and quietly said to those inside, "This man's name is Francis and he will be staying with you until such time as we can figure out what the hell to do with him." Not a very inspiring welcome or introduction. Three or four days later, I realized that the crew I had been bunking in with was the Squadron Commander's [Major Vic Jewkes] tank crew.

As fate would have it, a bottle of the CO's rum had gone missing from the stowage bin inside his tank. As this had never happened before, and as I was a new addition to the crew, it was naturally assumed that I was the perpetrator of this dastardly deed. The fact that I had no idea which tank belonged to the CO appeared to be of little consequence, and as punishment for this transgression I was told that I would be joining a tank crew in the front lines, a punishment that I would never regret.

At long last the previous eight months of service was all to come together as the young trooper was to join his first tank crew: two tank drivers, one gunner, one radio operator and a crew commander. The radio call sign, or identifier, of the tank was 4 Charlie. The four tanks in the troop were 4, 4A, 4B and 4C. The "Charlie" tank was commanded by Corporal Len Camponi assisted by troopers Penney, Lajombre and Peterson. Four Troop was then providing direct fire support to D Company of 2 R22^{e}R. Ron quickly came to realize just how green he was:

This first trip to the front lines was only to last a few weeks, as the Brigade was due for rest. It was sufficiently long enough, however, [for me] to realize how inadequate the training had been in Canada. The crew commander was not thrilled to learn that I had never operated a wireless set, fired either the master weapon or the .50-calibre machine-gun, or tactically driven a tank on a major exercise. In fact, I had never been on a tactical exercise of any size, in any capacity. There was obviously much to learn during these first few weeks in the forward defence lines, with every mistake having the potential of being not only my last one, but also that of the crew's. The incentive and encouragement from everyone concerned was sufficiently strong enough for me to learn well and quickly. It was indeed a learning experience.

The problem of Armoured crewmen not being qualified for more than one trade in a tank was caused by the time factor more than anything else. Unfortunately, in action this policy could have dire results if, say, the gunner was wounded or sick and another crewman had to take on the job. To be sure, there were other skilled tradesmen in the echelon, but finding replacements could be difficult. Ron describes those early days in the front lines:

> The war was nothing like I had envisioned it to be. The tank was dug in alongside the infantry trenches and bunkers and our role appeared to be that of providing direct sniper fire support for the endless infantry night patrols. The nightly turret/radio watches were particularly nervewracking, although one would never admit to it. The noise of patrols going out or returning through the wire, the constant thumping of Vickers and .30-calibres firing on fixed lines, the frequent lighting of the sky by some equally nervous infantryman firing off flares, the shadows created by the searchlights providing the artificial moonlight, and every shrub exposed by the flares appearing to move — all had the tendency to make one rather anxious. These two-hour watches were the longest and loneliest times that I have ever experienced.

One of the wonderful things about soldiers is their unfailing sense of humour. At one time, Major Jewkes had broken his leg and was in a walking cast. Ron recalls,

> While on guard duty one evening talking to a fellow guard, we observed Major Jewkes, complete with leg cast, hobbling from a tent which had been designated the officers' mess, proceeding up a very slippery hill toward his bunker. He was in pain from the effects of a broken leg.

105

Remembering a lecture from Major Jewkes regarding the strict observance of issuing a challenge only three times before opening fire, we waited until he had almost reached the top of the hill, then issued the challenge. Obviously the CO was not aware of the password, as we had suspected, and he shouted back, "It's me! Major Jewkes!" We replied to "advance and be recognized", to which he again shouted, "It's me, damn it! Major Jewkes!" Again we challenged, only this time we indicated that it was the second challenge and next time we would shoot. Upon his arrival back at the bottom of the hill, we greeted the CO with "Good evening, Sir. We had no idea who it was, and one cannot be too careful given the circumstances." He eyed both of us very carefully, knowing he had been taken. In my own rather immature mind, I suppose, my less-than-cordial welcome to the squadron had finally been vindicated, and the reputation gained by the incident had guaranteed my acceptance amongst the other soldiers.

The whole procedure of moving single tanks into an infantry area had its pros and cons. As a pro, the infantry had instant fire support on call. A con was that the tank might invite enemy fire of a much larger calibre than normal:

The troop was to be situated on the extreme left flank of the Canadian Brigade and the Commonwealth Division, with an American Marine Company to our immediate left. The nameless feature we were to occupy overlooked the Sami-ch'on Valley, which was several hundred yards across with a river in its centre. On the opposing feature, soldiers of the Chinese People's Volunteer Army were dug in. Like our previous tour in the line, this tasking was to man a static defence. On arrival, we dug in the tank up to the trench leading under the tank to the escape hatch located immediately behind the co-driver's seat. Having completed this, we started building a crew bunker. Having completed the digging in process, we went about the task of registering on enemy trenches, likely observation posts, roads and trails. Retaliation by 122 and 152 mm gunfire soon followed, much to the annoyance of the infantry. There were odd minor probes by both sides. The rule seemed to be "If you don't shoot at me, I won't shoot at you." On most occasions when we engaged targets of opportunity, the retaliation would be on the American Marines to our left. This did not endear us to our American cousins.

In every group of soldiers are people who by their actions become legends. Ron remembers one such soldier:

Soon after our arrival in the line a member of the crew left, to be replaced by a legendary character by the name of "Tiny" Dixon. This man was huge. The story of him being able to span the top of a fire pail and lift it with one hand was no exaggeration. Late one night while I was standing in the turret on turret watch, two hands gripped me by the shoulders, lifted me clear of the hatch and set me down on the rear deck. Tiny quietly said, "I'll take over now young fellow." My heart by this time had almost stopped. I had neither seen nor heard [anything to indicate that] Tiny [was near].

One of the more laborious tasks of each late evening was meeting with the ADREP [supply] truck at the bottom of the hill, offloading our fuel, ammo and supplies and then carrying the lot up the hill to our position. The most 76 mm ammo that was normally carried by one human being prior to Tiny arriving was four rounds. Tiny would carry one lengthwise on each shoulder and five or six across these two rounds. He called them bullets!

C Squadron's tour was almost at an end, but seven reinforcements, including Trooper Francis, would remain to join the incoming B Squadron. Ron was "delighted to learn that the new group had many of my friends from Panda Force". When B Squadron moved into the line for the first time, this story of war and its cost in human lives emerged:

When 4 Troop reached the bottom of the feature they and the 1st Battalion R22ᵉR would occupy, we pulled off to the side of the road and waited for nightfall before moving up onto the crest of the feature [Hill 210]. Sitting on the edge of the road beside the vehicle, listening to incoming shells landing somewhere up on the feature, and periodically watching jeep ambulances with litters across their hoods taking away casualties did little to elevate the spirits of the first-timers. A jeep carrying what appeared to be a wounded soldier came to a halt close to our tank, and the driver leapt out, moving quickly into the back of a larger medical van. Seeing this, one of our crew members went over to the young soldier and offered his reassurances that everything would be alright and that he would be back with his unit in no time. He was still there when a medical officer came to the vehicle, checked the young soldier's vital signs and then slowly pulled the blanket over the head of the body.

The new squadron had not arrived at a quiet time in the war. Ron recalls,

It did not take long for the Chinese to make us aware of their presence. They started their bombardment of the hill at daybreak of our first day in the line. This was obviously not going to be a repeat of the Sami-ch'on Valley area, which was a rest camp by comparison. The shelling of this position was constant throughout our three-month tour in the line, and we all became very adept at vacating our bunkers, getting into the vehicle in record time and getting a round into the breach in the event the shellings were to be a prelude to an infantry assault. It was during this tour in the line and while in this location that I learned of the stupidity of entering the vehicle through the turret during a shelling. While climbing up onto the top of the turret, I became puzzled by a buzzing and chipping sound. After the shelling had ceased, I inspected the outside front of the turret to discover chips in the armour from rounds fired by a sniper. The Chinese had obviously watched us climbing up onto the vehicle during a shelling, and had decided they would teach a lesson.

On one occasion, following the explosion of an incoming shell, myself and Henry Wyatt, who had recently replaced "Pop" Thivierge to become our co-driver, had quickly left our bunker for the safety of the vehicle. After the shelling had ceased, we returned to our bunker only to find it had suffered a direct hit from a mortar. This hit did, however, support the theory that the safest place to be during a barrage was in the vehicle. This lesson was learned too late by the crew of one squadron vehicle, who sat in the S-trench during a bombardment and suffered the effects of the blast and shrapnel from a near-miss mortar following up the trench. One of the crew was killed, the first killed in action for B Squadron.

By the time Trooper Francis came close to the end of his tour, his feelings had changed: "Gone was the casual attitude of 'what will be will be'. I was now more cautious as each day passed."

War is never about the efforts of one man, one tank or one squadron alone. Warfare is teamwork from all components of the combat arms team plus by the thousands working in support, some well behind the lines. Ron's last tour in the line describes the efforts, during one battle, of the entire team:

> From the sounds of gunfire and noise coming from the hill to our immediate left (Hill 355), it was obviously the large-scale attack anticipated. We were later to find out that the attack had been of battalion strength, and by the time the signal flares were observed, the enemy was on the wire. This attack gained complete surprise, and the initial success of the Chinese went far beyond their own expectations. Had it not been for the

Artillery and their relentless fire sealing off the valley and preventing the reinforcing of the initial wave, the results would have been much more disastrous. To me, the gunners with their 25-pounders were the heroes on that night. With the confusion of soldiers running about in the half-light of flares and the enemy on the friendly positions, there was little direct fire support that we could provide without the risk of firing on our own troops. We could only wait to ensure the attack did not spread over into our area. It was a long, nerve-wrenching night. The shouting of troops from 355 was clearly heard through the noise of small arms and artillery fire, which was both incoming and outgoing. It was obviously hell for those up on the hill, as the Chinese were up into the trenches and the bunkers. The following day, after the withdrawal of the Chinese, a Welfare Officer brought cigarettes and goodies to our position and informed us of the enormity of the attack. Through it all the Patricias had held their ground, but they certainly were in debt to the gunners. On the day following the attack, troops were totally exhausted and the infantry were given hot fresh rations, a treat which the squadron could not provide for the tankers.

The long road home was about to take place: a new uniform, a hot shower, a flight from Korea to Japan and finally a train trip to Yokahama. The American ship that Ron boarded for the journey home was the *General Hugh Gaffey*, which contained not only soldiers, but a large number of Japanese wives and families of US servicemen. The ship arrived in Seattle on December 20th, 1952. Four days later, Ron Francis arrived home a much different person from the young soldier who had left home a year earlier:

> I was more nervous waiting to face my welcoming family members than I had ever been during my time in Korea. Finally, we were making our way through the station, to be greeted by a packed crowd of well-wishers, a band from one of the local militia units and banners of all sorts hanging all over the station. It took several minutes before I saw my mother break through the rope barriers and come running through the crowd. It was a very emotional moment, one that was shared by many troopers as they were also greeted by their loved ones. I was finally home, and Korea was behind me. It was an experience that changed my outlook on life and certainly my immature thoughts of how glamorous and exciting it must have been for those who took part in the First and Second World Wars.

An Oral History From Those Who Were There

Ron Francis went on to have a long and eventful career. He became a helicopter observer, served in other Armoured regiments and became an assault trooper. He was chosen to serve with Canadian naval sailors training officer candidates in Esquimalt. He was a Regimental Sergeant Major for various bases, including the Lord Strathcona's Horse (Royal Canadians). (Another soldier serving the LdSH (RC) at the time was Clifford Brown, who had been responsible for the burning tank on the night of Ron's arrival in C Squadron. Brown gave RSM Francis a bottle of rum — he was the one who had stolen the CO's rum, a crime suspected of Ron back in 1951.) Ron was awarded both the Member of Military Merit and the Officer of Military Merit. His rewarding career spanned the years 1951 to 1988. Ron now works for the federal government. He and his wife Alice live in Nepean, Ontario.

Ron Francis greets his mother on 24 December 1952.
(Toronto Telegram photo)

Captain Jack de Hart is awarded the Military Cross on 2 October 1953 by the Commonwealth Division Commander, M Gen MM West.

SUPPORTING THE NETHERLANDS BATTALION

John de Hart could never find the time for me to interview him but, fortunately, he did put some ideas down on paper before his death on November 8, 1992. This reluctance to tell of his actions in Korea was typical of this man, who never sought praise or recognition, yet deserved both in large measure.

Jack, as he was known, joined the Canadian Army in 1943 as a gunner. He was commissioned and served in England until the Second War ended. Having a Bachelor's degree in law, he worked for a year with the Judge Advocate General, but his first choice was the Artillery. Thus, it was in the 81st Field Regiment that his Korea story begins:

> I was a member of the 81st Field Regiment in Petawawa, but because one of the FOOs [Forward Observation Officers] in 1 RCHA [Royal Canadian Horse Artillery], Korea, had been burned in his tent and evacuated to Japan, I was rushed over from Canada to replace him. [Jack sailed on the USNS *James O'Hare* on 15 January 1953.] The Regiment was commanded by the well-known Teddy McNaughton, whom I had never met. My introduction to him was somewhat unnerving. He asked me what I knew

about Field Artillery, and when I replied, "Not much, Sir," he looked me in the eye and said, "I'll give you one month — one month, do you understand? In one month you'll either know everything or you're finished — absolutely finished. I'll come and give you a test in a month. That's all."

Jack's first exposure to the war was as the FOO directing the artillery fire from the 25-pounders of 1 RCHA. He worked from an observation post (OP), from which the FOO could observe the front and provide fire support to the infantry, in this case the Royal Netherlands Battalion. One feature of the artillery is that they seldom went out of the line to rest. In Jack's words,

> The Canadian Brigade had been pulled out of the line for a six-week rest but the artillery carried on and we were attached to the Second American Division. I had been there for almost four weeks when I received a radio message at about two in the morning from my Battery Commander informing me that the CO would arrive at my position at 0900 hours to test me on artillery procedures. Naturally I was quite worried, as he could not give me any idea of what to expect. This worry was intensified at 0855 hours when I received a terse radio message from the CO, which said, "I'll be at your location in five minutes. Have the teapot boiling. Out." My OP crew, whom I had inherited on my arrival, had been in position for some time and were quite used to the CO. When I said to one of them, "Perhaps we should put on the hot water," he laughed and replied, "Don't worry, Sir; we've already got it boiling."

Jack's future in Korea and maybe as an Artillery officer was at stake:

> When the CO arrived he put me through a gruelling test of various artillery procedures, commencing with a standard barrage, which I had never fired in my life although I had worked them out on course in Shilo. After the CO pointed out where I was to lay down the barrage he put his hands behind his back and paced up and down behind me where I was working with my assistant and said, "Don't worry about me, Jack. Pretend I'm not here at all." Eventually the barrage began, and no sooner had we fired on the second line when he got very excited and gave me a Mike target, which is what we called regimental targets in those days. Once the Mike target got under way he pointed out another area which also required a Mike target, and as I began that call for fire he said, "Don't worry, Jack. I'm not only testing you, I'm testing the Regimental Command Post as well to see how they distribute the fire." This test went

on for four hours and included such things as my having to place an officer under arrest for a large Command Post error, several cups of hot tea for the CO, the firing of a single gun target by the CO and the rest by me. Finally, at 1000 hours, he smiled and said, "Well, Jack, thank you very much. That was a most pleasant morning." He said goodbye to my OP party and left. I waited a week, and having heard nothing called the Battery Commander one night to ask him how I had done. His reply was, "You're still there, aren't you? So don't worry. If you had not done well on the test you would have been on your way to Canada by now."

There is no doubt that Jack's entire career was affected by Lieutenant Colonel Teddy McNaughton. One incident remained vivid in his mind:

He gave much sound advice to me and at times seemed somewhat surprised that I followed it. For example, I had a well dug in OP with twelve-inch by twelve-inch timbers and railway tracks holding up the overhead sandbags and earth. He said I needed several layers of additional sandbags on top of that. I asked the Sergeant Major to get me a thousand sandbags, and in two days he delivers ten thousand bags. I said, "Sergeant Major what am I going to do with these? I only need a thousand." He smiled and said, "The Americans charge the same for ten thousand as for one, Sir — they're all worth one bottle of Scotch!" When the CO arrived a few days later he expressed surprise that my OP had already been reinforced with the sandbags, and I said, "Well, Sir, you told me that it should be done so I did it. Why are you surprised?" He replied, "Well, I guess I'm not really surprised, but people don't always listen to me." Anyway, it proved to be a most valuable piece of advice, and I'm sure it saved my life a week or two later when we came under heavy attack and had several direct hits on the top of our OP. When a large shell landed, we were all knocked to the ground by the shock wave, and I guess we were unconscious for a few seconds or minutes. When I came to I experienced the strange sensation of thinking I was dead and floating around in heaven or some other place. I remember thinking how strange it was, and how I finally knew what it was like to be dead. Of course we couldn't see anything because of the dust in the OP, but I was suddenly returned to my senses by the voice of my Bombardier saying, "Are you all right, Sir? Are you all right?" Fortunately we all were.

The leadership of the Commanding Officer permeated down to the most junior member of the Regiment:

There was something about Teddy that endeared him to all whom he met. He got quite annoyed one New Year's Eve because the radio net, which to him was sacred, was disrupted at the stroke of midnight when one operator began to sing, "One Able, One Able for all stations three; Mike target, Mike target he chortled with glee. All the CPOs shudder, the GPOs shake; the Number Ones quiver, the Gun Numbers quake." This song had a verse for each Battery and sure enough an operator from each Battery came on in turn until the song was completed. Naturally the CO was unable to discover which operators had done the singing, although he did make an attempt. We all knew that in spite of his outward anger, he was secretly pleased with the tribute from his troops.

There were certain moments of Jack's Korea experience that he would never forget, like the time he loosed his wrath on a single member of the enemy:

I noticed a small enemy machine-gun firing at one of our air OP planes which was circling in the air in front of my OP. I was determined to put an end to that machine-gun and began firing non-stop with my troop of four guns. ... [On hearing the commotion], the CO ordered the whole Regiment to man the guns, calling them out of a movie which had been showing. ... He was convinced that an attack was coming in. After some eight or nine hundred rounds, all fired by my four-gun troop in some forty minutes, everything subsided and I was ordered to report to the CO. When he asked me what was going on, I said, "Sir, that little machine-gun made me so mad firing at one of our planes that I decided to wipe it out. ... My gunners were absolutely delighted that they had been able to fire such a large number of rounds in such a few minutes. The CO was not amused.

The FOO did not work all alone but had a small team of driver, signaller, technical assistant and so on to support him. When the Dutch Company Commander, Ber Kamavarr, whom Jack had been supporting, was killed on 18 March 1953, an incident followed that justified Jack's admiration for his OP crew:

We came under very heavy attack, which was not unexpected as we had been severely shelled for several days. The young Dutch officer who took over immediately from Ber was able to speak only a few words of English when he was not under stress, and we had a most difficult time for the first hour as the attack was still being pressed. Finally I insisted on having an interpreter, even at the risk of losing one rifle, because the artillery fire which we were able to produce was absolutely vital for the security of the Battalion. This was finally arranged and a rifleman was assigned as our interpreter. By morning things had slowed down, and the position was, at least temporarily, secure. It was during that night that most communications along the Brigade front were out, but I was lucky enough to be able to communicate all night, and to provide information for both the Commanding Officer and the Brigade Commander. At one stage I was the only link from the front.

This act of professionalism resulted in Jack being awarded the Military Cross. The citation reads as follows:

> Captain deHart [sic] has successfully manned exposed artillery observation posts for long periods and frequently under intensive enemy fire. During the period 16 to 28 March 1953, A Company of the Royal Netherlands Battalion, 2 United States Division which he was supporting was occupying a position known as "Nudae" and became subjected to heavy Chinese attacks, preceded by intense bombardment. ... Throughout this time Captain deHart directed artillery fire in support of the Royal Netherlands Battalion. The Company occupying "Nudae" was relieved by another Company of the Royal Netherlands Battalion, but Captain deHart remained as the Artillery representative throughout the period. On the night 16/17 March 1953, at 1215 hours, fifty to sixty enemy attacked and again at 0200 hours a further fifty to sixty enemy launched another attack. ... Enemy casualties caused by Artillery fire directed by Captain deHart were heavy. On the night 17/18 March 1953, at 0200 hours, a large ambush inflicted heavy casualties on our own troops. The position was heavily shelled and mortared and the Company Commander was killed. Again, in spite of the enemy shelling, Captain deHart directed Artillery fire with outstanding success. On the night 28/29 March 1953, at 2200 hours an intense enemy bombardment commenced and at 2230 hours an attack by two to three hundred enemy was launched. For one-half hour the only communications were those of the Artillery, which were maintained in spite of two direct hits on the observation post. Captain deHart coolly directed Artillery fire, and the attack was driven off with enemy casualties officially estimated as fifty killed and seventy-five wounded. During the intense bombardment prior to the attacks and during the attacks themselves, Captain deHart directed Artillery fire, maintained communications and passed information with such steadiness and with such disregard for his personal safety that he made a magnificent

contribution to the successful defence of the position. His conduct in these trying circumstances, and in the light of language difficulties, was an inspiration to all those intimately concerned with the battles.

Life in Korea, the war, and the very demanding work as a FOO all went a long way to building Jack's military professionalism, a professionalism that never wavered. The uniqueness of one aspect is covered in this final quote from Jack's account of what happened forty years ago:

> We experienced strange things at night. [One time] we were holding one side of the Sami-ch'on River valley which was about two thousand metres wide, and the Chinese were in the opposite hills. On a dark evening when nothing much was happening we would often hear a Chinese female voice speaking in reasonably good English to us through tremendous loudspeakers across the valley. She would remind us of our loved ones at home, telling us not to get ourselves killed, but to lay down our arms, leave the positions and go back to Canada. Other propaganda was showered on us from artillery propaganda shells in the form of leaflets, all with the same message — Canadians go home. It was uncanny how quickly the Chinese knew when one of our units had been replaced. One could understand it when the Van Doos came in the line because of the French accent on the radio nets. But it didn't seem to matter what unit had arrived. Invariably, that same evening, we would hear over the loudspeaker, "Welcome to the Royal Canadian Regiment," or whatever unit it was. "Why did you come here? You are wasting your time. Your loved ones are waiting for you. Go home while you still have the chance."

Jack de Hart came home to the Artillery School, then Staff College. He held a series of staff appointments, spent a year in the Middle East as a United Nations observer, was promoted to Lieutenant Colonel and finally retired from the Army in May 1971. Jack went on to work with the Canadian Corps of Commissionaires in Ottawa for almost twenty years, fourteen as Executive Secretary. In a eulogy for Jack at his funeral in early November 1992 Lieutenant Colonel Jerry Donahue said, "Many of us knew him as a quiet, gracious gentleman who had a unique understanding of human nature and concern for the individual." Perhaps these are the words that best describe this courageous, determined veteran of Korea.

Gordon Owen on returning to Canada.

WOUNDED SIX TIMES, TAKEN PRISONER

Gordon Owen had attended the University of British Columbia in Vancouver and served in the Militia before transferring to the Active Force on May 17, 1951. Gordon became the Pioneer Officer (a regimental engineer responsible for mines, demolitions, flame throwers and engineering projects) for the Third Battalion, Royal Canadian Regiment (3 RCR). Almost two years later he was en route to Korea, arriving on March 23, 1953.

Gordon's unit, C Company, was part of the Jamestown Line on the Sami-ch'on River. C Company was in the most forward position with A Company to their right, B Company to the left and rear, and D Company in the reserve position. As mentioned in Herbert Wood's, *Strange Battleground*, "One of the significant features of this layout was dispersion." The layout of C Company is described as having "the trenches, fire bays, weapon pits, shelters, command posts and observation posts ... [linked by] a communications trench ... from five to seven feet [in depth]."

Gordon describes one aspect of the layout:

> I was detailed to take my pioneers to C Company's area to deal with an unexploded shell which was on the top of a platoon bunker. There were

vast amounts of barbed wire — for instance, the area surrounding Number 8 Platoon's position had seventeen rows of double concertina wire. This should have made the position very safe, but the Chinese would overcome all of the defences. I arrived with my pioneer sergeant, three pioneers, four South Korean soldiers and two privates from the Nathan Hale Counter Bombardment Unit of the US Army. We took up residence in 8 Platoon's area in the centre of C Company's position.

The Pioneer Platoon was near C Company clearing a path into a mined area to allow the Strathcona tanks to get forward into a better firing position. Gordon recalls, "We had just finished at first light in the morning. ... [While we were] expecting the tanks to come up, there was the familiar sound of mortars ... so I jumped into ... an old Korean well. The mortar shell landed right where I had been standing."

On the night of May 2–3, C Company of the battalion was hit and hit hard. When Gordon came up to the front he was "just in time to see Jerry Meynell leaving with a twenty-five — man fighting patrol." A mere twenty minutes later the word came over the radio that Jerry's men had been ambushed by the Chinese. Doug Banton, Number 8 Platoon Commander, was ordered "to take ten men on a fighting patrol to go and see what could be done to help them, leaving just four men behind." Gordon was the only officer left in the position, so he told Doug, "I've got three pioneers with me; we'll hold this position." Like Jerry's group, Banton and his ten men were ambushed. Banton was killed. Now the Chinese were all over the position:

> When the Chinese saturation shoot ended I was already wounded. I ordered Corporal Pero of 8 Platoon to assess damage and group any survivors at Platoon Headquarters. ... The only shooting from the RCR that I could hear was from my 9 mm Browning pistol. ... It was a busy night. My first wound was from shrapnel in my right arm, my right arm was now broken. [In all Gordon was hit six times.] I was knocked out by an explosion and when I came to, there was a Chinese soldier standing over me.

Second Lieutenant Gordon Owen gave his last order in the war when he told Corporal Pero, "You go left to the trench and get the men out, and I'll go right." It is explained in *Strange Battleground* that Corporal Pero "won the Military Medal for his work in the defence of Number 8 Platoon after Lieutenant Banton's death."

Losses that night for 3 RCR were twenty-six killed, twenty-seven wounded, seven taken prisoner. Gordon had a broken arm, broken leg and head wound from which "a piece of stuff was hanging out". The Chinese took Gordon prisoner and moved him back into an underground bunker with "six or seven other people they had picked up that night". In spite of his wounds Gordon walked to an area close to Panmunjon [the site later chosen for the peace talks]. The treatment was harsh and when Gordon refused to tell his captors what they wanted, they "had him stand on the edge of a grave ... moved out a firing squad and demanded some information." It was merely a staged threat, for at the last moment the firing party would leave.

The weeks passed:

> I eventually ended up at a place close to Wosan, and I never did get into a prisoner-of-war camp. I was not considered a safe person and had my own platoon of guards all the time. One interesting time was when they put me in a spot during the rainy season (May and June, or longer). The rain was just pouring down, through the roof of this tiny cell I was in (which was a little bigger than a table). I thought, Jiminy Christmas, I've got to do something about this! What I did was ask for a bucket to collect the water so a blanket I had would not be destroyed. It worked, I was moved to a dryer place to save a blanket.
>
> My wounds had started to heal, and I was still using my first field dressing, the same one that I had used for weeks. My leg had healed fairly well, and later I took the splint off my arm.

There was nothing Gordon could do to improve his situation. The weather, lack of food and less-than-comfortable surroundings all took their toll. When the armistice was signed on July 27, 1953, Gordon was still imprisoned. Another month passed:

> I got some medical care just before I was released. A Chinese soldier came along with two tubes of sulpha ointment, put it on top of the wounds, and put it in the top shrapnel hole, pushing it through until it came out the bottom hole, then pushed it into the next hole until it came out there. That was fine, I was willing to go along with it, but it was a little painful. I had splinted my own arm, and had looked after myself. Eventually a piece of shrapnel in my head wiggled out. I figured I was dying of malnutrition by the end of August. By this time the fighting had stopped, and I was put in with eleven Americans and one Australian. There were still no camp amenities. We never saw a Red Cross parcel. We were lucky to get a few peanuts every two or three days.
>
> One day I was paraded out the door to see a line of nineteen ambulances, Molotov models, complete with red stars, all of which were filled

with [wounded] UN soldiers [who, like me, had been captured]. There was a Chinese general there, a big ceremony with cameras, and a large scroll written all in Chinese. They said, "Sign here. You can be in charge of this convoy; take it to Panmunjom!"

I was quite surprised, but didn't question what I was signing. Both sides had declared that they had sent back all the prisoners thirty days before. We were non-people. I had not been declared a prisoner, neither had the people that were with me. Everyone of those people on the ambulances had been badly wounded and was not expected to live.

I arrived at Panmunjom with Chinese drivers and about ninety UN soldiers, all in bad shape. I arrived at the checkpoint on the UN side, and an American soldier refused to let us through because there wasn't anyone due on this road until next morning and he had no communications to the rear. I told him that if he didn't open the gate, I was driving through. He said that if I did he would have to shoot us. The Chinese drivers all understood English, especially the lead driver with me. He was a little apprehensive, but I said, "Go ahead, drive through!" We were dressed in Chinese uniforms (at least I was) meaning a white cotton shirt, blue jacket and trousers and a blue cap (I was still wearing my RCR scarf). At the last minute the guard opened the gate and let us through. I drove into the UN camp as they were demolishing it. The exchange area for Canadians was called Beaver Camp. I saw the duty officer, Lieutenant Colonel K.L. Campbell (my CO), who recognized me immediately. I informed him very quickly what the situation was — that these were Chinese ambulances and that they had to go back — I had agreed with the Chinese to do this before my departure. I also mentioned the problem we had had with the guard and so on. We were quickly moved to a safe area and the ambulances returned to the North.

Gordon was temporarily hospitalized at a Norwegian Mobile Army Surgical Hospital (MASH) and then flown to Japan for another week's hospitalization while he waited to be flown back to Canada.

Back in Canada, Gordon Owen served with 1 RCR and 2 RCR and later in various staff positions. He was in Cyprus from 1976 to 1979. He retired from the Army in 1979 and spent seven years as the Rehabilitation Coordinator for the British Columbia government. Gordon Owen is now retired and lives in Victoria, British Columbia, with his wife Fabiole. Gordon now works full-time on his stock market hobby in gold and precious metals.

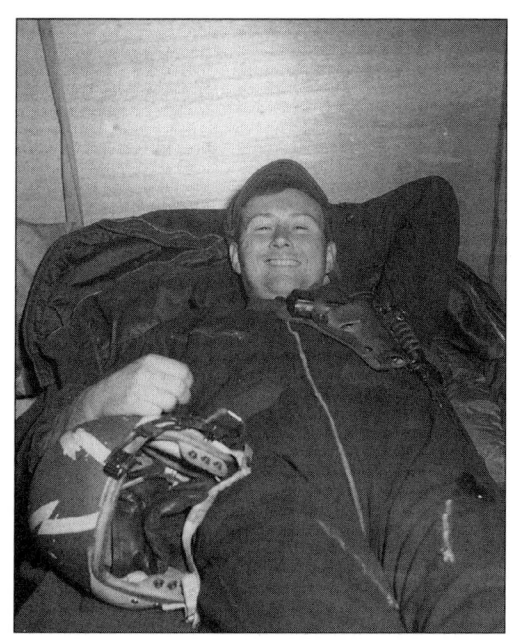

Bill Ward just before a mission. Note his pistol and helmet. Despite the grin, Bill was superstitious and was not keen on having a photo taken at such a tense time.

IN TANKS AND AIRCRAFT AGAINST THE ENEMY

Bill Ward had just completed his academic training at Queen's University and was serving in Camp Petawawa when he volunteered to join the Special Service Force. The establishment was full at that time, but eventually he did get to go to Korea. "There was pressure on the system to get the reinforcements overseas as we were Special Force, only serving for eighteen months."

On 12 November 1950, Lieutenant Colonel Dean Freeman called Bill into his office and asked, "Do you still want to go to Korea?" Just a few weeks later the draft, including Bill Ward and his buddy Rick Allen, was aboard the *S.B. Buckner* en route to Japan. Bill was seasick before the ship left Puget Sound. Some of the people on the draft with Bill were Vic Johnson, Ramsey Withers, Russ Gardner and Don Pruner. Seventeen days later, after a very rough crossing, the ship arrived in Yokahama just in time for Christmas dinner: Australian mutton.

On Boxing Day, Bill and other Canadians set off for Pusan in a very old Chinese freighter. The trip was uneventful until the troops found there was beer in the hold [see Charlie Hamilton's story]. Bill remembers,

An Oral History From Those Who Were There

Just prior to reaching Pusan we learned that the draft was to assist the crew on our arrival in Pusan. We were asked to canvass the soldiers to see if one of them could run the donkey engine to lift the cargo out of the hold. The Australians, New Zealanders and Canadians discovered that part of the cargo was Asahi beer on top of the ammunition. We arrived off Pusan and anchored awaiting our turn to go alongside — this was on 29 December. We waited because we were to unload ourselves. The troops were getting restless. On New Year's Eve the troops were allocated two cans of beer each, but that night the party continued without the officers' knowledge. By three in the morning the soldiers were having the best party possible. No one could control the soldiers. We were in trouble. I got ashore and told the Canadian Movements staff that they had to get the ship alongside at once. The Australians were not pleased with the British Merchant Navy crew, who had made the big mistake. They turned the fire hoses on the soldiers, who in turn threw the pumps overboard. I saw all this as I was returning to the ship. The whole bay was covered with empty beer bottles. A US Navy landing craft came alongside filled with US Military Police armed with submachine-guns. The soldiers pointed their rifles at the MPs, who left in a hurry (we carried no ammunition). The ship was docked and the soldiers went into the camp through a line of British Military Police. Anyone who was drunk went into detention. As I was leaving the camp I was handed a wad of papers which I put in my kit bag [and promptly forgot].

It was New Year's Day 1951 when they took the eighteen-hour train ride to Seoul. When the train arrived and the soldiers unloaded, they were surrounded by Korean urchins looking for food. Hal Wyant met the reinforcements to take them to C Squadron, which was then in the line. Next day Major Vic Jewkes, the Squadron Commander, had a surprise for Rick Allen and Bill Ward, the new boys. Bill recalls, "He took us on a complete walking tour of the entire squadron front. I can't even remember eating dinner that night, I was so exhausted!"

The time had come to put into practice all the theory leaned in Canada. Bill went to Bob Neelin's troop as a spare crew commander on Hill 159. As the newcomer walked into the front lines, the first thing he saw was "a burned-out ambulance, ambushed the night before by the Chinese". After a month Bill was given command of 4th Troop, which had been Strath MacDonald's troop (see Ron Francis's story).

We operated as individual tank crews, sometimes more than 600 to 800 yards apart. We were in sniping positions and, of course, we strengthened the infantry position in the defence. When we went into rest I dug down in my kit bag looking for clean socks. I came across the wad of papers I had been given months before at Pusan. They were charge reports on the Canadian soldiers. I went to the garbage dump where a fire was burning and I tossed in the whole lot! A few days later Vic Jewkes came and saw me. He said, "What do you know about paperwork concerning the ship you were on?" I told him and he said we had to go to Brigade Headquarters. Vic did all the talking with Brigadier General Rockingham. The General said, "Alright. You are here to do a job, Ward." I agreed with him and we got out of there fast. There were shifts in the line as the R22ᵉR took over a larger section of the front. They were replaced by the King's Own Scottish Borderers [KOSB]. My French was not good, but I could understand the R22ᵉR French Canadians better than the KOSBs with their broad Scottish accents!

After six months, C Squadron was replaced by B Squadron, and Bill went to Squadron Headquarters. After a while Bill joined Ron Steven's troop in, as Bill put it, "a very tricky part of the front". The Chinese hit that particular troop position with 120 mm mortars. Bill said, "One 120 mm round hit the bunker — it blew all the urinals down." The Squadron came out of the line and Bill and Rick were the two spare officers. Rick went to the Junior NCO School and Bill went on course as a student at the 8th Army Gas School at Taegu. Later, Ron Stevens broke his ankle, and Bill remained with 1st Troop supporting 1 PPCLI.

Bill's time in Korea was drawing to a close in November 1951 when he went to Brigade Headquarters. It was here he learned that volunteers were needed to join the Mosquito Group, flying as observers. Before Bill left B Squadron he and Bruce Rutherford planned and executed a night counter-attack:

> The PPCLI platoon commander we supported was Peter Worthington. ...On 31 December 1951 Peter Berry of the Royal Tank Regiment [British] and I went to the rear to an American Airfield at Chun Chon where the Mosquito Group was situated. We reported in on January 1, 1952, to commence our indoctrination with 6147 Tactical Control Group, part of the 5th US Air Force. The Group's role was to control and direct all Allied fighter bomber strikes. We covered the territory from the enemy forward defence line back 10,000 metres. The US force integrated we "foreigners" right into the team. We had three days ground school:

> which side of the aeroplane to jump out of; radio procedures; escape procedures and the briefing system used to tell pilots (all Americans) and the assorted observers how to bring ordnance — machine-gun fire, rockets, bombs and napalm — onto the target. It was then that the flying phase began. The first trip was orientation near the actual front lines, theirs and ours. On my very first trip we ended up putting in a strike, replacing another plane that had gone unserviceable. There was a major psychological change from sitting behind three-and-one-half inches of armour in a tank to Alcan-thickness aluminum in an aeroplane. The moments of action were short but violent. We would acquire the target, mark it with rockets and then direct the attack aircraft. We were flying the Harvard single-engine aircraft, the T6, G Model, nicknamed The Terrible Texan. My pilot was experienced and he did everything for those first missions. I was busy being airsick for most of that first trip. After twelve missions you had to do everything but pilot the aircraft. At this point the experienced pilot took on another new boy, and the teaming up of two inexperienced crew members then began.

Bill flew all of January until May 1952, completing eighty-eight missions over hostile territory. (The record was 230 by a Scot, flying for almost a year.) Bill recalls,

> On one occasion we flew through a salvo of 37 mm anti-aircraft fire which dinted the fuselage but didn't break the metal. Our problem was that once a target was acquired we had to stay over it until the attack aircraft hit the target and we had completed a post-strike assessment. We also flew through our own artillery barrages when we had no choice, as well as the ground fire of all calibres from the Chinese. The most difficult weapon to face was the Quad 50 — four .50-calibre machine-guns being aimed by determined Chinese crews.

When one realizes that the Harvard was unarmed except for the target identification rockets, one cannot help feeling admiration for the Mosquito Group. Bill was awarded the United States Distinguished Flying Cross on 19 March 1952 for his time as an observer. Bill's final story concerns his fourth mission: "I was sitting on my parachute and we were aloft. I said to the pilot, Jack James, 'It's the right side we jump out of, eh?' He said over the intercom, 'Jump? Jump? You can jump out of the right side if you want! I'm going to ride the biggest piece down, if it comes to that!'"

For their work the Mosquito Group received the United States Presidential Unit Citation and the Korean Presidential Citation.

*The single-engine Harvard, known as the Terrible Texan.
Bill Ward flew eighty-eight sorties in this type of aircraft*

Bill returned to B Squadron and the much slower pace on the ground: "I took over Clint Cowan's troop position just as Brigadier Allard's new policy came into force. The tanks were to be kept back and only move forward when attacks came in." Two nights later, "The Chinese bombardment really came in on 3rd Battalion Royal Canadian Regiment. It was a long, hard night, and we fired a lot of high explosive, machine-guns and white phosphorous to break up the attack."

The Squadron came out of the line in mid-May 1953, when Bill Ellis's A Squadron took over. Bill Ward's extra-long tour in the Far East was over.

Bill returned to Canada and served at Camp Borden and 1 Canadian Division in Camp Petawawa. He served in Germany twice and then returned to regimental duty in Calgary. Bill attended Staff College and in 1968 went to Indo-China. Major Bill Ward retired in January 1974 from the world of writing intelligence summaries about the Far East. He then began a fifteen-year career with External Affairs until 1990, when he retired. Bill and his wife Eleanor live in Ottawa, Ontario.

Harry Pope joins Bruce Rutherford in a Strathcona tank to perfect infantry and tank cooperation. Shooting at a Chinese tunnel across the Sami-ch'on River, January 1953.

HARRY POPE
— THE SOLDIER'S SOLDIER

When I started to interview soldiers who served in Korea after April 1952, time and again I heard, "You must get Harry Pope's story." Even General Dextraze said, "Then there was the event at Fort Lewis concerning Harry Pope, but that is another story." In the summer of 1993 Harry agreed to allow his story to be put in my book, and here it is.

In March 1939, having just turned sixteen, William Henry Pope joined the Canadian Militia. He graduated from the Royal Military College in 1942 and served with the Royal 22^e Regiment in Italy and North West Europe. He became a regimental legend when on 19 May 1944 he went back, unarmed and slightly wounded, into the German lines to rescue two of his severely wounded soldiers at the Hitler Line. He was taken prisoner, escaped after eleven days and joined a group of British paratroopers, Italian Partisans and other escaped prisoners who laid mines on roads and blew up German trucks. On 25 July 1944, after fifty-one days on the loose behind the lines, Harry Pope finally rejoined his regiment. Not surprisingly, Harry remained in the Army and volunteered to join 2nd Battalion R22ᵉR to go with Lieutenant Colonel Dextraze to Korea. Fighting was what Harry was good at. When Dextraze insisted he be allowed to handpick his officers, Harry was one of them.

The story of Fort Lewis is recounted here in Harry Pope's own words:

> On Good Friday 1951 I spent a good part of the day in a Seattle Rathskeller [German beer-hall], rather wishing I had a blonde with me. On re-entering my hotel, I passed a meeting room with about fifty people in it and a big sign up on the wall: "Hands off Korea." Being slated for Korea in about three weeks, I asked the young woman at the door if this was a Republican meeting. "No," she replied, "It's the Socialist Workers Party of America."
>
> Not having had a good political discussion for a long time, I then asked, "May I sit down with the proletariat?"
>
> [She replied,] "Yes, for fifty cents."
>
> After about two hours of Comrade Joe Hansen's speech, he being the leader and a former secretary to Trotsky, I turned and noticed a very young blonde with glasses sitting at the back of the room. "A beauty with brains!" The only way to get to know her was to stick around. I was not able to get Colleen's address, and then could not do better than find out where the Trotskyists would be meeting the next evening. I remember very well Colleen's last name but suppress it here — she is likely a sedate grandmother now!

For the Trotskyist social, Harry polished the buttons of his service dress and went to the party, Sam Browne and all. Things were going well with Colleen when her fiance turned up looking for her. Nothing for it but Harry had to go to a Unitarian Church next morning, Sunday, to hear Comrade Joe's lecture "The Agrarian Reform Movement in China: Mao Tse-Tung's Takeover". But it paid off–Colleen agreed to a date the next Saturday evening.

> Next morning, back in Fort Lewis, I said to my CO, Lieutenant Colonel Jacques Dextraze, DSO, "I'd better tell you what I did over the weekend before the FBI or the CIA tells the Adjutant-General." The most prophetic joke I ever made in my life.
>
> The next Wednesday, Colonel Dextraze called a mess meeting and told the officers that the mess would throw a thank-you party on Saturday for our American hosts in view of 2 R22ᵉR's imminent departure for Korea. "All officers will attend," concluded the CO.
>
> "All officers?" I asked, horrified.
>
> "No, no, all except those that have a date with a Trotskyist blonde."

The date went well. Two or three days later, Colonel Dextraze told me he had been told by Brigadier Rockingham to parade me to him immediately. "I think you're in trouble," said the CO.

Though most of 2 R22ᵉR had heard of my two Trotskyist weekends, Brigadier Rockingham was hearing of it for the first time. "I think you've been a little indiscreet," he said. "I'll phone the Adjutant-General [AG, in Ottawa] and see what can be done." However, the AG had not yet heard of it either — it had been handled at Ministerial level. I was ordered back to Ottawa to become adjutant of No. 1 Army Administrative Unit.

Before [I left], Colonel Dextraze and I agreed that the affair would probably cost me my commission. "Come back as a private," Colonel Dextraze said, "and I'll keep a Company Sergeant Major's vacancy open to which I'll promote you as soon as you get back."

Major Pope, promoted at last! Korea 1953.

On arrival in Ottawa, Harry was at once up before the Adjutant-General. Before Captain Pope had had time to salute, Major-General Macklin had let fly: "God dammit, Pope, when I used to work for your father I never thought I'd have a son [of his] parading up before me like this." Colleen was not mentioned. It might have lightened the atmosphere had she been, but probably not.

After a couple of weeks, on 25 April 1951, I wrote Lieutenant Colonel McClelland, CO 1 AAU. "My Battalion is en route to Korea. From newspaper reports of the battle now going on there, it is obvious that it will have a hard and bloody fight. I feel that being removed from my Battalion ten days before it sails for the Front brings dishonour upon me. I can only be vindicated by serving with my Battalion, and that as soon as possible. I therefore request that I be reposted to the 2nd Battalion, Royal 22ᵉ Regiment immediately, if possible before it makes contact with the enemy. If it is felt that my continuing interest in political questions renders me a liability in my present rank, I am willing to serve His Majesty in action in any inferior rank that may be decided upon."

The letter came back with the Adjutant-General's minute on it: "The Americans would find him a liability in any rank."

After six weeks at 1 AAU, Harry was reposted to 1 R22ᵉR in Valcartier. His former CO, Lieutenant-Colonel McClelland, wrote him, in part, as follows:

> I want you to know that when you first arrived at the unit I had some misgivings about the effect your natural annoyance at the unfortunate turn of events would have on your work. However, my fears proved to be unfounded and I can say, without reservation, that I was very glad to have you and that your move was a definite loss to the unit.

Naturally, on arrival at 1 R22ᵉR Harry became the adjutant—his sixth time in the appointment. He arrived in Korea with the advance party of 1 R22ᵉR and continued as adjutant until August 1952 when, a major having left the battalion temporarily, Harry was given command of C Company. He retained command even when the battalion had all its seven majors back on strength. Harry, of course, was still a captain — Colleen had cost him fourteen months of seniority!

At last Harry was again in command in action — his first time since a German bullet broke his arm on the Senio River, Italy, on 1 January 1945. Harry was determined to keep his command, and, in the words of the citation for his Military Cross,

> throughout this period he remained continuously with his men, refusing periods of rest that were offered to him. Through his own resolute manner and his eagerness to strike back at the enemy at every opportunity, he has developed a fighting spirit of the highest order in everyone under his command. And his unceasing attention to the welfare of his men and the needs of others has endeared him to both officers and men alike. Major Pope has shown qualities of leadership of the highest order. His enthusiasm, competence and coolness under fire have been an example to all.

Captain Pope's wartime experiences were put to good use in Korea. In his paper "Infantry Defences in Korea", he wrote this about all round defence:

> We applied all our techniques without variation to the Korean hills we occupied. ... As the enemy shelling increased and with it nasty-minded probes, we remembered the stories of our fathers and began digging in and wiring in the positions we had first occupied in the 1940–45 pattern. We were overwhelmed at our own sagacity in thus applying the lessons of two World Wars.

The question Harry soon asked about this type of defence was "Have we applied the lessons properly?" The Chinese were not the Germans. They did not have the air power, sophisticated target acquisition or communication network of the UN forces, so they resorted to a different battle plan. In Harry's word, "the enemy increased his patrolling in front of the locality to be raided. Our routine recce patrols and so-called fighting or ambush patrols would be engaged and defeated on our side of the valley by enemy forces of up to company size. Our static, nighttime outposts would be raided or destroyed."

Trench warfare developed a "sit tight and stay safe" mentality. Time and again the UN forces took large losses despite their superior equipment. It seemed that the reason for being there was so different from the First and Second World Wars. The forces had the psychological feeling of "a one-year tour and then rotate home". This attitude produced a "soldier-saving" feeling amongst all ranks. Harry recalls, "Many majors and lieutenant colonels with Second War experience were most concerned not to get themselves killed in a sideshow like Korea."

Harry also has a few words about Chinese shellfire and mortar attacks, which he believes were to neutralize the front-line soldiers:

> It was intended to keep our heads down, disorganize our defences, depress our morale and, most importantly, discourage us from doing any daylight detailed reconnaissance of our forward slopes. The enemy often prepared caves in which his raiding party laid up. It became second nature for us to surrender the initiative to him. The enemy appears to have been successful in all the raids he carried out against the Commonwealth Division in the last year before the armistice.

Harry's thoughts on the above were really driven home when he wrote, "Every attack must be repulsed before even one hill — one platoon position — falls."

Joseph Goulden's *Korea: the Untold Story of the War* tells of President-elect Eisenhower's secret visit to Korea in November 1952:

> Ike reviewed the troops near the front, talked to the wounded at an American mobile army surgical hospital (MASH) and at a press conference said it would be difficult to end the fighting with a "positive and definite victory without enlarging the war". In his memoirs he wrote, "We could not stand forever on a static front and continue to accept casualties without any visible results.

In retrospect, who could blame the leadership for waiting for an armistice to preserve the soldiers from death in a foreign land? In the last paragraph of *Strange Battleground*, Herb Wood writes, "In this light, the many gallant actions fought by the soldiers of the Commonwealth in spite of such conditions, seem all the more remarkable."

Harry Pope thinks that the "sit tight" mentality was taken advantage of by the Chinese. During the winter of 1952–53, C Company, 1 R22^{e}R, was temporarily under command of a British battalion on The Hook. In Harry's words,

> We spent two very quiet weeks like that [sitting tight]. Too quiet, in fact. So one day I suggested to Sergeant Bruno Bergeron, MM, who commanded 7 Platoon, that he accompany me on a recce towards the Chinese position directly in front of us. About 1,500 metres from our position and thus about 500 metres from the presumed Chinese position, we saw what looked like a white spot in the middle of what looked like the entrance to a cave. Having a rifle with us, as well as a submachine-gun, naturally, either Sergeant Bergeron or I fired at the centre of the cave. The white spot disappeared, which indicated to us that it had been one of our enemies who had been watching us.
>
> Back with C Company, I phoned Battalion — to be told by a major that we had come damn close to having the fire of the twenty-four guns of the divisional artillery regiment come down on our heads. Apparently, one of their observation posts had seen us and it was only at the last minute that they had realized that it was a couple of Vingt-Deux strolling like that in the fresh air and not the Chinese. I said that our recce had been worthwhile because it showed that the enemy defended very badly on this part of his front. Therefore, I proposed to the major that I make further recce patrols in front of my company with the aim of determining exactly the locations of the enemy positions so that I could then lead a strong fighting patrol into the enemy lines to take prisoners. The British major replied that his battalion already had enough to do to defend itself on The Hook. "Don't go waking them up in front of you." Impossible to make him understand that the tactical advantage in front of C Company was entirely ours: If the enemy tried a counter-attack across a valley that had no cover and was two kilometres wide, it would be a massacre. Our artillery, our mortars, our tanks, our air power would permit none of the enemy to get out alive. There's a principle at play here, not merely a particular method: Defend yourself where the enemy attacks; attack the enemy where he gives no indication of wishing to make war. Why leave to the enemy the choice of the field of battle? We ended up with higher casualties because of the "sit tight" mentality.

An Oral History From Those Who Were There

Major Harry Pope's opportunity to ensure more skilful patrolling came after his promotion in January 1953 and Brigadier General Allard's arrival three months later on 21 April 1953. The Brigadier General took little time to appoint Harry to command a Brigade Patrol School. Allard had been Harry's commanding officer in Italy in 1944 and knew that Harry himself had led every patrol that his platoon had been ordered to carry out–as well as every unauthorized one that he had not been ordered to carry out! In *Strange Battleground*, Wood quoted from Pope's "Infantry Patrolling in Korea":

> The ambush would consist of a subaltern or NCO and five to twenty men. ... Ambushes were usually ordered from forward companies [who were] incapable of reinforcing their ambushes without denuding the entire company position. ... Our men knew the enemy patrols were specially trained for the job ... whereas they themselves were simply out in the valley for a routine task that came around to their platoon every third night. ... In other words "the basic sense of mission" was lacking.

Before the Brigade Patrol School could make made its specialized training felt, Brigadier Allard "limited the forward movement of patrols to the river line in front of the Canadian positions" *(25 Brigade War Diary)*.

Harry spent eighteen months in Korea, twelve with 1 R22ᵉR and six with 3 R22ᵉR, and commanded C Company from August 1952. Having been selected to attend the 1954 Staff College course he relinquished command to return to Canada at the end of September 1953. The armistice had been signed two months previously. The Company organized a party for him on 19 September and presented him with a testimonial drawn up by one of the soldiers:

> Dear Major,
>
> We are all gathered here this evening to celebrate your departure, which will take place in a few days. We are all very happy that you are at last going home for a well-deserved rest. But at the bottom of our hearts, joy and sadness are conjoined, because in you we are losing a great friend and almost a father. How many times, through your good counsel and your explanations, you have renewed our confidence at the moments we most needed it. For us under your command we have lived a beautiful experience, which perhaps for us will never occur again, and for others will help them in the future to become good leaders. But always, even after we have returned to civilian life, we will never be able to think of Korea without thinking of you. You are leaving, but your memory will remain with us. All of us here, officers, non-commissioned officers and

soldiers, wish you a good voyage and we hope that you will take a well-deserved rest and in thinking of us you will think what all will say and that is: Je me souviens [I remember].

This letter amply testifies that Harry Pope was indeed a soldier's soldier.

In 1959 Major Pope became Second in Command of 1 R22^eR but, not agreeing with NATO's first-strike nuclear policy, he resigned from the Army he had served for twenty years. He then became executive assistant to Hazen Argue, parliamentary leader of the Co-operative Commonwealth Federation (CCF, the forerunner of the New Democratic Party). The following year he became president of the CCF of Quebec. For twenty years, from 1967 to 1987, Harry was a full-time lecturer in economics at Ryerson Polytechnical Institute in Toronto. He has written books on economics and has been published in countless publications. Twenty-six of his columns on "Souvenirs de guerre" (Memories of war) were published in La Citadelle, *R22^eR's regimental journal, between 1986 and 1993. The second of these, dealing with the Hitler Line, was republished in French and English in the autumn 1993* Canadian Military History. *Since 1969, Harry Pope has lived in the round house he built on twenty acres north of Uxbridge, Ontario, in the midst of 15,000 conifers he planted. His wife Sheila Kathleen shares the gardening chores.*

An Oral History From Those Who Were There

Ramsey Withers (centre) and friends in Korea.

1 R22eR "TELEPHONE" COMPANY

Ramsey Withers was a fourth-year cadet at the Royal Military College in Kingston, Ontario, when he learned he was going to serve in Korea: "The graduating class was mustered and told that the Army types were to go to Korea. This was about two months before our final parade."

Ramsey had completed three summers at the Royal Canadian School of Signals in Kingston in what Ramsey calls "a well-developed officer training system". The emphasis was on the field army communications system, the very thing for the young officer going to Korea. What made it even better was that sixty per cent of fellow trainees who began with Ramsey were Second World War veterans who were attending civilian universities. To add even more experience in the final summer's training there was an "infusion of former non-commissioned officers (NCOs) who were now taking their commissions." One of these was Ron Routledge, who had won a Distinguished Conduct Medal at Hong Kong. These former NCOs worked very well with the cadets at the Royal Military College and they all became "a very close team". As well as learning the officer's role, Ramsey and his friends assisted in training the signalmen for the NATO Brigade. Ramsey comments, "This all combined to give an excellent grounding on all Second World War equipment and radio procedures, plus, thank goodness, a detailed knowledge of telephone and switchboards."

As soon as graduation was over Ramsey was outfitted at the College, issued a 9 mm pistol and shipped off to Vancouver. He flew to Japan by commercial air and on arrival was given no specific assignment other than being a reinforcement officer.

> We sat up late that first night talking to an officer just in from Korea. Just hours later I was awakened to be told, "You are going." It was off to the Commonwealth Air Force Base at Iwakuni and, along with the sacks of mail, we flew to Korea. This was early July and it was so hot. The perspiration poured off Andy King's nose in a steady stream!

On arrival the small group of reinforcement officers were taken to the Commonwealth Base Maintenance Unit for lunch and to be assigned to units. Ramsey left by jeep for the Brigade Signal Troop. Don Pruner, Second in Command of the troop, greeted Ramsey and told him he was to go to 1 R22^{e}R, where Ray Fleurey had been doing the Battalion Signals Officer's job assisted by Bill Smale. Ramsey comments, "Ray was suffering from an old parachute injury and would not leave until a reinforcement could be found. Bill replaced Ray, and I replaced Bill as the Second Signal Officer in 1 R22^{e}R commanded by Lieutenant Colonel L.F. Trudeau." Ramsey explains the division of responsibilities between the two signals officers:

> The junior officer looked after all the telephones and wire and the senior one looked after everything else including the signals office and the radio net [the common frequency to which all wireless sets were connected]. In reality, as there were only three duty officers, Bill, the Intelligence Officer Jean Fournier and myself, I worked at night in the Battalion Command Post [CP] on duty watch and by day my major task was keeping the telephones in operation. The Commanding Officer and his artillery officer remained in the CP until the battle quietened down or all patrols were back, then the two of them left the duty officer to handle things. The CO was always close by and ready to take over.

Ramsey says that the infantry net was never very active, but that the artillery net "was a beautiful thing to listen to. Under Lieutenant Colonel Leslie [in *Strange Battleground*, Herb Wood explains how Teddy McNaughton changed his name to Leslie to satisfy the terms of a will], the gunners had fantastic radio discipline, and when a call was made it was always answered at once."

An Oral History From Those Who Were There

The Regiment was in a reserve position in Gloucester Valley when Ramsey reported for duty. From there, they re-entered the line in August. The Brigade was deployed two battalions forward and one back; 1 R22ᵉR was "on the left, Hills 159, 169 and 210, and 1 RCR on the right on Hill 355 [see Dan Loomis's story]. Between us was the low ground known as the Bowling Alley." The telephone line situation was a signal officer's main challenge. Across from the Canadian Brigade were three Chinese Divisions on "the Apostles" — hills code-named Matthew, Mark, Luke and John. Chinese patrols from the Apostles repeatedly cut the telephone cables, as did the Chinese harassing fire of artillery and mortar shells.

In *Strange Battleground*, Wood says,

> Lieutenant-Colonel Trudeau began to run seriously short of reinforcements. In March ... there were insufficient trained soldiers available to keep the Royal 22ᵉR at full strength. ... At the end of the first week of September [1952], the unit showed a total posted strength of 687 ... short nearly 300 officers and men. ... "C" Company, on the very vulnerable Hill 159, had a total strength in the line of 55 all ranks. ... "A" Company was broken up and its men distributed

Ramsey saw this shortage as critical. The Signal Platoon was composed of Royal 22ᵉ soldiers employed in all telephone-line duties. "The platoon establishment called for fifty-three soldiers but we had in fact just twenty-one." Ramsey and his men manufactured pipe from mortar shell casings, buried the pipe beneath the ground and pulled the signals cable through it. This stopped shell splinters from cutting the wire as often. Each cable was tagged so that a break could be traced.

How important was the telephone line? It was vital to communications. The radio net could not be relied on, for the Chinese had so many captured US radios that they could jam radio frequencies. Ramsey recalls,

> The war establishment of an infantry battalion called for thirty-six telephones: 1 R22ᵉR had 200! The additional had been obtained by scrounging. 2 R22ᵉR had gone to Korea with all the proper Canadian equipment including the old crystal set and WD 10 switchboards and the WD 10 telephone line. 1 R22ᵉR had the US BD96 switchboard, which gave Battalion Headquarters ninety-six telephone lines. We had a US Divisional-level switchboard and we had US twenty-four — line switchboards in every Company. We also had, thankfully, acquired a substantial number of Double E8s, the US field telephone, a fantastic set, and we used US WD 1 telephone cable, which was vastly superior to the Canadian cable.

The extra equipment meant that the Signal Platoon could put in surplus circuits to accommodate any requirement, be it a forward listening post, a tank troop from the Strathcona's or an additional line in the battalion area. At one time Ramsey had "200 miles of WD 1 cable forward of Battalion Headquarters and 200 telephones." This network meant that anyone could call for artillery support when a battalion was so light in manpower that it needed extra firepower. Ramsey gives an example:

> Bob Tremblay's platoon was bothered by Chinese mortars at 144178 [the grid reference], and I would call for counter bombardment fire from the guns at the target when the artillery battery commander turned in for the night. One night I got overenthusiastic and fired 1,400 rounds at the offending Chinese mortars, forgetting to enter it in the gunner's log.

Because the war had been static for some time, each side knew where the other was located. All one had to do was to listen in on a given frequency; the accents of the different UN troops were a giveaway. At one time, a massive deception was planned, but it was doomed to fail:

> The Canadian Brigade was to sound like the 3rd US Division and to deceive the Chinese into believing that there had been a major troop move on the UN front. All the tactical signs on vehicles were changed to the 3rd Division sign. US steel helmets were issued to replace the Canadian ones. Most importantly, the radio voice procedure was to be replaced by US Army procedure, including identifying call signs and so on. I asked the Brigade Signal Officer if 1 R22ᵉR had to do this, for our net was all done in French. I explained that the ruse would fail once our battalion went on the air. We retrained all the R22ᵉR radio operators and we used as much English as possible. The "great deception" lasted twenty four hours, for the Chinese appeared in front of 1 R22ᵉR with signs [that read] "Welcome back to the line, Royal 22nd Regiment!"

The Regiment performed well in Korea, even though they had "so few men that even a Chinese shelling caused casualties we could not replace". On one occasion, a direct hit from Chinese rounds landed at Battalion Headquarters on a mess tent, killing several soldiers lined up to get their food. Patrolling was active, and often the line parties had to go out, find breaks in the line and repair them. A favourite trick by the Chinese was to cut one of the lines and then lie in ambush for the line party. Nonetheless, Ramsey points out, "We never lost one of our men despite the conditions. By scrounging we had Thompson submachine-guns for our line parties; they were well armed."

At long last, sixty reinforcements arrived from Canada. Ramsey and Bill Smale were away that day; when they returned, all but one of the new soldiers had gone to the rifle companies. That one soldier was very small — the line party equipment was bigger than he was. Despite the difference, he "became one of the best in the platoon."

The Regiment left for Canada in late April 1953, but Ramsey still had to do four months to complete his year. He asked to go to the Commonwealth Division Signal Regiment or to become a Liaison Officer at Brigade. Forty hours before his move he was sent to the Commonwealth Division Battle School in Japan at Haramura, a village in the hills about twenty-five miles northeast of Kure. This tour was, in Ramsey's words, "the most interesting four months I've ever had in my life". The Commanding Officer was British, Colonel R. Hammish Tait, DSO and Bar, MC and Bar, Royal Liverpool Regiment. He was an "acting Lieutenant Colonel, temporary Colonel — during the Second World War he had been a Brigadier in North West Europe."

There were three rifle companies, one each from Canada, Britain and Australia. The school's role was to train the individual reinforcement soldiers for Korea. The Support Company had mortar, pioneer and signal platoons; Ramsey had the latter but on occasion commanded the Company. The signal platoon had both a training and an operational function. Regimental infantry signallers from all Commonwealth nations were trained at the Battle School. Ramsey taught voice procedure to the French Canadian operators. Some of the students in the Support Company had Korea experience but were now spending time in Japan upgrading their training.

In 1993, Ramsey reflected on his year in Korea:

> One could not have had a better preparation for life. The platoon level command experience in a war has no equal, for it is the ultimate responsibility for an officer. The lives of your people is consideration number one, I could never lose sight of the men in my line party and the danger I exposed them to. On 23 October 1952 for instance, we provided as much support as possible to 1 RCR on our right. Our mortars fired 10,000 rounds. Our Vickers machine-guns burned out barrel after barrel as they fired to support the defence of 1 RCR on Hill 355 [see the Dan Loomis story]. 1 R22^{e}R took a heavy pounding from Chinese artillery, and the lines to C Company were cut. As I prepared to send out the line party, the Battalion Second-in-Command, Major Georges Sevigny, said, "You are not sending one until I say so," thus saving the lives of my men. I was so glad he said it. The gods were with us — the radio worked that night. In essence, the officer had to train his men, lead them in battle and look

after them when out of the line. All other tasks were subordinate to caring for the soldier.

As with most who served in Korea, Ramsey hold one even strong in his memory. It surfaces each year on November 11, Remembrance Day:

> Art Herman was in my Royal Roads class, and he was commanding a platoon in D Company. I had just visited his position to check the communications [August 19, 1952] and was returning along the track back to Battalion Headquarters. I passed Art's resupply group as they moved forward. Later, at the point where the platoon parties split left and right, they must have paused, and Art, seeing this, came back to help them or get them moving. A Chinese 152 mm shell landed on the fork in the track, and Art Herman was killed outright. It is his face I see on Remembrance Day and I raise one and drink to his memory.

Ramsey Withers at Royal Roads Military College receiving an honorary degree.

When the armistice was signed July 27, 1953, Ramsey's plans to visit Australia and go on to Malaya all came to an end. Ramsey was told that he and ten other Korea veterans were to go to Queen's University in Kingston, Ontario, to continue their education. A year later, Ramsey received his degree in Electrical Engineering.

The career that followed in both Command and Staff positions culminated in 1980 when Prime Minister Trudeau appointed him Chief of the Defence Staff. He retired from that post in 1983 to become the Deputy Minister of the Department of Transport, from which he retired in 1988. He is now a consultant and also chairs The Canadian War Museum Committee. Ramsey and his wife Alison reside in Ottawa, Ontario.

RSM Jim Holland with the Mayor of Hiro, Japan, and schoolchildren, 1952.

CANADIAN PROVOST CORPS IN KOREA AND JAPAN

Jim Holland was a thoroughly experienced Warrant Officer Second Class (WOII) when he sailed for Korea in April 1952. His previous wartime experience saw him rise in rank from Staff Sergeant to WOI, and his career continued in the Canadian Army after the war. Jim was serving in Edmonton when he was informed he was to go to Korea. On arrival in Korea he served with the Commonwealth Division Provost Company until he was promoted to Regimental Sergeant Major (RSM) of 25 Field Detention Barracks (FDB) in Seoul.

RSM Holland was pleased with the quality of the police officers in the Canadian Provost Corps:

> You could rely upon them — there were many Second World War veterans and they could impart their wartime experiences to the younger members. Our Canadians had no difficulty fitting in with other Commonwealth military policemen. We had no adverse incidents of any kind while I was RSM.

> The routine in 25 FDB was tough, not only on the inmates but on the staff as well. The excess shouting and the constant doubling had its effect on everyone. The daily routine was as follows: All inmates had to be up at dawn and all vigourous routine completed before the heat of the day. The physical training was done in the hills near 25 FDB, as all inmates had to be in top physical condition when they returned to their units.

In the 1950s, it was well established the Canadian Provost Corps was an extension of the Unit Commanding Officer's power of command. Time spent in detention was used to improve one's attitude toward the Army and was not just punitive. Many fine soldiers served in detention (the "digger"), and the time spent in incarceration ("digger time") often resulted in a much more professional soldier.

Jim Holland's observations about the other Commonwealth police are interesting:

> The British, Australians, New Zealanders and Canadians all worked well with the Japanese civilian police. When a discipline problem arose within the police community, each country tried their own people. Often the other three national groups waited to see what the Canadians did before they tried their own people. The Canadians usually gave the maximum punishment. In one instance Canadians got reprimands and the others [just] got cautions.

The co-operation between police officers was very good, and patrols always contained a Canadian and a British MP (Military Police Officer) or an Aussie or New Zealander. There were differences in dress, methods and style, but the result was always professional police work. Jim recalls the rules for newcomers to the unit: "Always travel with a partner; never go out alone. Ensure that the area to be patrolled is well known and be prepared to handle any situation which may arise. Never put yourself in a compromising situation. Take all precautions so that you will survive any situation."

RSM Holland returned to Canada in 1953 after ten months in the Far East. Back home, he did eleven more postings as a Chief Warrant Officer; his last was in the security section of Air Command Headquarters.

An Oral History From Those Who Were There

When Jim Holland retired in 1978 he had the distinction of being the most senior Chief Warrant Officer in all the Canadian Forces with twenty-six years in rank and more than thirty-eight years of continuous service. He and his wife Hannelore moved to Winnipeg, Manitoba, where he worked in the insurance business for Maritime Life for ten years. He has acted in movies and television commercials and is now the advertising manager for Voxair, *the 17 Wing Base Winnipeg newspaper.*

Lieutenant Dan Loomis, MC, 1953.

FLIP A COIN: HEADS, MILITARY COLLEGE; TAILS, MCGILL UNIVERSITY

It was with incredibly detailed planning that Dan Loomis became a soldier! Dan remembers,

> After I had graduated from Ottawa's Lisgar Collegiate in 1946 I obtained a job as a lab technician with the National Research Council at their Atomic Energy plant in Chalk River. It soon became obvious that a degree was required. Accordingly, I applied to go to McGill University in Montreal.
>
> I had not saved enough money for four years of engineering at university, and as an alternative I applied to the Royal Military College in Kingston, where first year cost some $1,100 and the three subsequent years $750 each. I had the $1,100 for the first year and knew I could make the rest of the money in the summer as a military trainee. The day before I was to leave for McGill I received a letter saying I had been accepted

at RRMC [Royal Roads Military College, Victoria]. I stood in the mall outside the post office at Deep River and flipped a coin — it came up heads, and two days later I left on the train for British Columbia. Atomic Energy said they would hold a job for me for four years, since the wartime policy of holding civil jobs for servicemen until they returned to civilian life was still in effect.

After two years at RRMC, Dan went on to Kingston to finish his military education. His summers in the West were spent in Calgary training with the Princess Patricia's Canadian Light Infantry and in the East at Valcartier just outside Quebec City.

As Dan's fourth year came to a close, he made up his mind to go to McGill to add a Chemical Engineering degree to his RMC diploma; however, a visit from Colonel Moogk changed all this. Colonel Moogk announced that all fourth-year cadets who were entering the Regular Army would join units then fighting in Korea.

Bob Peacock came rushing into my room and told me the news, and I said this was too good an opportunity to miss. I raced to Colonel Moogk's office to say that I had changed my mind and that I wanted to go to Korea. After a heated discussion I signed up for the Regular Army. Since Bob and I were both joining airborne regiments we volunteered to spend our embarkation leave qualifying for our parachutist wings to ensure we were "properly dressed" when we joined our new units in Korea.

With my good friend Bob Peacock going to the Patricia's and no one from our class originally slated for the Royal Canadian Regiment [RCR] I said I would join it to share the wealth. In August we flew first class by air to Japan and then on to Korea. At Brigade Headquarters all the reinforcement officers were briefed by Brigadier Bogert, who explained to us the seriousness of the operation and that we were expected "to perform well and be officers and gentlemen". It was right out of Kipling.

Dan joined 1 RCR and was assigned temporarily to be a platoon commander in D Company under the command of Major Richardson, a "former Indian Army officer with lots of war experience". The platoon sergeant was a huge Australian who had joined the Canadian Army as a soldier of fortune. He had fought the Japanese in the Second World War. The platoon already had battle experience, and there were men in the ranks who had experienced from fighting in the Second World War. Says Dan, "I was the only one who had no experience. I asked the Sergeant to tell me if I made a mistake. He said with a broad smile, 'Don't worry, Sir. I will.' And he did."

After a month Dan joined C Company and was assigned his own platoon. Two people who impressed him were

> Company Sergeant Major Lewis, who was a pillar of strength in the company and big help to me, [and] Company Quarter Master Sergeant Anderson, better known as Dogface. He was a down-to-earth, brave fellow who daily came forward with our rations and ammunition and all too often evacuated my casualties. Both these men took the time to show me the ropes, ensuring I knew what was expected of a greenhorn officer leading troops in combat.

Battalion Headquarters was far back, but Lieutenant Colonel Peter Bingham (the Commanding Officer), Second in Command Klink Klenavik and Operations Officer "Uncle" Don Holmes often come forward to platoon trenches. The Company Commander, Captain Bob Mahar, was always there.

Within a month the Korean War would put Lieutenant Loomis through the most difficult test, a fighting patrol. Dan recalls,

> It was 27 September [1952] when I was detailed to take a fighting patrol to Hill 227 far across no-man's land from our positions on Hill 355 [Little Gibraltar]. The objective was an old British position. The British had withdrawn and the Chinese now occupied it in what was thought to be as an outpost. Higher headquarters wanted to find out exactly what was on the top of the feature. Russ Gardner had been to its base a few days earlier and, in classic infantry action, captured a prisoner. As we climbed up Hill 227, my patrol went through rows of old rusted barbed wire — at night this is not easy — and when we stopped we heard rustling in the brush behind us. The Chinese were moving in and setting an ambush on the path we had used and would be waiting for our return. This was hairy, in that other possible withdrawal routes were through old British minefields.
>
> I dropped off half my patrol of twenty-two soldiers to form a firm base on a small ridge to provide direct fire support as we advanced to the top. Some fifty paces further I heard many clicks as heavy weapons were cocked. This was no outpost.
>
> We looked up the hill and could see heads silhouetted against the moonlit sky looking down on us. A vicious firefight began with weapons firing, grenades being thrown, a lot of noise and people being hit. Everyone in my entire assault group was wounded. We were in a jam.
>
> We would not have got away but for one Strathcona tank [John Bell's troop]. It had been previously laid [aimed] on one of the suspected

Chinese positions near the top of the hill, which turned out to be a heavy machine-gun that had pinned us down by its fire from its pit about thirty yards off our left flank. [The Strathcona tank] got the machine-gun with its first round! We took out its mate providing crossfire from the right with a well-thrown phosphorous grenade. At the time we were barely ten paces away from the central Chinese fire position, but we were below them on the steep hillside. They mostly shot over us. While we could see them, luckily they could not see us. With some of the Chinese heavy weapons destroyed under a hail of fire from our firm base, we were able to withdraw after fifteen minutes. With my assault group wounded we still faced a serious situation. We were still deep in no-man's land and a long way from home.

Major Don Holmes was patrol master that night. [He] had taken up a position to direct the patrol from a forward company observation post. He ordered us to withdraw and coordinated the covering fire. Salvoes of artillery hammered the Chinese as we went down the side of the hill through ancient British minefields. With nearly half the patrol tied up carrying two wounded and assisting others, we stole single file through rows of old barbed wire and minefields churned up by previous artillery bombardments and, amazingly, never set off a single mine.

The barbed wire was a real obstacle. The teams carrying the badly wounded in ponchos kept getting caught in it. However, we surprised the Chinese by taking a different route and managed to slip away. The artillery fired on targets where I thought Chinese had established their ambush position on our inbound track. Finally we made it across the valley and back to our own trenches on Hill 355.

By that time I had given morphine to the two most seriously wounded to kill the pain and stop them from making a noise. Fortunately, the Medical Officer [MO], Major Jaffee, had moved his medical team forward so that he could begin treatment as soon as we got to Company Headquarters. On the evacuation back we staged through the Regimental Aid Post at Battalion Headquarters, where I was able to brief Lieutenant Colonel Bingham on what we had found. However, the debriefing was cut short by the MO, who was concerned by the wound in my lower back caused by an exploding grenade. Soon I was on my way to the Norwegian MASH for surgery.

For this action plus others Dan Loomis was awarded the Military Cross. The citation reads, in part,

During the period 8 August to 2 November 1952 C Company 1 RCR occupied the centre forward position on the Kowang San feature. Lieutenant Loomis was a platoon commander during that period and commanded two reconnaissance patrols and two fighting patrols in a most gallant manner. On the night 26/27 September Lieutenant Loomis, while leading a patrol, ... was wounded by fragments of enemy grenades as he assaulted their positions. Despite his wounds, he ... continued under heavy shell and machine-gun fire to assist in the evacuation of three ... who were wounded in the assault, and during the entire encounter with the enemy he succeeded in keeping his commanding officer informed ... by wireless. ... This officer made certain that all casualties were safely in and all personnel of the patrol accounted for before he allowed himself to be evacuated by stretcher to the Regimental Aid Post, where he gave a clear, concise picture [briefing] to his commanding officer. ... He and his patrol are credited with destroying an enemy medium machine-gun and crew.

The citation also says, "He showed outstanding qualities of leadership and above-average proficiency ... and a feeling of confidence to his men."

In her first Honours and Awards List, announced at her 1953 Coronation, Her Majesty Queen Elizabeth II, awarded decorations to several Canadians for their service and gallantry in Korea, one being Lieutenant D.G. Loomis, RCIC, 1 RCR.

After two days at the Norwegian MASH, Dan was sent to 160 the British Military Hospital in Seoul. The powers that be decided to evacuate him to Canada, but Dan was not having it. He argued, "I've only just got here! I don't want to go back." Dan won out, and some weeks later he was sent back to E Company, a composite group of cooks, clerks, mechanics and the like gathered from the rear echelons and hastily formed into combat sub units to fill a gap in the front line.

Dan spent the nights with the Company and the days having his wounds treated. As it turned out, E Company had been positioned on the critical route to Seoul. Next door, B Company received the brunt of a major Chinese attack in the left forward area of 1 RCR as the battle for "Little Gibraltar" reached its climax.

The men had been taught to count the enemy shells for an estimate of the weight of an enemy barrage. Recalls Dan, "I counted 700 rounds in just the first ten minutes. The cordite smoke was so thick you couldn't see your hand in front of your face." As the attack intensified, all telephone and radio contract was lost. Dan said he could talk to no one except "Don Patterson from the

Strathconas, who said if E Company was in danger of being overrun, he'd come forward with his troop of four tanks." It did not come to that, for 1 RCR held on and the Chinese withdrew. *Strange Battleground* mentions that "the casualties sustained by the whole of 1 RCR on 22 and 23 October 1952 amounted to 18 killed, 35 wounded and 14 prisoners of war,"

In March 1953, 1 RCR was relieved by 3 RCR under the command of Lieutenant Colonel K.L. Campbell, but Dan Loomis still hoped for further action with his former platoon in C Company. But the senior staff had other plans for Lieutenant Loomis. The Division Commander, Major General Michael West, had just fired his British aide-de-camp (ADC). He asked for a Canadian replacement, and Lieutenant Loomis was accepted. Says Dan, "Getting that job was one of the best things that happened in my life." Dan learned a lot of things in Korea, but, he says, "I learned most of the valuable lessons from General West."

West had served during the Second War and was a seasoned formation commander. He taught Dan

> how the Army functioned in the field, all parts of it including workshops, field hospitals, supply and of course the combat arms. He regarded an ADC as an acolyte in training for senior command later in life. As we jeeped on our daily rounds in the divisional area he quizzed me on his rationale for his divisional plans at all levels. However, the greatest thing I learned from him was people. I kept a list of all the officers in the Commonwealth Division from major on up. When we visited a unit I would review all the personalities and the General then knew who he would be meeting at that particular unit. Afterwards, as we drove back to Headquarters, he would give a synopsis of the officers he had just met, emphasizing how he expected each would perform during battle. He was a fine judge of character, a very able commander.

As a young officer right out of Military College, Dan found Korea to be one big learning experience. All the lectures in the world could never cover the experience he obtained. For example,

> [The first lesson was that] even under the pain of death people will not do the logical thing to preserve themselves. We took over a trench system on Hill 355 that needed deepening. Try as I might I could not get the soldiers to dig as fast and as hard as they potentially could. I tried everything to increase their productivity without much success until one day I set a goal — four inches more in depth and then the rest of the night

relaxing with only those on guard duty being fully vigilant. It worked. Now, rather than take the trenches down an inch or so over the whole night, they went down four times as fast with the soldiers getting an extra hour or so off every night. The grumbling ceased. Measurable goals and incentives are superior to generalized motivation, even in life and day situations. The second lesson has to do with bravery. This came out in patrolling. You had to ensure that your major firepower such as machine-guns were in the hands of the soldiers you could depend upon to fire during a fire fight. Experience showed me that only about half of the men were fully effective in any given fire fight, but they were not always the same half. Some days Private X is a very brave fellow and does all sorts of wonderful things but on other days he is not. Remember that bravery, fear, courage and dependability are not constants. The key for a good leader is to pick the right people on the right day. This is an essential lesson for any young officer going into combat.

One fact of life in Korea in the front lines was that injuries and casualties would be suffered. Dan recalls, "Writing to the next of kin to explain the loss of a son or husband was a very difficult task, but one that had to be done with empathy." It was also important to go to the dead soldier's friends in the platoon and "put in some words of comfort".

Another difficult lesson that every officer must learn deals with finding the right balance between personally leading in battle and being in the best place so that the battle can be controlled. The officer has the wherewithal to call on other help: artillery, tanks, airpower or unit support weapons, and for that officer to be hit at a critical time could result in a battlefield failure. Dan recalls his first Sergeant's advice: "It helps to lead up front the first couple of times to show the troops you can do it, but the soldiers understand that the officer and radio operator have to be in a position to affect the battle. Their lives depend upon his ability to orchestrate direct and indirect firepower with their movements".

Dan Loomis left Korea the day the cease-fire came into effect, and he did it in style. He took the General's light aircraft to Seoul then flew to Vancouver via Japan: forty-eight hours from the war zone to home. Dan was all set to take his release when a message arrived saying that he was to go to Queen's University for a Chemical Engineering degree. Once again the job at Atomic Energy was put on hold — in fact. one of Dan's friends was given the job when Dan decided to remain in the Army.

An Oral History From Those Who Were There

As the years went by, Dan Loomis became qualified as both a technical and a general staff officer. Staff and Command appointments in Canada, Germany, Vietnam and elsewhere followed. The highlight of Dan's career came in 1970, when he took his original unit, 1 RCR, to Cyprus as their Commanding Officer. During the mid-1980s, after thirty-eight years' service to Canada, Major General Dan Loomis retired. He now lives in Ottawa, Ontario.

KOREA VOLUNTEER

Flora Baptist on leaving the Far East in 1953 to return home.

TWO WARS SERVING THE RED CROSS AND HUMANITY

In April 1994, Flora Baptist of Three Rivers, Quebec, now retired in Ottawa, gave me the one and only female veteran's interview for this book. To do justice to Flora's story, one has to go back to 1940, the year she served as a civilian medical technician in the Royal Canadian Air Force. When told she would not get to serve overseas, Flora resigned. She volunteered with the Canadian Red Cross in Montreal, and her sheer persistence took her overseas as an administrator.

Her first job for the war effort — at Red Cross House in London, England — was the painstaking work of trying to locate Canadians who had been taken prisoner by the Germans. Once these Canadians were found, the next of kin was informed and Red Cross support began.

Flora had joined to see more of the world than the inside of an office, so she volunteered to go on a secret assignment. The assignment turned out to be a voyage to Sicily and thence to Italy. Flora's new work was to provide special comforts to the troops in hospital: library services, arts and crafts, and letter-writing for those who were wounded and could not handle a pen. As Flora is bilingual, much of her work was with French Canadian patients. One of her young patients was Belgian:

> The patient, John Claeys, had a bad head wound which, after surgery rendered him unconscious. His mother tongue was French, so I was asked to sit with him night after night [in case he came around]. I kept speaking to him. One day he became conscious, and I was there to greet him. We remained in touch for some years. I was so pleased to have been able to be there when I was needed.

As the war in Italy came to a close and the Canadians left for North West Europe, Flora's unit moved to Belgium and then into Holland, where she worked in a hospital in Nijmegen until the end of hostilities.

After an interval at home, Flora rejoined the Red Cross, this time in the capacity of driver. This venture took her out West with the Blood Transfusion Service, working with teams to set up depots across the continent. Flora's experiences in driving large, cumbersome trucks through the Rockies — come sleet, blizzards or raging fires — are stories in themselves.

Flora eventually returned to Montreal and in 1950 was appointed to establish and direct a Volunteer Department at The Montreal General Hospital. But the wanderlust had not left this dedicated Red Cross worker, and in 1952 she was delighted to be asked by the Canadian Red Cross if she would return to duty, this time in Korea. The contract signed by Flora on July 4, 1952, would have been unacceptable by today's standards:

> *Whereas* the Society has been requested by the Minister of National defence to provide Canadian Red Cross workers [for] ... the Far Eastern Theatre of Operations ...
> [Be it agreed]
> *That* the Society hereby retains the employee to act in the capacity of a Red Cross Worker. ...
> *That* the Society is to remunerate the employee at the rate of $2,040.00 per annum.
> *That* the employee shall serve ... for a minimum of twelve months.
> *That* the employee shall wear a uniform at all times whether on or off duty. ...
> *That* the employee shall take the oath of allegiance [and] accept inoculations and vaccinations. ...

That the employee shall execute a release of liability to the Society [and] its successors ... absolving the Society from any liability for injury or illness, however incurred, arising out of performance of the terms of this agreement.

Just before Flora's departure for overseas she served as an attaché for the delegation from North Korea in a meeting in Toronto. The North Koreans had refused to accept Red Cross supplies or to allow the Red Cross to inspect prisoner-of-war camps.

On August 12, 1952, Flora was given her letter certifying her as a member of the Canadian Red Cross Welfare team, and she was on her way via commercial airlines.

As soon as Flora arrived in the Far East, she began full-time duties as the welfare officer affiliated with the Maple Leaf Club, Tokyo. This club had been formed when administration recognized the urgent need for a club for Canadians on leave in Japan. Following her duties at the Maple Leaf Club, Flora was posted to the British Commonwealth Hospital in Koyoto. In April 1953 she travelled on to Seoul to the British Commonwealth Communications Zone Medical Unit (BCCZMU) in Seoul, run by Australians.

Flora's scrapbook contains numerous photographs of the airport car parks filled with ambulances, converted buses and helicopters — they formed a major part of the medical evacuation system. Patients from the battlefield were either sent back to Japan or held until the soldier could return to his unit at the front. Photographs of litters being placed into a DC3 for the trip over the sea of Japan speak many words. Flora retains many memories of those days:

> At BCCZMU the statistics for Canadians were Admissions 204; Discharged 70; Transferred to other facilities 97. The Commonwealth patients were visited by three Red Cross members: one Brit, one Australian and one Canadian. During the month I visited Canadian patients at two other hospitals: the American 121 Evacuation Hospital at Yon Dong Po, ten miles north of Seoul, and the American 48 Surgical Hospital or Haemorrhagic Fever Hospital, eighteen miles east of Seoul. I visited Canadians at the 25th Canadian Field Dressing Station and the 38th Canadian Field Ambulance. One felt most elated and ready to venture on because of the warm and enthusiastic welcome given by the patients and staff; in fact, it was so genuine that it was difficult to tear oneself away. One time I boarded a launch to visit the American Hospital Ship *Consolation* at Inchon. The wounded were landed on the deck in helicopters, which picked them up at the front and about 10 minutes later landed them at this first-class

hospital. On May 28th I was posted to the 38th Canadian Field Dressing Station under canvass at Uijongbu.

Also in Flora's scrapbook is a letter from Captain Landymore, Commanding Officer of HMCS *Iroquois*, concerning shipmates from HMCS *Iroquois* who had died on 2 October, 1952. Flora and a co-worker, Louise Guerin, had gone to the cemetery and placed floral wreaths on the graves. Captain Landymore wrote, "I know their next-of-kin would feel deeply indebted that you have taken the time and trouble." Taking time and trouble was and is the trademark of the Red Cross women who have served whenever and wherever wars have been fought. This special care was the normal day-to-day life for Flora and her group.

Flora Baptist's time in Korea then drew to a close. She looks back all these years later with many memories of a time in her life when she was able to make a big difference to countless patients, Canadians and others.

On 3 September 1953, Flora received a letter from The Canadian Red Cross in Toronto. It said, in part, "Enclosed is a cheque for $163.22, being one dollar for each day you served in the Far East Theatre, less prepaid income tax at the basic rate of 17%. ... On behalf of our National Executive Committee [I] assure you that your fine contribution to our work in the Far East is deeply appreciated."

While in Korea Flora had been on a leave of absence from the Montreal General Hospital, to which she returned in 1953. Twelve years later she moved to the Rehabilitation Institute of Montreal. Flora's career then took her to Vermont, where she worked for seventeen years. She now lives in Ottawa, Ontario. I am proud that the one woman whose story is told in this book had a career of such distinction, spanning two wars and a lifetime of devoted service to humankind.

KOREA VOLUNTEER

Pat Carew at the Squadron Headquarters bunker, Korea.

COMMANDING GREYHOUNDS IN THE SAMI-CH'ON VALLEY

Pat Carew joined the Royal Canadian Armoured Corps through the Command Contingent method, wearing the badge of the British Columbia Dragoons. After six months' training he was commissioned in Lord Strathcona's Horse (Royal Canadians) and reported to snowy, rainy Wainwright, Alberta, in June 1951. In Pat's words:

> Panda Force [27 Brigade for Germany] was in full swing. I was given a troop of 126 names but twenty-six per cent were AWOL [absent without leave]. Y Squadron was made up of newly joined militiamen, and we spent three and a half months in Wainwright that year. Over eight months of my first year as a Strathcona were spent away broadening my military education.
>
> In the spring of 1952 I was slated to go to Korea with B Squadron [Major J.S. Roxborough] but was removed, allegedly because I was under twenty-one years of age. The Squadron left in June and six months later

155

I was sent to Korea halfway through the Squadron's tour. I subsequently became the Intelligence Officer, Liaison Officer in the Squadron and Welfare Officer at the Commonwealth Division Junior NCO School in Uijongbu.

What happened to Pat Carew was not unusual. Tank troop leaders guarded their command jealously to avoid getting the Joe jobs that Pat had been handed.

B Squadron left for Canada in May 1953, leaving behind soldiers who had not completed their full twelve-month tour, Pat being one of them. But Bill Ellis's A Squadron, which came in to replace Pat's group, was fully up to strength; once again Pat Carew was surplus to establishment.

Not for long, however. A new Armoured troop was formed, with Lieutenant Pat Carew as its leader. Bill Boss, a public relations officer, wrote this article about the new Greyhound Troop:

> The Canadian Army has a unit over here that Ottawa doesn't even know about yet!!
>
> It's an armoured car troop, attached to the newly arrived "A" Squadron of Lord Strathcona's Horse. It's probably the only one in Korea.
>
> "Actually, it was a caesarean operation," says Lieut Pat Carew of Kelowna, B.C., the troop commander. It was born of the brigade itself.
>
> The Strathcona's provided the men and six units in the brigade provided the armoured cars which had been standing unused in vehicle parks more than 18 months.
>
> Useful in mobile operations as command vehicles, the eight-ton greyhound "Light" armoured cars became unfashionable when the war froze to a halt in September, 1951.
>
> Equipped with wireless, they are relatively heavily armed, carrying a 37-millimetre cannon with which is co-axially mounted a .30-calibre Browning machine-gun plus a separately-mounted .50-calibre Browning on the turret. Each of the four crew members carries his personal weapon — either a Sten gun or a pistol — and there is a stock of grenades in the turret.
>
> After getting to know his front, and after studying lessons of the May 2 battle when an enemy force overran a position of the Royal Canadian Regiment, Brig Jean Allard decided he wanted a mobile reserve of fire power.
>
> A senior brigade officer said: "The need was for a weapon to bring greater fire power quickly to bear on vulnerable areas and on possibly enemy forming-up places when they appeared threatened."

The armoured cars–scattered among infantry battalions, the engineers, the Strathcona's and the ordnance field park–seemed the answer.

Pat explained how the troop was used to strengthen the firepower in the infantry company positions. In practice, Pat explains, "I never fired my vehicle weapons in anger, but we filled in the gaps between the battalions in the front line." The other bonus was that the excellent wireless network gave the Brigade Headquarters yet another link in the information-gathering process. Pat served as a Liaison Officer at Brigadier Allard's Headquarters, and in June he finally got command of a Sherman tank troop for five months. They were "an excellent group of men who kept the heavy machinery rolling without a breakdown". The Sherman M4A3 had a 500-hp gasoline engine that gave the tank great success climbing the Korean hills to get into positions where the 76 mm gun was used to blast enemy strong points. This tank outperformed the British Centurion as a hill climber, but the British 20-pounder gun was superior.

In the spring of 1953, the UN action along the front was mainly an artillery and mortar battle. There were some aggressive long-range patrols — for both fighting and reconnaissance — on the part of both sides. Pat recalls,

> Occasionally (fortunately), the enemy launched limited attacks along valley floors, along battalion boundaries or on positions between formations. Enemy propaganda broadcasts across the front occurred almost nightly. Under these semi-static circumstances, the Squadron Commander [Bill Ellis] used to call routine Orders Group every Sunday morning. In my case, I was required to walk out of my position along an access route about two kilometres in length before reaching an embussing area. The route included [the traverse of] a camouflage road [large camouflage nets were suspended vertically on the side of the road facing the enemy or horizontally on top], which covered open ground in the 3 R22ᵉR area where I was located. On this particular O Group morning, there had been a considerable amount of what I believed to be heavy mortar fire in and around the camouflage road, which was about 1,000 meters from my position. As I approached the near end of the road, which was about 100 to 150 meters long, the firing seemed closer. I reached the near end and the firing ceased. I stopped. I listened. I removed my beret and put on my steel helmet. I checked my pistol (why, I'll never know). I listened again. Nothing. I took a deep breath and stepped out briskly on the camouflage road. Nothing. I continued stepping out and reached the other end quite safely. I sat down on a rock and, suddenly, I started to laugh. I realized that with every brisk step I had taken, I had been

quietly whistling the chorus from the movie *High Noon* as I went to meet the bad guys. The steel helmet was removed, the black beret was replaced, and I continued happily on my way.

In *Korea War Almanac*, Harry Summers Jr says,

> Since there was no declaration of war to begin the Korean War, it is perhaps fitting that there has been no peace agreement to end it. As it now stands, there is still only a "truce", ... brought about by the military armistice agreement between the United Nations Command and the military forces of the North Korean People's Army and the Chinese Communist Forces, that went into effect on July 27, 1953.

When the armistice was signed the entire Brigade deployment began to change. Pat explains:

> The Brigade retired to assembly and concentration areas in the rear of the Jamestown Line. Areas that had been occupied by infantry battalions were now to be filled in an emergency by companies with a tank troop in support. Lieutenant F.M. [Marsh] Wright and I had our troops fulfilling these tasks. In Aug/Sep '53, while nude bathing in the Imjin River, I noticed Marsh doing a lot of underwater swimming in that half-mile-wide waterway. When I asked him why, he said, "Carew, if anything ever happens up there this is the only way you and I are going to get across this river in one piece." Marvellous morale builder!

During my interview with Pat, I raised the subject of decorations. Pat's answer might well have been given by countless people who served in Korea: "I don't think everyone who deserved recognition received it ... but if I was recognizing a contribution under very trying conditions I would have to single out Captain E.C. 'Skinner' Brumwell and Squadron Sergeant Major E.J. 'Squint' Armer of B Squadron and Staff Sergeant 'Red' McIndoe of A Squadron."

Major Bill Ellis was awarded his Military Cross for, in Pat's words, "his unflagging, unfailing concern for his soldiers and for his countless visits by day and night to the forward areas regardless of the intense action or regard for his own safety." In the eyes of the troops, Ellis's MC was well earned.

Pat, an officer who was in Korea during the war and afterwards, has this final comment: "People used to play up the 'police action' in Korea, but when they're using live ammunition it changes your whole perspective."

Pat Carew returned to Canada to a series of regimental and staff appointments in Canada and in Germany. Pat commanded both the Strathcona's and the Royal Canadian Dragoons in Germany. He retired as Brigadier General in 1985. He was appointed Honorary Lieutenant Colonel of the British Columbia Dragoons from 1986–89 and, in 1990, began his three-year tour as Colonel of the Royal Canadian Dragoons. He and his wife Dianne now live back home in Kelowna, British Columbia.

This photograph was taken just prior to Herb leaving for Korea.

WHY MEN PUT THEIR TRUST IN EACH OTHER

Herbert Pitts was a trained Armoured officer in Lord Strathcona's Horse (Royal Canadians) when he left the Royal Military College, Kingston, but his regimental affiliation was to change.

> Immediately after graduation from RMC on 3 June, 1952, all 24 Army cadets who had taken regular commissions were destined to go to Korea after thirty days' embarkation leave. We did not take any additional training prior to departure. However, about half a dozen were sent to 2 PPCLI in Calgary for orientation, which lasted about five or six weeks between exams in late April and the graduation parade on 2 June. My time there was also spent doing pre-para training with a jump serial of about thirty men as 2nd Battalion was converting to the parachute role. This was inherent in the Mobile Strike Force tasking of the day, which this unit had assumed from 1st Battalion, then in Korea.

> When Lieutenant Pitts and his classmates arrived in Korea, the five Armoured officers found that they would serve as platoon commanders in the Infantry, as B Squadron could not absorb five new subalterns all at one time.

KOREA VOLUNTEER

Herb Pitts served eight months with the PPCLI before transferring to the Infantry. In Herb's own words,

> I commanded 11 Platoon, D Company, in both battalions for five straight months in the line, except for a short time when we were withdrawn for the battalion changeover in November 1952. This initial period of my service saw a great variety of activities. Included were recce and advance parties to the Royal Norfolks of the British Army in preparation for our relief of them; many different and frequent patrolling tasks (some quiet and some not); reinforcement to 1 RCR during the October 1952 attack on Hill 355 (Little Gibraltar), when our D Company with only two officers became "Peter" Company, 1 RCR, for about ten days on that battered feature; counterattack preparation and rehearsal for The Hook; and wiring tasks in front of that feature.

The one constant theme throughout those months in the line was shelling. Daily work was needed to improve field defences, to carry out patrols and to learn essential lifesaving techniques. As a newcomer to the Infantry, Herb soon learned the skills in the best way possible.

> My period out of the line was roughly early January to end of March 1953 when I was our unit's instructor at the Commonwealth Division's Junior NCO School at Uijongbu, a village about twenty miles south of the front. I was busy boning up on the lessons when I thought my fellow officers were having a good time in reserve. Seriously, it was a great break for me and I learned a lot from the students and the others on staff at the school. It was reminiscent of the 1950 summer spent at Aldershot, Nova Scotia, when I learned much about basic infantry tactics while instructing Militia Senior NCOs and Warrant Officers. The course was memorable, and I owe a debt to both Captain Harry Harkess (Course CO) and Sergeant Eric Rowsell (my Platoon Sgt) for their patience and willingness to share experience and knowledge with a zipper head [nickname for Armoured soldiers]. Little did any of us realize that one day we would have to put all this theory to the test.
>
> Following the tour at Uijongbu, I rejoined the Battalion as the Mortar Platoon 2IC or baseplate officer. This was, to my way of thinking, just about the best job a subaltern could have. Besides — I was now a real Patricia — my transfer having been approved. Lieutenant Colonel "Tony" MacLachlan, having taken Command from Major Charlie McNeil and Lieutenant Colonel Herb Wood, sent me off happily to the "tubes", where giving fire orders in support of a great many different demands was

extremely satisfying. The platoon was good, fast and accurate — due in large part to capable NCOs and the Platoon Commander, Captain Barney Barnett. Ours was a baseplate that had "brigaded" six 81 mm, six 60 mm and two 4.2-inch rifled US mortars on one gun line. We could not man all weapons at the same time. The 81s were the weapons of choice but the 4.2s were used for sniping at bunkers, fire trenches and observation posts. The 60s were used for illumination and close work (they were manned by the Company crews who came with them). Lieutenant Joe Momberquette was my opposite number in 3 RCR, and we had liaised at his baseplate so that we could support each other if the need arose. It did — on the night of 2–3 May 1953, we had our most memorable shoot ever. The Chinese attacked 3 RCR and probed us, and as a result we were in action from early dark to dawn drawing a great deal of counter-battery fire in the process. We were well sited and escaped without casualties, but when dawn broke I looked outside the bunker to find we were in what looked like a garbage dump. There were ammo boxes, tubes and packaging everywhere. We had fired nearly 4,000 rounds, been resupplied and had a full day's work ahead of us to clean up and restock our bins.

Young officers had a variety of opinions of the men they commanded, led in action and lived with in trenches and bunkers for days on end. Some of the soldiers were excellent, could be trusted and would fight bravely when called upon to do so. The odd one just acted the part and could not be depended on when the shells started exploding. One person was singled out for being a great professional, namely a Sergeant who came to 11 Platoon with 3 PPCLI. Herb writes of Sergeant Peter Mann and his section commanders:

Peter Mann stayed on after I left for the NCO school. He was, in my view, a gem. We got to know each other well, established a mutual respect and developed a friendship which I still cherish even though Peter is now dead (he died of cancer shortly after we both retired). Pete was an older man than I, or so it seemed, was a veteran and liked people. He had a fierce loyalty to those he worked with and this showed in his concern for his men and in the straightforward way he would represent them.

My Section Commanders — Grant, Girard, Connelly and Wellsman — were all young, energetic and reliable. I felt fortunate in having them on my team for I know not all young platoon officers were as well served. My regret is that we have not had any contact subsequent to our time in Korea.

KOREA VOLUNTEER

The War Diary of 1 PPCLI for 3 October 1952 is repeated below, for it is the official record of an event:

0900: A patrol briefing took place in the morning. The patrol planned for 29 Sep 52 will go out the night of 4–5 Oct 52. Another briefing was required because one officer was replaced by another. The plan for the patrol remained the same, a firm base of one officer and thirty other ranks under Lt Pitts and an assault group of one officer and thirty other ranks under 2/Lt Rhodes. The object was to capture a prisoner and the limit of the objective was just short of Little 217.

This impersonal mention in the War Diary conceals the drama of what actually happened. Bill Boss, a Canadian Press staff writer serving in Korea, wrote more excitingly:

Oct. 25 — Chinese grenades "poured down like rice at a wedding" when a patrol of Princess Patricias encountered the enemy in no man's land earlier this month.

That was the way 29-year-old Sgt. Rhodes (Rocky) Prentice of Calgary described the clash. ...

Two Lieutenants
Prentice was on a patrol led by 2/Lt. Neil Rhodes of Brockville, Ont., and Lt. Herbert Pitts of Castlegar, B.C.

Pitts' men had just established a "firm base" more than one mile ahead of the battalion's position and those under Rhodes had gone deeper into no man's land to try for a prisoner when Chinese were spotted 500 yards ahead.

They were the first enemy a Patricia patrol had seen in months. ...

Rhodes decided to try for a prisoner, despatched Prentice with Pte. R.B. Macdonald of London, Ont., to reconnoitre a route up to the hill on which the Chinese were working. "We reached a point 75 yards from them and they didn't seem to notice us," Prentice said.

"We went back and brought up the rest of the patrol. We were within 20 yards of them before the Chinese spotted us. We charged, and the whole thing seemed to break loose. ..."

Prentice noticed a machine-gun just above him. "I could see the silhouette of the gunner's head and shoulders in the moonlight," he said.

"He would come up, fire a burst, and then duck down again. I dropped into a shell hole beneath him and waited for him to come up again. When he did I nailed him. There was another man to the left who

163

kept popping up with grenades. I got him too."

Despite the closeness of the clash, Canadian casualties were slight — one killed, one wounded.

Rhodes withdrew to regroup, intending to assault again but the CO (LCol J.R. Cameron) said "no".

"It was apparent that all along that portion of the front the enemy was alert and it would be impossible for so small a patrol to capture a prisoner," said the CO.

The event that will remain forever in Herb Pitts's memories of Korea, however, is the one in which a wiring party he commanded in 1952 produced a wire barrier extremely close to the Chinese lines. Herb's account, written forty years later, is reproduced here in its entirety:

> I was selected by the CO for the job based on reasons known only to him! The rest of the crew were volunteers chosen from the four Rifle Companies. We were thirty-five strong. We met at our B Echelon and immediately started training under the Engineer WOII. We mastered the job (building triple-concertina barbed fence) and started our first fences on 29 November. The wire for the start of the work was carried in by us and we were to be kept resupplied by South Koreans. This involved an exhausting climb at the rear of the hill and a careful steep descent to the worksite on the enemy side.
>
> I took the three team leaders on a recce before the party started down with the stores and we selected the starting point, which was marked by a tree stump. We chose the places where each would start and the axis of the fences before returning to bring down the teams with the stores needed to start. The aforementioned tree was the point where the near-side fence would start and the four of us had tramped around it a fair amount while we got our bearings. I then led the group down to start building the fence but just before we got to the tree a noise behind caused me to turn back and investigate. One of our men had fallen and Corporal Mullin, the first team leader, took over the lead from me. Almost immediately after he set off, an enemy mine at the base of the tree [exploded and he] was killed instantly. The man behind him, Private Batsch, was hit with one piece of shrapnel in the centre of his chest. He died in my arms before we could move him. Both casualties were moved back into the nearest company position and we got on with our job, completing three rows of fence, each about 600 yards long.
>
> Looking back on the incident now makes me wonder about why or

how men put trust in each other under such circumstances. These men, in most cases, were brand new to the theatre. This was their first real taste of danger and many of us were strangers to each other. There was no question after we got the matter sorted out that they were going to get the job done. The Korean porters were another kettle of fish! Most of them were older men (thirty to sixty years of age), had been shuffled all over the place, and had been doing manual labour for many different nations and (I suspect) under many different officers. They refused to carry any stores for us until a young Korean Lieutenant drew his pistol and I'm sure not only threatened but was prepared to use it. The second night we laid about the same amount of wire in a similar location but closer to the enemy. All told, nearly 3,600 yards was put down in three parallel fences where none had been left because of the Chinese attacks and shelling which had gone on over the previous couple of months.

The two dead from our party were evacuated by my team to the rear of our work area and a stretcher party was called for by me on the radio and one was despatched from the closest rifle company. The bodies were taken to the Regimental Aid Post, where I saw them after we had finished the first night's work. I felt I had to spend a few minutes with them after I had been debriefed by the CO. I understood that arrangements were made for letters to go to next-of-kin from their parent companies — neither were from D Company. Their names have been sponsored on the Patricia's Hall of Honour in the Museum of the Regiments at Currie Barracks in Calgary. Further, both men are commemorated by a brass plaque in the Museum, placed there in the name of the Third Battalion Wiring Party, Nov–Dec 1952.

Canadian Press reporter Bill Boss also described this action. His story adds colour to Herb's modest account:

> Canadian Infantrymen have built barbed-wire barricades within 75 yards of Chinese communist outpost positions.
>
> Probably the most daring piece of defensive field work yet carried out here was accomplished by the newly arrived 3rd Battalion Princess Patricia's Canadian Light Infantry.
>
> It was a job to be done by men who wouldn't think too much about the accompanying hazards, tailor-made for the fresh troops.
>
> The Patricias were holding a position that has taken as much punishment as Little Gibraltar. It is a curved ridge known as "The Hook". The Hook is about 150 feet high, but so shaped that the enemy can observe

it both fore and aft.

Regularly shelled and mortared, it takes persistent work to keep its defence in order.

Lt.-Col. Herb Wood, of Toronto, Patricia's commander, decided there should be minefields and barbed-wire barricades ahead of it. Any there before had been blown to bits by enemy shelling.

He assigned Lieut. Herb Pitts of Castlegar, B.C., to supervise the job. Pitts took his men down to the battalion's rear echelon and drilled them for four days in wiring techniques. Sgt. Maj. Winslow of Cultus Lake, B.C., was loaned by 23rd Field Squadron, RCE [Royal Canadian Engineers], to teach them.

Pitts recalls, "We were to go out under our own artillery and mortar and we also had a supplementary noise program arranged to divert the enemy's attention.

"We were allotted 1,000 artillery rounds, available on demand, each of the two nights."

Standard engineer procedure calls for well-trained teams to build 100 yards of triple concertina fence by day in 30 minutes.

By the time Pitts considered his men ready, one crew could string 100 yards in 31 minutes — at night. The other two could do it in 33 minutes. Each team comprised 10 men and a corporal.

The area wired off the first night was 400 yards from the Chinese. The night was cold and moonlit.

Pitts: "The ground was frozen solid to a depth of one inch, and it was a bit of a problem to screw the pickets in quietly. But the men did it."

They were not yet at work when there was an explosion and Cpl. F.A. Mullin of Montreal was killed. Pte. J. Batsch of Swift Current, Sask., was wounded and died before he could be carried into the lines for treatment.

With presence of mind, Pitts, knowing they were in an old minefield said, "That was a mortar. Keep at it. We've got to finish the fence."

"Later I told them it was a mine," he said. "They weren't shocked. They accepted the fact that we had to take the risk to get the job done."

Having familiarized themselves with the "real thing" they were ready for their second assignment — a toughie. It was just below, a hill on which the Chinese were known to keep an outpost.

The hill extended two fingers toward the Canadian position and the job was to barricade just below the fingers. There was snow, the ground was frozen and it was cold.

The group was not bothered. It is assumed the Chinese either didn't man their outpost that night, or else were shivering within.

By the time they'd finished the Patricias had barbed-wire barricades right close to the enemy's positions.

A Military Cross was awarded to Lieutenant Pitts for his actions that night. The citation also refers to his control of the Battalion Mortar Platoon while under counter-battery fire during the incident.

Lieutenant Herb Pitts returned to Canada after one year in Korea. He was selected to attend McMaster University in the fall of 1953 to complete his baccalaureate. On graduation he was reassigned to the Queen's Own Rifles of Canada. He served that Regiment until it was removed from the Regular order of battle in 1970. Herb was posted to a wide variety of command and staff appointments in Canada, Germany, the United States and Great Britain until his retirement in 1978 with the rank of Major General.

Since retiring from the Forces, Herb has been honoured by the Royal Military College with the honorary degree Doctor of Military Science. He has completed the appointments of Colonel of the Regiment, Canadian Airborne Regiment, and Colonel Commandant, Infantry Corps. Currently, he is serving as the Colonel of the Regiment, Princess Patricia's Canadian Light Infantry.

Major General Pitts has been active in many community, veterans', regimental and national organizations. He is a Life Governor of The Dominion of Canada Rifle Association. He joined the National Council of Scouts Canada in 1981, for which he has been President (1986–88), International Commissioner (1990–92) and National Commissioner (today). Herb and his wife Marianne live in Islington, Ontario.

An Oral History From Those Who Were There

Gordon Peacock balancing books, Korea, February 1953.

BOOKS BALANCED, DUTY DONE, HOME AGAIN

Mention of the Royal Canadian Army Pay Corps prompts one to think of lining up, saluting the Paymaster, being paid, saluting a second time and marching off to count one's wealth. Gordon Peacock served in the other part of pay services — Accounting and Regulations pertaining to all Non-Public Activities (NPF): messes, canteens and the like.

Gordon's employment in pay services came after a Second World War career as a clerk in the Canadian Army and as an air bomber in the Royal Canadian Air Force. Released in 1945, he rejoined the Canadian Army and by 1948 was employed in NPF. Says Gordon,

> This was a most fortunate career move for me, as mathematics was always my strongest subject and I enjoyed the work from day one.
>
> At the time of being advised of my posting to the Far East, I was a

> Sergeant employed with the Institute Inspection Section of the Area Pay Office at Headquarters, Eastern Ontario Area, in Kingston. We were living in PMQs [married quarters], and my wife decided she would prefer to spend the time, while I was away, living with her mother in the hamlet of Tyvan, Saskatchewan.
>
> I arrived in Japan in mid-July 52 and took over the accounting responsibilities for the institutes at 25 Canadian Reinforcement Group located in Kure. The activities consisted of a unit fund, the usual officers', sergeants' and junior ranks' messes, and a central warehouse operation. The Central Warehouse handled all the liquor, beer and other merchandise sold in the messes, plus the messing supplies, so it was fairly complicated. A lot of the merchandise was purchased locally, in addition to the items from Canada, e.g., almost all liquor came from Canada. Fortunately, American scrip money was used for about ninety per cent of transactions, so money exchange did not pose a problem.

Soon after his arrival, Gordon realized that the accounting records were not up to standard. He spent many hours trying to capture lost information, balance books and, most of all, reconcile the stock levels in the warehouse. In the summer months the humidity resulted in working hours from 6 a.m. to noon. On days that Gordon did work late into the afternoon, "the main problem was keeping the sweat from my brow from falling on to the pages of the books of account."

Gordon became a "Father confessor" figure to the young reinforcements. He often listened to their concerns about what it would be like in action.

One experience remains crystal clear in Gordon's mind today, forty-one years later:

> I visited Hiroshima, which was close to Kure, and I will always remember seeing the pictures of devastation caused by the bomb. There were a number of Japanese people in attendance at the shrine to the event — which was located at the centre of the bomb impact — who had been injured by the bomb and whose bodies were badly disfigured. Strangely enough, they did not hold a grudge against the Americans for dropping the bomb and were rather ashamed of their country's record of attacking the Americans at Pearl Harbor. It is a very sobering place to visit (or was at that time) and to know now how fortunate we are that, other than the two bombs dropped on Japan, man has not since attacked his fellow man with such a horrendous weapon.

Sergeant Peacock's time in Japan came to an end in February 1953 when he reported to the Field Cash Office in Korea.

> The Institute Inspection Section at Field Cash had an establishment of three, Captain, Staff Sergeant and Sergeant. The Captain position was not filled at the time, so the Staff Sergeant and I were it. Fortunately, the Staff Sergeant was a very capable and experienced chap and he thoroughly outlined what I could expect when visiting units in the field. Unfortunately, the officer who had headed our section and had since returned to Canada, although very experienced, was far too much of a book man and did not seem to understand that institute operations in the field were different from at static units in Canada. COs were not worried whether every institute regulation was followed to the letter, but were concerned that their troops obtained the amenities afforded by their mess operations and that the NPF funds were adequately controlled. The Staff Sergeant and I fully agreed that our approach would be to ensure that proper accounting records were maintained and that no one was "cheating" as far as the handling and accounting for funds was concerned. We were well received by the units, who appreciated our help, and were quite satisfied that the institutes were as well controlled as possible and that no unacceptable deviations from the rules were being permitted.

Five months passed. The Staff Sergeant returned to Canada, and Gordon was promoted to fill the vacancy. Staff Sergeant Peacock's pay at that time was $350 a month, which included separated family allowance of $70 a month. Gordon was due to rotate back to Canada in July, but he waited another month to train the Captain who came to take over the Institute Section. Gordon was then "able to fly home in August 1953 and spend a wonderful sixty days' leave with my family."

Gordon Peacock's career took him first to Winnipeg and then, in 1956, to the Directorate of Pay Services in Ottawa, Ontario. In 1962 he was commissioned and went to Camp Borden to be the Accounts Officer at the Royal Canadian Army Service Corps School. He later became one of the key people in the Canadian Army Welfare and Benevolent Funds. When he retired in 1979 he became a civil servant with the Canadian Forces Central Fund, for which he worked until 1988. Gordon and his wife Dorothy live in Ottawa, Ontario.

Bill Campbell views the Korean front from his "hole in the ground", 1953.

MEDIUM MACHINE-GUN OFFICER WITH THE VAN DOOS

Bill Campbell of Toronto joined the Canadian Army and began his officer training at the Officer Candidate School at Camp Borden, Ontario, in 1951. On graduation he was told he would take a short French course and then report to the Royal 22nd Regiment in Valcartier, Quebec. There was a shortage of French-speaking officers at that time so the expedient of hasty language training for English-speaking officers had to be used. Bill's regimental training period consisted of two challenges: to learn to speak to his soldiers in their mother tongue and to learn how to command an infantry machine-gun platoon of some thirty soldiers and six Vickers machine-guns.

In January 1953, 3 R22ᵉR left Valcartier by train for the first part of their journey to the Far East.

> We left on a cold and snowy day for the long train ride to British Columbia and then went south to San Francisco. The Unit embarked on the USN *General E.T. Collins* along with the 81st Field Regiment Royal

Canadian Artillery and US troops. The voyage was a long one, some thirty days. One American officer said it was because of antisubmarine tactics: I didn't know there were Chinese submarines! The ship landed the Canadians at Yokahama, Japan, and then it was a train ride to Kure. After two days, 3 R22ᵉR was airlifted to Korea in a US Globemaster, some two hundred fully equipped troops at a time. The Third Battalion then relieved the First Battalion. Our year in Korea had begun.

Second-Lieutenant Campbell soon found that his Unit had the Third Battalion of the Royal Australian Regiment (3 RAR) to their right. The geography of the position was such that Little Gibraltar was to the right and The Hook to the left. Bill recalls,

> It was damp and cold with the long hours of darkness, the preferred time for the Chinese to attack. Here I was at the age of twenty-two commanding the Vickers machine-gun platoon. My platoon sergeant was a month younger than me. My soldiers, mainly from rural Northern Quebec, were the salt of the earth. Our guns were tried and proven [the author's father had used similar guns in Palestine in the First World War]. They had a range of 4,500 yards, had a water-cooled jacket around the barrel, were belt-fed and were very reliable. The barrels could be changed quickly for, despite the water jacket, they did burn out.

As already recounted in Gordon Owen's story, the night 2–3 May, 1953, saw fierce action for C Company of 3 RCR. Herb Wood's *Strange Battleground* sets the scene:

> The area fronted on the Sami-ch'on [River]; the highest ground, Hill 187, lay in the north-east corner ... depressions made it difficult — and in most cases impossible — to cover the slopes running down from any given locality by direct small arms fire. Medium machine guns [Vickers] from neighbouring localities might have covered these difficult areas, but none was sited for this role.

Bill's guns "fired 70,000 rounds in support of 3 RCR". So many barrels were burned out that, as Bill recalls, "It took a truckload to bring up replacement barrels the next day." Brigadier Jean Victor Allard, the Brigade Commander, called his three medium machine-gun platoon officers to his headquarters the next day. He was not pleased and told the three officers, "Never again will the Canadians be put in the position of not being able to cover their entire front." The Commander then turned to the most junior of the three, Second-Lieutenant Campbell, and said, "Only medium machine-guns firing along with mortar fire and artillery fire will stop these mass Chinese attacks. You, Bill, have just twenty-four hours to produce the medium machine-gun defensive fire plan for the brigade." Bill had to coordinate with the RCR officer, a lieutenant, and the PPCLI officer, a captain. Bill remembers that, "This was do or die, as J.V. Allard knew machine-guns." But young Bill passed the test: the fire plan was delivered on time.

During a visit to 3 RAR at about that time, Bill questioned a particularly violent fire fight of medium machine-guns, guns, mortars and flares. The Aussies said, "I say mate, if the Chinese will not come and pick up our laundry, we deliver it to them."

On another occasion, Bill was told by Battalion Headquarters that he had a sixteen-year-old in his platoon who had to be returned to Canada because he was underage. When called in before Bill, the young soldier, with tears in his eyes, said, "I have no home. This is my home, this platoon and the regiment. You are my father." Bill was shaken to be regarded as a father image at twenty-two, but the sixteen-year-old was allowed to remain with his "regimental family".

Bill Campbell's leadership as the medium machine-gun platoon officer did not go unrewarded, for he was Mentioned in Despatches. Bill's brother in Toronto received a letter, which said, in part, "It gives me a great pleasure to inform you that Her Majesty the Queen has approved the award of a Mentioned in Despatches to your brother. ... This well merited honour was granted in recognition of gallantry and outstanding service in Korea."

Soon afterward Bill returned to Canada. In 1957 he reclassified to the Royal Canadian Armoured Corps, in which he served in regimental and staff appointments, later beccoming the Commanding Officer of his regiment. When he retired he formed his own company, W.R. Campbell, CD, & Associates in Orleans, Ontario. Bill lives in Orleans, Ontario. His wife Gisele died in October, 1994.

Chris Snider, 8 Platoon Commander, after an all-night patrol, May 3 1953.

OF SOLDIERS DYING AND KATCOMS SERVING IN 3 PPCLI

Chris Snider had just left the Officer Candidate School in Camp Borden when he was assigned to 3 PPCL1, then located in the same camp. The Battalion's prime duties were to train reinforcements for 1 PPCL1, which was fighting in Korea, and to train soldiers for 2 PPCL1 in Calgary. Chris explains:

> The original concept for the training of platoon commanders was that, as an officer cadet, one would be an understudy to a fully qualified and experienced lieutenant platoon commander. The concept failed badly, as there was a decided lack of qualified platoon leaders. Almost all those individuals were in Korea, thus, almost without exception, each of us as a novice was assigned to a platoon as its commander and left to sink or swim. A rough introduction to a new world, but one that provided a fast learning curve.

The major complaints of many Korea veterans were the shortage of kit and training ammunition and the constant make-do situations. Fresh into an infantry unit, Chris remembers,

> The lack of proper equipment was a real problem. Shortages extended through all items including vehicles, weapons and ammunition and even uniforms. One expedient was the issuing of mechanics' coveralls to all new arrivals, which, with whatever webbing was available and with black leather ankle boots, the dreaded khaki puttees, berets and a weapon, became the standard training uniform. It was not uncommon to see twenty shades of colour and style on the weekly battalion parades. It was not uncommon for departing drafts to remove equipment from the soldiers under training. At times one would see recruits under training wearing a mixture of civilian clothing with whatever military kit was available.

Any expansion of a military force takes time. In the case of the Canadian Army, there had been undue haste in cutting its size and capability at the end of the Second World War. When raw recruits joined with no prior military knowledge, the lack of experienced veterans put a premium on instructors. There were never enough.

> At one point while stationed with the Third Battalion in Camp Ipperwash on the shores of Georgian Bay, I was in charge of a platoon of 110 recruits, assisted by Sergeant Little, who spent his whole time trying to unravel incorrect enrolment documents, taking the individuals in small groups through Q stores to get kitted and completing the myriad of documents required by the system. Meanwhile, those recruits with the required minimum of equipment would go with me and our one corporal and two lance-corporals to do as much of the basic training as we could manage. It was a succession of eighteen-hour days, with Saturdays highlighted by a commanding officer's parade and inspection. This effectively killed Saturday morning and left each junior officer with a list of points that had displeased the battalion commander and that had to be corrected immediately.

Policy changes abounded, pouring from both Army Headquarters in Ottawa and Central Command in Oakville, Ontario. One such change was the rank required to go to Korea.

> Army Headquarters in Ottawa issued an order to the effect that second-lieutenants were to be considered officers under training and not qualified to proceed overseas, regardless of the fact that some second-lieutenants were already serving abroad. Sadly, a dozen of us who had spent a full year training new soldiers to fully trained status watched our battalion

leave by train for Seattle to board a troopship for Korea. Lieutenant-Colonel H.F. Wood, the CO, suddenly had lost all his rifle platoon commanders because of a bureaucratic decision.

To make the situation even worse, the officers left behind were sent to 2 PPCL1 in Calgary, who were not only Korea veterans but were paratroopers, "strutting their stuff with their cherry berets and brown jump boots". It meant that 2 PPCL1 was now in the position of having to train recruits plus reinforcements for Korea. Chris soon found that

> The shortage of equipment in the Second Battalion was as bad as in the Third Battalion. However, in this case, since the training base was on the edge of the City of Calgary, access to the war surplus stores was easier than it had been for the Third Battalion. It always amazed me that new water bottles, bayonets and scabbards, field packs and webbing along with every size of battledress uniform could always be obtained from the war surplus stores, but these items were always "under backorder" or not available through the regular supply system. I also wondered why most of the equipment available from the surplus stores was new, while that coming from the Army supply system was refurbished and often had the previous owner's name and unit stencilled on it. If the shortage of equipment was as severe as it appeared to be, the country would have been in serious trouble if mobilization had ever been ordered.

The Army had many phrases in those days of the early fifties: "Hurry up and wait." "If you can't take a joke you shouldn't have joined." "You might have broken your mother's heart but you won't break mine." "Things will keep on changing back to the way they were." This last one hit home with Chris:

> On a Friday in early November 1952, Geoff Pilcher, a second lieutenant from Bobcaygeon, Ontario, and I were hastily summoned to the Adjutant's office and told that Army Headquarters had reversed the policy of not permitting second lieutenants to go to Korea. In that only Geoff and I were up to date with the typhus, cholera and other inoculations, we were to proceed by the fastest possible means to Vancouver, and from there to be flown to Korea as reinforcement officers. We were given air tickets to our home towns in Ontario and forty-eight hours to get there and back. Two days later, we were at the Vancouver Personnel Depot where, to our amazement, they had never heard of us. Despite the information contained in our personally carried travel and other documents, we remained in Vancouver for eleven days. Finally, more

than two weeks after the rush trip from Calgary to Vancouver by air, we joined a draft of miscellaneous troops bound for Korea and departed not by air but by bus for Seattle where we boarded the US troopship *General H.B. Freeman*. Some 150 Canadians and 1,500 US soldiers were aboard on a twenty-one-day voyage across the Pacific.

Chris was to be delayed once again, this time in Japan, where he remained for several months to train reinforcements. Chris was finally able to escape to Korea because of a last-minute requirement for a substitute as the draft was passing through Kure from Haramura in Japan. The trip to rejoin the Third Battalion in Korea required an overnight voyage through the inland sea to Pusan in Korea:

> It was a beautiful trip through a series of lovely islands and along coastlines. As we neared Korea and Pusan, the effects of war became obvious. Pusan was a monster refugee camp, with open sewers, miserable hovels for houses, and hundreds of thousands of homeless, displaced persons. The smell reached several miles out to sea.

By train, the Canadians moved closer and closer to the war:

> [When] we entered what had been Seoul, the ravages of war became very obvious. There was scarcely a building left standing, unless it was burned out or badly damaged. The draft was taken from the train to a Commonwealth transit camp located in several refurbished buildings augmented by some quonset huts. A meal of stewed mutton and unrecognizable vegetables along with some sort of pudding accompanied by tea did not go down too well with most of the Canadians. [Nonetheless,] most ate with little complaint since they could remember the lines of destitute Koreans with expressionless faces who had watched the draft pass through the devastation of the city outside.
>
> The following morning at dawn saw the draft en route, again by truck, back to the train, and on again for hours at a snail's pace to the Commonwealth Division rear area railhead. This time on disembarking we were met by Brigade staff and, to my delight, a Patricia guide. Loaded into Canadian trucks we wound our way up to the Battalion area, which was in a tented camp in Divisional reserve. I was welcomed by my comrades, who were now veterans with three months' experience. I was assigned to 8 Platoon, C Company, under the command of Major "Oop" McPhail. We spent our days installing a great belt of barbed wire in the third line of defence, called the Kansas Line, across the front of what had

been the site of the great Kapyong battle. The area lay astride a natural route for the Chinese and North Korean army to retake Seoul. As well as laying minefields, digging in reserve positions and increasing the barbed wire fences, the unit undertook numerous field firing exercises, ran patrol training courses and practised all the procedures that were necessary to co-ordinate activities in a Division.

Chris was about to take part in a social interchange, a military training program called KATComs — Korean Augmentation Troops Commonwealth. The first encounter was memorable for both sides:

> They were young South Korean conscripts with less than six months' service and only rudimentary training, and that was mainly US-oriented. The major problem for them was their lack of understanding of the English language. Eight Platoon received eleven KATComs and only one was able to understand even the most basic English. We decided to pair off these KATComs with Canadian soldiers as it was the only way we could envisage getting them to understand what was happening and to establish a means of control. These bewildered individuals, who had never been exposed to much outside their previous village life, suddenly were thrust into a completely new culture. They had to conform to orders issued in a language they didn't understand and eat food they had never seen before. The first few days saw some very amazed Canadians watch the new arrivals dump sugar and milk and ketchup and whatever else was on the table on top of whatever had been dished out by the cooks, and then shovel that directly by fingers into their mouths. Fortunately, they learned very quickly to emulate the Canadian style of eating. I often wondered how they managed some twelve months later when most were returned to Korean units and had to revert to their former ways.

Chris considered himself fortunate. He had made it to Korea and was commanding 8 Platoon. But his fortunes were to change, much to his dismay:

> Shortly before the battalion was due to return to the front lines, our company commander departed to run the Brigade NCO school. C Company was then placed under the command of Captain Arthur Kemsley. At this time I also lost my platoon sergeant as he had completed a year in Korea and was returning to Canada, as did several of the men and one corporal. To make it worse, another soldier with driver's training was transferred to B Echelon. My platoon had suddenly disintegrated to under thirty all ranks with a corporal Second in Command and only two

corporals commanding sections. Of the total, eleven were KATComs who didn't speak English. It was not the image I had in mind while I was in Canada training to go to war!

The war now began in earnest for the young platoon commander. He and his men slept by day and patrolled by night. It was while patrolling that the new officer had to prove himself. Chris learned how to do it the hard way:

> My first patrol was leading a ten-man group forward to block the gap between the two forward companies and to provide a firm base for three-man reconnaissance patrols from each of the forward companies. To do this I was briefed by the Battalion Intelligence Officer, Lieutenant Peter Worthington [later of Toronto *Telegram* and *Sun* fame]. The patrol was briefed at four p.m. and had an equipment check at six after the evening meal. At dusk we wound our way to the rear of A Company and departed on the path out between the forward companies. We moved very slowly, watching in all directions. On reaching the barbed wire boundary of the barrier minefield, we walked along the wire to find the gap.
>
> Much to my horror, after two right-angled changes of direction, I realized we had walked through the minefield to the forward edge. We then moved out across the valley to the Naechon River lying between the Brigade front and the enemy. Using every known crawl, and dropping half the patrol to the ground while the other half moved forward and then repeating the manoeuvre, took us another hour to get to our position. On reporting "in location" on the Battalion wireless net, I received an angry retort that I was very late and thus was holding up the reconnaissance patrols. A request by me to be allowed to move forward to search the area was refused because of my primary mission to provide a firm base for the reconnaissance patrols. I moved the patrol with permission to the right and spent the remainder of the night motionless and freezing. It was the last patrol I made which saw me dress in the afternoon temperatures for a night patrol. I also learned to move much faster when proceeding out. Almost twelve hours after we had started out we were back at the minefield and confirmed that we had indeed walked all around the inside looking for the gap. Shortly thereafter, we were back at A Company and then made our way back to our own lines. I had to proceed back to the Battalion Command Post to be debriefed. That added a couple of hours. Near noon, I was back in 8 Platoon lines. My first live patrol had been completed. I was exhausted but I had learned a great deal.

It is safe to say the infantry officers matured very quickly. They were responsible for the lives of their men in an intimate way never experienced by other combat officers. The most sobering experience was having a soldier die:

> My first casualty came only a few days after we had moved into the lines when an enemy mortar round exploded on the parapet of one of the weapon pits while we were on stand-to and killed one of the riflemen. The other occupant of the weapon pit, although not injured, was extremely distraught and had to be evacuated to the Battalion Aid Post along with the dead soldier. He returned to the platoon after a day's rest but would never stay alone in a trench after that incident. My first letter to the next of kin was very difficult to write and my first attempts were rejected by the Company Commander. It was not a subject that had ever been covered in any of the training, and strangely, I do not recall it in any syllabus later. [Note: This subject is covered in detail in *The Legacy*, written by this author.]

Chris was to run afoul of newspaper correspondent Bill Boss. At one time Chris said of the KATComs that "physically they were equal to or better than Canadians". Boss misquoted young Snider, reporting his words as "KATComs (Koreans) made better soldiers than Canadians".

Chris had further problems involving the KATComs:

> I was on a night patrol and part way through the night was alarmed to hear loud snoring. It was a KATCom who had fallen asleep. He was awakened and quietly warned to stay awake. The next day, back in the platoon area, I was told by my NCOs that this had not been the first time this particular individual had fallen asleep. After trying to tell him of the danger of doing what he had done, I could see I was not being understood. I asked for the Battalion interpreter, who was a Korean lieutenant, to visit the platoon to ensure my concerns were understood by the KATCom. He lectured to all the KATComs that sleeping on patrol or on duty was not acceptable and dangerous to all the members of the patrol. Imagine my dismay when several days later the same individual again fell asleep and snored loudly while we were on a standing patrol. Since the lectures had had no effect, I filed a charge against him, with the intent of giving him a really good scare. A day later, the Korean Liaison Officer appeared along with a Korean captain and a Korean sergeant. They informed me that my soldier would be taken for trial by the Korean military. Several hours later I was awakened by one of my NCOs who had been back to B Echelon for a shower and a change of clothing. En route

back to the platoon he had passed a small group of Koreans in a re-entrant and had observed one digging while those around him watched. It was the KATCom who had been charged for sleeping on patrol. The NCO stated that he had seen one Korean draw a pistol and fire a round into the back of our KATCom soldier's head and that [our soldier] had fallen into the hole. I got nowhere with my incident report. I was informed that Brigade was also sceptical about an execution but that they were investigating. My reply was that if the incident was not true, all that had to be done was to produce the KATCom. A few days later I was informed that the incident was true but was the result of an overzealous Korean officer and that Canadian authorities had received assurances that never again would such a thing be allowed to happen in the Brigade area. However, for the next while, the Koreans in my platoon were very subdued and more than slightly uncooperative.

There is an object lesson here, still valid today. One must consider the social behaviour of non-Canadians when employing them alongside Canadian soldiers. If life is believed cheap, it may be "spent" easily.

As the months passed, Platoon Commander Snider changed:

> Familiarity may breed contempt, but not necessarily lack of care, and I was no longer the same person I had been on my first patrol, creeping and crawling slowly along the ground so as not to be seen. I reasoned that if our patrols left the forward positions just as light was fading, that it would be some time before enemy patrols would be able to cross the valley to intercept us if we moved quickly under the fading light. I was proven correct as we never had a problem getting the patrols into position, although newly arrived reinforcements on their first patrol were visibly nervous when they realized how quickly we moved in the forward area after dark. During one of these nightly excursions I discovered some hand-dug caves at the edge of the valley floor in which, we believed, it was possible for the enemy to hide and lay-up during the day. We thought the caves could have been used by the enemy when they attacked the position when it had been held by the RCR. Several attempts by my men to collapse the caves with shovels failed and the Pioneer Officer, Geoff Pilcher, came forward with some of his pioneers and packs full of 808 explosives and destroyed the caves. The enemy responded to the blasts with a bombardment of mortar rounds, which fortunately caused no damage.

An Oral History From Those Who Were There

As the infantry watched the enemy hour after hour, the forward observation posts sometimes struck it lucky. One such event occurred when 8 Platoon reported that an enemy observer with binoculars was watching them from a position on the opposite hill. The observer appeared to be wearing a white hat.

> I went up to the observation post and confirmed the target observing us from one of the three rings of trenches running around the enemy hill code-named Luke. A quick call to the Battalion Fire Control Centre (FCC) revealed that there were no guns available nor was it policy to fire artillery at a single enemy. The FCC was being manned by Lieutenant Barney Barnett, who commanded the Battalion Mortar Platoon. His deputy was Lieutenant Herb Pitts. Barney stated that enemy soldiers were a legitimate target for mortars and undertook a quick fire task on the enemy trench. One of the first rounds landed directly in the trench occupied by the enemy observer. The resulting explosion sent a white helmet rolling down the opposite hillside. We can only assume he had been wearing it and was now hors de combat. We did not ever see that position occupied in daylight again and were never able to explain why anyone would have worn such a visible piece of headgear. We wondered if it might have been an attempt to attract our fire to pinpoint the location of our guns, but the mortars' quick reaction and exceptional accuracy did him in.

After some Chinese bombardments, the damage was so great that additional help was needed. One solution was to bring forward Korean labourers from an organization called the Korean Service Corps. These individuals were used as porters to carry forward defence stores such as steel fence pickets, rolls of barbed wire and rolls of concertina wire. At times they carried forward the daily cooked meal, prepared in the company kitchen at A Echelon and transported forward in large insulated containers called hay boxes. This meal usually arrived at midnight, which was the middle of the normal "working day".

> Individuals would break off from their sections in pairs and would quickly eat, then return to their duty and be replaced by another pair, until everyone had eaten. The Korean Service Corps would then eat any leftovers and depart back up the communication trench. Those on patrol would miss out on the hot meal. All other meals were prepared individually using hard rations. Usually, fresh eggs, canned bacon and bread would be available as the morning meal, consumed after all weapons had been cleaned.

Sad events stay in the mind forever, and Chris recalls an incident concerning a reinforcement:

> Most reinforcements came up with the night's resupply run. One night two individuals were added to the strength of the platoon to replace two others who had completed their tours of duty and had departed. The normal procedure was for new individuals to be taken directly to the platoon commander, who would interview the individual and note down all the particulars for the platoon commander's notebook. It was decided to interview the new men in the morning after first light.
>
> At the time of the morning stand-to, the platoon was subjected to enemy mortar fire, with the aim, presumably, of catching men in the open. One of the new replacements was struck and instantly killed by a large mortar fragment which had burst directly on the parapet of the section commander's trench which he had been sharing. The death of a comrade is hard on all members of a platoon. In this case it affected the platoon more than usual because the new man was killed on his first day, dispelling the commonly held belief that the greatest danger befell those with longer service in the front lines.

Death was a constant that had to be accepted and it came in strange ways and at strange times. Eight Platoon's third casualty came when one of the patrols came under rifle and small-arms fire from an enemy patrol:

> Almost immediately, mortar fire struck the forward trenches. One of the patrol members was hit in the chest with a rifle round which penetrated his flak vest. Carried back to the platoon, he was given first aid by the platoon stretcher bearer, Private Hutchinson, and a team of stretcher bearers was readied to carry the wounded man back to the Battalion Aid Post. As Hutchinson was placing a shell dressing on the injured man's wounds, a second series of enemy mortar rounds fell on the platoon area, with an 81 mm round landing directly on the injured man while he was being tended by Hutchinson. The concussion, immediately outside the platoon command post was intense, but amazingly, although the wounded man was instantly killed, Hutchinson was untouched by shrapnel and appeared to suffer less from the concussion than other nearby individuals, several of whom were hit with multiple pieces of shrapnel. Hutchinson was closely examined by Platoon Sergeant Evoy and myself before being evacuated along with the wounded so that he could be seen by the Battalion Medical Officer. Hutchinson returned after a day's rest and resumed his superb efforts with the platoon. He performed not only the

first aid role, but was, as well, the telephone and radio operator. Much to everyone's delight, he was later Mentioned in Despatches for his sterling efforts, although we believed he deserved a more significant award.

Patrolling became 8 Platoon's forté:

> On one occasion I led a twenty-man patrol across to the enemy hills with the object of capturing a prisoner. We laid up all one day nearer to the enemy than to our own lines and then moved to occupy an ambush site the following night, where we stayed until the next day. Although there was evidence that the enemy had used the area extensively, no contact was made, and we returned unscathed but empty-handed.

Chris developed a deserved reputation for being cool under fire. Indeed, the citation for his Military Cross reads, in part,

> This officer was commanding a standing patrol in front of "B" Company on the night of 25 April 1953. Enemy soldiers were spotted by him moving toward his area. At about the same time the area of the standing patrol was subjected to intensive mortar fire. With great coolness this officer continued to observe the enemy's movement and directed very accurate artillery fire onto the main body of twenty to thirty enemy soldiers. The enemy continued to move forward and was not turned back until friendly artillery fire was within twenty-five yards of the standing patrol. During this period the enemy mortar fire increased in volume and, without regard for his personal safety, Lieutenant Snider moved throughout his patrol area checking on the safety of his men and reassuring them. ... Due to this officer's courageous action no casualties were suffered by the standing patrol and the enemy were unable to accomplish their aim. On the night of 13 June 1953 a standing patrol in front of No. 8 Platoon of "C" Company reported enemy moving in their area. This officer organized a fighting patrol and proceeded to the area of the standing patrol. ... Without regard for his personal safety he proceeded alone to the standing patrol and brought them back to the main body. ... He repeatedly exposed himself in an attempt to draw enemy small arms fire and personally searched the suspected area of the enemy. ... This officer's prompt, efficient, and aggressive handling of all situations was responsible for the lack of casualties and the continuation of the domination of no man's land.

After peace talks had been going on for months, 8 Platoon came to realize that the last position they would occupy was on the highest hill on the

KOREA VOLUNTEER

Divisional front — Hill 355, or Little Gibraltar. This feature had been fought over several times before finally remaining in Allied hands. It dominated the surrounding land for many miles in every direction. The whole of the Commonwealth Divisional front could be seen lying to the west of the Platoon. To the east, most of the Republic of Korea 1st Division area could be seen, as well as part of the US 1st Marine Division area. On the very top of this hill lay 8 Platoon. The platoon was strung out, three sections in a row, along the crest of the ridge, with company headquarters and the other two platoons slightly below and to the northwest.

Chris remembers the end of the fighting clearly:

> On the 26th of July 1953, we heard that a ceasefire was to take effect on the next day at 2200 hours. There had been previous such announcements, which had not come about, so we were somewhat sceptical. The instructions were that all activities would carry on as normal, except that under no conditions would anyone fire any weapon after 2200 hours on the 27th without Brigade approval. I took a small standing patrol forward to the right front of the Battalion that evening and we lay waiting. Just short of the time the ceasefire was to take effect, a large number of artillery guns fired across the front, from the 25-pounder close support batteries to the 8-inch mediums and others. We all thought it was the end of the ceasefire, but later learned it was the artillery method of unloading guns. However, exactly at 2200 hours, the whole front as far as we could see or hear became strangely silent and dark. Within an hour, our patrol was instructed to return to the platoon area but [warned] that everyone was to remain on full stand-to.
>
> Back in the platoon area we were able to look out over the front. No firing was taking place. It really was a ceasefire. On the enemy hills, bonfires were started, and we could hear singing and bugles blowing. The enemy loudspeakers called for the "friends of liberty" to join them in toasting peace. The Chinese had another surprise in store for us when daylight broke. The hills occupied by the Chinese were covered with tens of thousands of soldiers in quilted uniforms, some waving flags and others waving banners. Our soldiers were dumbfounded at the extraordinary numbers, as they exceeded us by a ratio of four or five to one. We explained to our troops that it was a propaganda ploy as there wasn't room for such numbers in the tunnels that we knew existed in the Chinese defence works. The Chinese had evidently brought forward all their reserve and support troops for the occasion. They had huge

bonfires and remained on the forward hills for most of the morning and then began to disperse to the rear, confirming our explanation.

Korea was to become a memory for Chris Snider and his platoon. The Army does not stand still but is forever changing. Chris's summary follows, a fitting ending to an officer who was awarded the Military Cross for his leadership as a brand new officer, learning his trade with men who will always be part of his memory.

> The 3rd Battalion PPCLI returned to Canada in late fall. We boarded a troopship off Inchon on 29 October and sailed for Vancouver. Halfway home across the Pacific, our Battalion took part in an emotional Remembrance Day service. A few days later, to everyone's surprise, the Battalion was informed by message that it was to be disbanded and deleted from the order of battle. Those personnel who were not scheduled for release were to be posted to the newly created First and Second Canadian Guards. Lieutenant Colonel MacLachlan, our commanding officer, was to be the founding commanding officer of 2 Canadian Guards. Some of us with strong connections to the PPCLI were posted to the 1st and 2nd PPCLI. However, there were heavy hearts for the remainder of the trip back to Canada, as there was a unanimous conviction that 3 PPCLI had become an exceptionally efficient, effective and cohesive unit and undoubtably had the best morale and spirit of the Brigade, if not the Canadian Army, and that it was a terrible shame to destroy the unit at the peak of its form. The last parade of the Battalion as a whole took place after we disembarked at Vancouver.

As the first major unit to return to Canada following the Korean armistice, we marched in triumph through the city streets before boarding a railway train to take us to our individual homes on leave. The Patricias had done well in Korea, as they had done well in both World Wars before, and the individuals who had taken part would never be the same persons they had been before they had taken part in the most recent adventure.

Chris Snider served in Canada and overseas. He commanded 2 PPCLI and 3 Canadian Mechanized Commando. His final posting as a Brigadier was as the Commander, Canadian Defence Liaison Staff in London, England. He retired in 1987. Chris and his wife Maurine live in Nepean, Ontario.

KOREA VOLUNTEER

Lieutenant Duncan McDougall, July 1952.

THE ROYAL CANADIAN ELECTRICAL MECHANICAL ENGINEERS AT PARUN-NI

Duncan McDougall's story is the only Royal Canadian Electrical Mechanical Engineer's (RCEME) account in this book. It is only correct that RCEME's story include far more detail than just one person's experiences. To this end, *Canada's Craftsmen* by Murray Johnston was of great assistance for, in just six pages, he gives an excellent synopsis of the period May 1951 to July 1953.

Dunc's service in Korea began in October 1952:

> I had elected to take RCEME training at Barriefield Camp, Kingston, Ontario, during the summer months while I was a cadet at the Royal Military College (RMC). I began this in the summer of 1949 when artisan training [hands-on mechanical skills] was conducted. In 1950 I went to 202 Base Workshop in Montreal and worked in the shop learning more in-depth mechanical skills. We rotated from section to section throughout the summer. One job was changing GM diesel engines in the M10 anti-tank tracked vehicle that was supposed to go to Korea [see Jim Quinn's

story]. In 1951 the training was in 205 Minor Base Workshop in Camp Borden. One of the more interesting phases was working on the heavy engine rebuild line (the same type of engines we had installed the year before). The summer of 1952 came but I could not leave RMC until late summer, for I had to write a supplemental exam in thermodynamics.

With the exam passed and behind him, Lieutenant McDougall was bound for Korea. At Vancouver he was given a draft of twenty-five Van Doo reinforcements en route to join 1 R22ᵉR (see Ramsey Withers' story). Recalls Dunc, "We were sent to McCord USAF base in Tacoma, Washington. The RCAF North Stars were flying from Washington to Alaska to the Aleutians and on to Japan. The trip was long, noisy and without creature comforts, but it was faster than a troopship."

Not too much time was spent in Japan, but Dunc was given twenty-five more R22ᵉR reinforcements, just one of them a lance corporal. While Dunc was waiting to travel on to Korea, a soldier in full US Army equipment came up one day and asked if he could join them to go to Korea. Dunc was taken aback, and said that this was a Canadian draft; the soldier should go to see the American authorities. The soldier retorted, "But I am an RCR, and here is my I card to prove it." The soldier had been discharged from an American hospital and equipped as one of their own.

On arrival in Korea, little time was wasted before Dunc was delivered by jeep to 191 Infantry Workshop at Parun-ni, described in *Canada's Craftsmen* as "a small village in the area of the town of Uijongbu. ... The front lines were some forty miles in advance of the workshop's location." Dunc described his new home as a "tented camp with accommodation, messes and repair shops all under canvas. There were paddy fields on one side and a high, hilly bluff on the other with South Korean families living nearby. In the summer it was one large dust bowl; in the winter mud and more mud."

The first job assigned to the new boy was unit Administrative Officer, responsible for all paperwork, for overseeing the South Korean indigenous labourers (carpenters, electricians, plumbers and metal workers), running the men's canteen and in general doing all the jobs not assigned to anyone else. One weekly task was to pay the twelve "laundry ladies" who had set up shop in the Workshop area. To keep the records straight, each woman had a numbered disc hanging around her neck. Before the woman could be paid, the disc had to be shown. Recalls Dunc, "The ladies wore very few clothes in the summer months and the pulling out of the disc quite often revealed more of the laundry lady than I was prepared for!"

The major task of the Workshop was the repair of vehicles, including tanks and weapons that required work beyond the capabilities of the unit armourer. These statistics from *Canada's Craftsmen* indicate the impressive output: "In the two years from May 1951 ... until the Armistice was signed in 1953 ... [there were] 22,000 field repairs including 440 combat vehicles, 3,500 trucks and engineer equipment, 160 guns, 320 small arms, 290 instruments and 4,200 miscellaneous equipments."

The problems with telecommunications equipment are still legend today. The workload grew to such proportions that all repair sections were combined to form the 1st Commonwealth Division Telecommunications Workshop. As Murray Johnston states in *Canada's Craftsmen*, "In one three-month period this workshop, which included ten Canadians, repaired nearly 1,400 radio sets."

The second area in which the task was too large for just one section was vehicle recovery. The team of six recovery vehicles in "one four-month period backloaded 2,500 vehicles to brigade workshops".

The neverending task of unit line security led to observation towers being built along the perimeter next to the hilly bluff. At night, sealed beam lights connected to vehicle batteries were used to illuminate the area. The unit Orderly Officer went from tower to tower to check on the RCEME guards. There were also weapon pits, which were fully manned if there was an enemy alert. This warlike role caused no problems for the Workshop staff for, as Dunc mentioned, "nearly everyone else was a Second World War veteran and they performed very well indeed".

The workload of the unit included a six-day week. If there were critical jobs to be completed and the spare parts were available, quitting time did not exist. Many of the necessary parts were made by the unit artisans. One item that made it into the history books was "Fernet's portable shower bath. ... This 'Heath Robinson' contraption conceived and built by WOI J.M. Fernets and WOII A.M. Rivers was capable of showering 200 men per hour." One day Dunc visited a US Chemical Corps Supply Company in Seoul to obtain a spare part for the shower. He says, "I asked the storeman if he had any one-inch copper pipe. He said that he did and asked how much I needed. When I mentioned the number of feet he said, 'You must be building the biggest still in Korea.' Even when I assured him it was for repairs to a shower, he winked, for he was sure it was for a still."

The Canadians were very popular with the Americans. They were considered a "dry" Army (no alcohol), whereas the Commonwealth Division had canteens and messes for all rank levels. One incident still makes Dunc laugh when he remembers it today:

One night two American Military Police (MPs) parked their jeep at our junior ranks canteen and went in for a nightcap or two. The jeep had a huge red light on top and a large chrome siren on the hood. A couple of our guys came out of the canteen and, you guessed it, took the jeep for a joy ride. They were picked up by the American MP 622 Company when our Canadians came roaring down the main supply route, siren howling, red lights flashing. The craftsmen were thrown in the clink and I was called to come and get them. When I arrived, the Corporal in charge, who was a typical "Radar O'Reilly" [the character on the television show *MASH*] had all the paperwork ready for me to sign. I took them home to the Workshop, very subdued!

As the war dragged on and the peace talks started and stopped, "a strange situation was created. There were all kinds of rumours, and when the armistice did come it was anticlimactic." It was just a coincidence that Lieutenant Duncan McDougall left Korea for Canada the day after Armistice Day in July 1953.

Dunc served in Kingston, Winnipeg, Calgary, Ottawa and Vietnam over the next thirty years. He retired as a Lieutenant Colonel in December 1983 to an engineering job in the Department of National Defence, a job from which he retired in May 1990. He and his wife Jean are now living in Nepean, Ontario.

KOREA VOLUNTEER

This picture looks like a set for the television program MASH. *The sign "You are Now Entering Sapperville — Welcome" indicates that Karl Snider is at the home of the Fighting 59th.*

THE FIGHTING 59TH

Karl Snider joined the 59th Field Squadron under the command of Laurie Schmidlin by a rather indirect route:

> I left the University of Toronto, following convocation, in June 1952, and was ordered to report to 59th Field Squadron in Camp Petawawa, Ontario. When I got there I found the unit was in Camp Wainwright, Alberta, on a traditional summer Brigade concentration. There was no hint about going to Korea. Instead I learned something about engineers in the field doing water supply, building roads and bridging. As a new second lieutenant, everything seemed to be as it should. It wasn't until some time after our return to Petawawa that we were told we would be going to Korea in the early spring of 1953.

I asked Karl about the nickname "fighting 59th". He said that Major Schmidlin named the unit that because "at the unit's favourite watering hole in Pembroke, arguments were at times settled by fights between unit members." The name stuck, and became of a matter of pride to the extent that when, in Korea, the unit was redesignated Fourth Field Squadron, Schmidlin was so angry that he dubbed the unit "the Furious Fourth"! One other officer recalled that it was "Schmid's way of creating pride in the unit".

When asked about Laurie Schmidlin, Karl reflected for a moment before this synopsis flowed forth:

> He was a special man whose nature was to get close to people; he never stood aloof. He could relate to any rank level, be it a sapper or a Divisional Commander. Laurie left the technical details of field engineering to his officers and NCOs and he knew when a job was being done properly. He was always present and, the biggest morale booster, he allowed people to use their initiative. He trusted his Troop Commanders to keep control and keep their priorities straight–his way was effective. He had an unbelievable memory; he knew everything about everyone in the Squadron. Laurie's recall of administrative detail was uncanny. He boasted, "I'll match my memory against a filing system any day." He seldom got angry and had a most cheerful disposition with everyone. He got along with all the other units in the Brigade and within the Engineer Regiment. The Fighting 59th was successful, and much of the credit has to go to its Commanding Officer. [Laurie passed away some years ago.]

Between the time of warning and the departure for the Far East, there was little time for preparations other than sorting out personal matters. Karl was left behind because there were officers from 23rd Field Squadron remaining in Korea and, at that time, surplus officers were not permitted. Recalls Karl, "I was disappointed about not accompanying the unit, but I learned I was to await posting to Korea at the Engineer School, Chilliwack, British Columbia." (Karl's wife Ethel was from Chilliwack, so the arrangement worked out well, for she remained there during his year overseas.)

Almost two months later, on 2 May 1953, Karl arrived in Japan. When he reported to his unit he found he was to be the Intelligence Officer (IO). Much to his relief, he only had to do that job for a few months, for he found it rather dull. Apart from keeping the War Diary and listening on the radio and telephone, an IO had little to do in this "static war".

At last Karl joined 3 Troop commanded by Dick Penney (one of the holdovers from the 23rd Squadron), where he remained until the Squadron went home to Canada. By joining 3 Troop, Karl found his life changed immensely:

> The field troops were the nuts and bolts of the unit. It was here that problems were solved and results were seen first-hand. ... During the hostilities

there were numerous jobs to be done, but the main task was route maintenance. In forward areas, for those roads under enemy observation, we had to keep the camouflage netting in good condition to hide troop and vehicle movement from enemy observation. South Korean labourers assisted the Canadian sappers in these tasks. Cover was not the complete answer: where dust was raised by vehicles it could be tracked and a skilful enemy mortar crew could provide a nasty surprise. Reconnaissance was done by day, but work was done after dark. Culverts and ditches had to be kept clear, for when the rains came, they came with a vengeance. After the May 2–3 attack on the RCR position, mine clearance became a big task. Chuck Carter's troop did a great job clearing one of the minefields in The Hook position in front of the RCR.

Chuck Carter was contacted by Karl in March 1994. Chuck's account of the mine clearance (along with photographs and diagrams) was written with such clarity that it deserves to be in this engineer's story. Here is the mine-lifting operation in Chuck's own words:

> The minefield had been laid by other United Nations troops in 1952. The record of the location of the mines was available but was not considered too accurate. The three NCOs I remember from that operation were Sergeant Lewis Evans and Lance Corporals Gordon Rapley and Jack Roberts. The entire team did an outstanding job. An infantry section had been sent out into no-man's land to provide us with a protective screen, but we still felt vulnerable. There was no moonlight, but artificial moonlight was provided by reflecting light off the clouds by using searchlights. Often rolling mists coupled with the silence of the night created images in the soldier's imagination. After practising in a dummy minefield in a rear area I led my soldiers into the minefield. We followed an infantry NCO into the minefield and then were left to fend for ourselves. I was leading but I felt we were on the wrong path. We stopped and retraced our steps and we started again, lifting the mines one at a time, locating them by prodding as the shrapnel made our electronic mine detectors useless. I would defuse each mine by inserting two safety pins and removing the fuses, all of this in the dark night with only the man-made moonlight to show me the way. After five nights the soldiers' morale was very high and even two cooks tried to join in our task! By the last night, 25 May 1953, half an hour before dawn we had lifted and recorded the last mines. Suddenly there was machine-gun fire directed at us. I called in on the radio to say, "Friendly fire is being directed at us." The response

was that it was not friendly but, in fact, Chinese machine-guns. We had just finished in time!

Lieutenant Carter received a Military Cross for this most difficult, 14 to 25 May operation carried out in darkness. Part of his citation reads,

> Due to careful planning and organization the operation proceeded smoothly from night to night and although the mine lifting party was frequently subjected to enemy mortar and machine gun fire Lieutenant Carter's steady calm direction and cheerfulness instilled a spirit of confidence in his team. ... The successful completion of this task, under very difficult conditions, was due to this officer's high qualities of tenacity, devotion to duty and leadership.

Chuck Carter went into business after he left the Canadian Army and now lives in Vancouver.

The work of 23rd Field Squadron is written up in *Strange Battleground.* Herb Wood explains,

> Work on tunnels into this feature started immediately. [When the attack came] on the Black Watch [British], they were able to take cover in the tunnels and bring artillery fire right onto the Chinese above. ... When the 3rd PPCLI and Royal 22^e took over the forward battalion areas on each side of the Sami-ch'on, engineers assisted them to restore and strengthen the position. ... A greater part of the squadron was employed on The Hook ... working three eight-hour shifts per day.

Karl is quick to point out that the infantry pioneer platoons did a lot of the defensive work. He explains how the engineer tasks changed once the actual fighting ceased:

> There were a myriad of jobs to be done; many of these would not normally have been carried out by a field squadron. Stress was placed on route maintenance and the Squadron operated a fifty-ton stone crusher in support of road repairs. Also, some routes were prepared for demolitions. These could be cratered if the truce failed and the Chinese advanced. The plan was that should the truce fail the routes would be blown as the UN Forces withdrew to prepared positions further south. When the Squadron was faced with the task of preparing these demolitions we used an American truck-mounted telephone post hole digger. At each demolition one or two holes were dug and plugged with a wooden stopper. All that was required was to pull the plug, insert the charge and wire it for

blowing. When the Squadron left in March 1954 the holes were still intact.

In remembering the NCOs and men in the Squadron, Karl says, "They were impressive, their morale was very good and they did a fine job. I was impressed with all of them in the troop, they used their initiative, assumed responsibility and took pride in their work." The radio operators in the Squadron were Newfoundlanders, and Karl remembers that they developed a radio procedure of their own: "There was never a need for codes!"

The equipment in the Squadron and Plant Troop worked well, but Karl mentions one new piece of equipment: "We got the first wheeled 'dozer. It was very effective as a bulldozer and most importantly we did not have to rely on a low-bed to move it, like a tracked bulldozer. It had front and back articulating wheels so it could turn on a dime."

When the cease-fire was announced, the actual document had to be read to all troops. Karl was ordered to go and read the necessary orders to some troops in a forward area. Karl drove forward in a jeep:

> I was getting closer to the area where the fighting had been going on the previous day. I passed a large sign which said, "Warning. Movement Beyond This Point Is Under Enemy Observation." I drove on, read out the orders and had a strange feeling of being watched by a large number of enemy eyes. A strange quiet existed throughout my visit to the actual front line. The next day those same hills were filled with enemy soldiers carrying large banners — an unforgettable sight.

After Korea, Karl Snider served at the Engineer School in Chilliwack, British Columbia, before going on to the United Kingdom. He was then posted to the Works Company in Winnipeg, Manitoba, where once again he served with Dick Penney (who passed away November 1992). As a major, Karl commanded the United Nations Emergency Force Engineer Company. His last appointment with the Army was for four years as the Engineer Officer Career Manager. After retiring from the Army, Karl became a civil servant working first for Public Works Canada and for the Treasury Board, where he spent seventeen years before he retired again. Karl and his wife Ethel reside in Ottawa, Ontario.

An Oral History From Those Who Were There

Paul Mayer with Brigadier Jean Victor Allard, 25 Brigade Headquarters, November 1953.

LINE CROSSERS AND RADIO INTERCEPTS

When I interviewed Paul Mayer in September 1993 he revealed an aspect of the Korean War that receives scant mention in other histories.

Paul's military career began in 1938 when he joined the Algonquin Regiment. A year later, one week after the Second World War began, he was commissioned. Paul's Second World War service included several months with Combined Operations, with which he was serving until just after D-Day. Paul then returned to the Algonquins just days before they went to France with the 4th Canadian Armoured Division. On the 9th of August 1944, when Paul's unit was part of a battle group with the British Columbia Regiment, they were heavily engaged by a force of Tiger tanks and suffered heavy losses. Paul was wounded in late September. After a stay in hospital he rejoined his unit on a stolen motorcycle, much to the anger of the medics who believed he was not ready to go back into action.

When the Second War was over, Paul Mayer became an instructor at the Royal Canadian School of Infantry in Camp Borden, Ontario. One Saturday, he was told that "he was to leave for Korea on the Monday to be a Grade Two Staff Officer (Intelligence) at Headquarters First Commonwealth Division." On

April 26, 1953, he became GSO II (Intelligence). Here is his account of what he found on arrival in Korea:

> I was not a trained intelligence officer, but when I arrived I found there was a good staff made up of an Australian, a South African, a New Zealander and two very good Canadian NCOs. There were also three excellent British NCOs who ran the "line crossers". This latter group was composed of South Koreans of all ages who would cross our front line and get information about the Chinese enemy. It seemed as if the information being gathered was of little value. I saw the chap at I Corps who had conscripted these people and said they had to become far more active. My feelings were that the crossers had to go well behind the lines, get information and then try to get back quickly. We reorganized the entire system, gave each crosser a camera and explained what I needed. Pictures of weapons, defensive works and troop concentrations and to know where the pictures were taken. The first one I put across was a young man of twenty-two. I took him to the front line of the Kings Liverpool Regiment, got him oriented at the barbed wire and away he went. Some of the photographs developed from his camera were very useful. These crossers were risking their necks for us. At one stage an agent came back and he had the photo of a Katyusha rocket battery and he knew just where they were — aimed at Hill 355 where the PPCLI were located. I got on to Corps artillery and they used the 240 mm cannon and just sixteen rounds destroyed the rockets.

The second intelligence gathering source available to the intelligence staff was the interception of radio messages. The radio operators were South Korean, Hong Kong Chinese and American Chinese. They listened in on enemy frequencies, recorded information of value and passed the raw information on to Corps Headquarters, who would try to interpret the information at once and then send it to all the Divisional Headquarters. Paul said, "They were concentrating on far too high a level and the intercepts were useless to us. I wanted to know what the enemy opposite to us was up to." So Paul changed things again. The interceptors now concentrated on the Chinese directly opposite the Commonwealth Division. The information began going first to Paul to be analyzed and then on to the front-line units. This system allowed prompt action to be taken to avoid a surprise attack; it also enabled action to be taken on targets of opportunity. One such action was the result of an intercept that told Division "that some senior Chinese officers would be visiting their Hill 346 position at a lookout at a specific time. We welcomed them with several rounds of 240s from Corps artillery. The third round found its mark and got fifteen people, including two generals."

The value of the information to the front-line units started to pay large dividends. Paul said, "We reaped a harvest the night the RCR got hit. I was able to call Lieutenant Colonel Campbell and tell him the time and place of the Chinese attack." On another occasion Paul informed the British 29th Brigade that they would be hit between eight and nine p.m. on their left flank. Indeed, he told them a lot more than that about the Chinese attack procedures: "I informed the units that the first two waves of Chinese will be unarmed but carrying satchels of explosives. They will throw themselves on the wire, detonate the charges tied to their bodies and by suicide, cut holes in the wire. The third wave will be armed, move through the gaps in the wire and overrun the British positions."

The information gathering had improved in just weeks to such a degree that Paul Mayer then used an American Chinese sergeant to translate simple phrases so that the intercept teams could pass back such information as, "A platoon is going to attack here and their route will be X." This speedy passage of information started saving Commonwealth Division lives and stopping attacks along the forward slopes well in front of the defensive wire. When Paul Mayer left the Division on 21 September 1953 to go to the Canadian Brigade Headquarters, he was awarded a well-deserved Member of the British Empire Medal (MBE) for his work as GSO II Intelligence.

Major Mayer then joined Brigadier J.V. Allard as his Brigade Major. Brigadier Allard had been in command since April 1953.

> The fighting was over but we had to reorganize quickly and re-evaluate our plans so that if the war broke out again we would be ready. The idea at the time was that if we had to pull back we would leave behind small, self-contained groups of infantry who could pass back information as to Chinese intentions and plans. We would disrupt the Chinese movement if possible. Lieutenant Colonel Ned Amy and Major General West had thought out this plan at the divisional level before I arrived at Brigade. These plans were perfected by Major General Murray and Lieutenant Colonel Mike Dare.

KOREA VOLUNTEER

October 1993: LGen Paul Addy, ADM (Per) presents Paul Mayer with his Voluntary Sevice (Korea) and Special Service Medals.

Major Paul Mayer returned to Canada in May 1954 and became the Chief Instructor of the newly formed Canadian Guards Depot. Later he served with the First Battalion of the Guards. In 1959 he went to Indo-China as a peacekeeper serving in Cambodia, North Vietnam and South Vietnam (where he met Pamela McDougall, who later became his wife). When Paul returned to Ottawa he became the Deputy Director of Canadian Army Public Relations. In 1963 he went to the Congo, again as a peacekeeper. It was during this mission that he was awarded the George Medal for bravery. In June 1964 he became the Executive Officer to Major General J.V. Allard and was subsequently appointed Assistant Military Advisor to U Thant, the Secretary General of the United Nations. Almost immediately he was dispatched to the Dominican Republic, once again as a peacekeeper. In 1968 Paul retired from the Canadian Forces, the same year that Pamela became Canada's Ambassador to Poland. Paul Mayer and Pamela McDougall were married in 1987. They now live in Pinehurst, North Carolina, in the winter months and spend their summers in Quebec.

An Oral History From Those Who Were There

Norm Crowder just before leaving for Korea.

TWO ORDNANCE STORIES FROM KOREA

The stories of Lieutenant Norm Crowder and Lieutenant Gordon MacDonald are presented here together as fine examples of the work of the Royal Canadian Ordnance Corps.

One of the most unusual tales I uncovered in my research described something that happened to the Mobile Laundry and Bath Unit of the Brigade Ordnance Company. It all began in May 1951 when 25 Brigade was first committed to battle in the area of the Kansas Line. At the time, the RCR, R22ᵉR and C Squadron were starting to advance in the area of Chail-li. As Herb Wood notes in *Strange Battleground*:

> During this advance, some Chinese positions were inadvertently by-passed with unexpected consequences to the Laundry and Bath platoon of the Brigade Ordnance Company. That energetic and devoted unit had been keeping pace with the advancing troops and on the afternoon of 28 May had set up shop some fifteen miles north of Uijongbu on a stream near the Brigade centre line. The Officer Commanding, returning from a search for a new location, found his men standing over two

Chinese soldiers whom they had flushed from a nearby Korean farmhouse. These were the first prisoners taken by the brigade [not including any taken by 2 PPCLI serving under British command]. Three days later, the platoon captured three more Chinese."

The Sergeant Major (Reid) at the Mobile Laundry and Bath Unit, had acted quickly when the Korean peasants reported that the Chinese were hiding in a hut. The Ordnance soldiers mounted an attack with a Bren gun and grenades. After they fired a few shots, the Chinese surrendered.

One of the Ordnance officers who served with the Mobile Laundry and Bath Unit after the above event was Norm Crowder. He describes the unit's equipment and operation as follows:

> The platoon HQ and the laundry section were situated together on a water source in the vicinity of Brigade HQ while the bath sections were located further forward behind the fighting units at the sharp end. Periodically the troops would be withdrawn and given an opportunity to visit a bath section, where they received a towel and an exchange of underclothing, shirts and socks after they had showered. The towels and dirty clothing were returned to the laundry section to be washed, dried and given minor repairs and eventually sent back to the bath sections for further service. When the forward units moved, the bath sections also moved to be reasonably close to the fighting units. While our bath sections were primarily for the use of Canadian troops, many other nationalities also made use of the facilities.

Norm had joined the Canadian Army in 1947:

> I was a lieutenant in the RCOC at 27 Ordnance Depot in London, Ontario, when I was notified in the summer of 1951 that I was posted to the Brigade in the Far East. I settled Ruth and baby daughter Patricia with my parents in Renfrew, Ontario — after they were in place I then let my parents in on the secret that another child was on the way. I left Renfrew on 11 November 1951 and flew to Japan by commercial aircraft from Vancouver — I missed the thrill of travelling by troopship that the earlier members of the force had enjoyed! I spent six months in Kure, Japan as second in command of No. 1 Sub-Depot (Mechanical Transport Stores) of the British Commonwealth Base Ordnance Depot, which had been set up in a former Japanese naval base in the Australian Occupation Zone. The depot was staffed with officers from Britain and Canada and other ranks from Britain, Australia and New Zealand. On the whole it was a pleasant

experience, apart from surviving on British rations — to this day I detest boiled mutton and boiled cabbage.

As I approached the mid-point of my tour of duty, I campaigned for a posting to Korea so that I could see that part of the Far East. My wish was granted, and in late April I went over to Korea to replace Bob Ringma, then Officer Commanding the Mobile Laundry and Bath Unit which was located in the vicinity of the 38th parallel.

The daily routine of the Mobile Laundry and Bath Unit soldiers was to provide laundry facilities and replacement clothing. The soldiers did not get their own clothing back, but rather received replacement clothes.

In *To the Thunderer His Arms*, by W.F. Rannie, it is explained that

Booze was important in Korea in more ways than one, reports Bob Ringma. The Canadians had the best of both worlds in that land: they drew rations from the Americans and had NAAFI [British Canteen] privileges as well. Result was that our chaps ate better than the British and drank better than the Americans. The RCOC bath section used American equipment and Ringma found it quite surprising how a bottle of Scotch or gin seemed to prove the catalyst in the US supply line when it came to procuring replacement electrodes for shower heads that otherwise were in very short supply.

Norm has the great capacity of seeing the funny side of life in Korea. This memory attests to his humourous bent:

About two a.m. one night, the camp was shaken awake by an explosion in a nearby minefield. A North Korean had stepped in the wrong place. One of our sentries thought he heard noises from the vehicle compound and shone his flashlight in that direction. Sure enough, there was a light! When his challenge went unheeded he fired off a round in a business-like manner. Daylight revealed that he was an excellent marksman — a bullet hole through the mirror of a truck that had reflected back the beam from his flashlight. Who says Ordnance types don't fire in anger?

Norm recalls another incident that is amusing in retrospect:

Shortly after I took over we had to move on orders from Commonwealth Division HQ, and I selected a new site. In the course of setting up it was necessary to pick a spot for my officers' latrine and I found a pleasant nook slightly downhill from the unit HQ. My NCOs tried to talk me out of it but, as a twenty-five-year-old lieutenant, I, of course, knew better.

A few weeks later the spring Monsoons hit and the little stream at the bottom of the valley below my latrine turned into a raging torrent. Soon the water level reached the hut. At that point I could claim to be the only officer in the field who had a toilet with running water.

Norm Crowder closes his story with the following comments:

OC Mobile Laundry and Bath Unit was the cushiest job in Ordnance in the field and had many perks. One was being on the chaplain's distribution list for films — we gave his laundry special treatment and made sure that it was all returned to him intact. In mid-June I even received a telegram from my father-in-law, announcing the arrival of son Douglas on 15 June 1952. Apart from having a North Korean infiltrator blow himself up in a minefield beside my camp, life was fairly uneventful, and so I have no war stories to relate. I arrived back in Renfrew on 22 November 1952 — Ruth had been keeping score and clearly remembers that I was away for a year and eleven days.

Norman Crowder served in the Canadian Army until 1958. He then worked as a civil servant in Defence Production, Treasury Board, and Manpower and Immigration until he retired in 1981. Norm is involved in researching genealogy and gives lectures on the subject at Elder Hostels in Canada and the United States. He and his wife Ruth live in Nepean, Ontario.

An Oral History From Those Who Were There

Gordon MacDonald's Second World War service with the RCAF is covered in *Fifty Years After*. By 1953 Lieutenant MacDonald was serving in the Regional Ordnance Depot at Lynn Creek, Vancouver, British Columbia. Lynn Creek was the main shipment point for Canadian stores going to Japan and Korea. In January 1953 Gordon was posted to Japan, where he began working at the Canadian Reinforcement Centre of the Royal Canadian Army Ordnance Corps. He also travelled to all Canadian Ordnance Units in the Far East, including the depot at Pusan, Korea.

It was in the summer of 1953 that Gordon came into his own in an unusual way. Gordon recalls,

Gordon MacDonald at age twenty-two: another war, another uniform.

> The Canadians who had returned from Korean prisons came to Japan to be made healthy to go back to Canada. I knew just how they felt, having been in the same boat when the Second World War ended. I worked with the chief cook and the hospital dietician to produce healthy meals. We kept the kitchen open twenty-four hours a day so that the ex-prisoners could eat lots of small meals.

Gordon worked with the Ordnance Field Park to set up "Camp Maple Leaf", a recreational centre for the Canadian Brigade (see John Saunder's story). This was his last task before returning to Canada in December 1953.

Gordon MacDonald continued to serve in the Canadian Forces until he retired in 1972 as the Base Logistics Officer at Rockcliffe Base (Ottawa). He then became a leading organizer for hearing-impaired people at the national level. His work in this area has been of great benefit to all in the organization. He lives in Nepean, Ontario; his wife Terry died in 1993.

KOREA VOLUNTEER

Ian Firstbrook in a screen position, Korea, 1953.

THE WATCH ALONG THE DMZ

Ian Firstbrook was a junior officer in Aldershot, Nova Scotia, in May 1952 serving in the 2nd Canadian Highland Battalion (CHB), under the command of Lieutenant Colonel R.M. Ross. This unit had been formed as part of the massive increase in the Canadian Infantry Corps. Before the Korean War there had been just three Regular battalions, but by the spring of 1952 there were fifteen battalions. Only part of this increase was due to the war; the rest was a result of Canada's commitment to NATO.

Initially the CHB had been raised from the Reserve Army. In Ian's words, "The Battalion was organized with representation as follows: A Company — The Black Watch; B Company — 48th Highlanders; C Company — Seaforth Highlanders; D Company — Canadian Scottish; Special Company — North Nova Scotias. The CO and RSM wore Cameron badges."

Aldershot was ideal for training the individual soldier but was just too small for more ambitious exercises. Recalls Ian,

> To describe the summer of 1952 as being long and very warm would be an understatement. I remember firing light mortars on the Peach Lake

205

Range and the start of a large brush fire which was quickly running out of control. When I called for assistance on the range phone I was informed with considerable regret that none was available as the officers' mess was also on fire. I suppose it was all a matter of priority.

It was after that long hot summer that 2 CHB was informed it was to replace 3 PPCLI in Korea. The armistice had been signed on 27 July 1953, but there was a plan to keep the rotation active until such time as there was no requirement for Canadians to serve in Korea. Accordingly, 2 CHB was sent to Wainwright, Alberta, for much-needed company and battalion training. Ian's recollections of Wainwright clearly explain the situation:

Our training in Wainwright was spent entirely in the field in a long succession of brigade level exercises with the full array of supporting arms and services. By this time, 2 CHB was at full strength, well organized and in fit condition. Although the standard of training was very good the same could not be said for the quality of some equipment. We were still wearing ammunition boots and puttees; the web equipment was essentially the same design as issued during WWII including bolt-operated rifles. One of the main complaints was the lack of reliable communications equipment. In Wainwright we were using 58 and 19 sets. We were equipped later with VHF radios in Korea. There is no doubt that UK and US combat clothing was superior to what we had available in 1953, particularly during the cold weather. Our parkas were adequate in the winter months providing the weather was dry. UK sweaters and US field jackets were highly prized.

As for most of the Canadian Army units, 2 CHB's embarkation port was Seattle, Washington. The unit went aboard the MSTS *Marine Lynx*. A surprise awaited all unit members when, "Shortly after our departure the announcement was made on the intercom system that effective October 16, 2 CHB was designated the 2nd Battalion, The Black Watch (Royal Highland Regiment) of Canada."

The voyage to the Far East included a full-blown storm with forty-foot seas. On October 25, 1953, the *Marine Lynx* arrived at Sasebo on the Island of Kyūshū, Japan. Ian recalls:

What was now 2 RHC disembarked and formed up on the pier led by the Pipes and Drums of the battalion. We proceeded to march to a park or playing field somewhere in the centre of Sasebo. After forty years I can remember this event as if it were yesterday. The battalion was halted and stood at ease, whereupon Major Logan, the Second-in-Command, addressed the battalion in his somewhat hyperbolic vocabulary. The gist of the message was that every member of 2 RHC would be back on board the *Lynx* by a specified hour October 27 and that the consequences of failing to do so would result in treatment that defied description. [Later] At about two o'clock on the afternoon of the 27th I checked with the RSM at the gangway of the *Lynx*. Unbelievable as it may seem, all 2 RHC personnel were accounted for and on board the ship. I duly reported this to a US colonel, who didn't believe a word I said. His response was that their people would be digging our soldiers out of the woodwork for the next six months. I saluted and left.

The Regiment landed at Inchon, was taken by vehicle across the Imjin River and then began its handover from 3rd Royal Australian Regiment. The twelve-month tour was about to begin. The operational deployment was north of the Imjin by 25 Brigade:

The general arrangement was 3 RCR left, 2 RHC centre and 3 R22ᵉR right. The Brigade screened the divisional front, the idea being that we would force deployment and delay while the division manned the main battle positions in the Kansas Line which was established on a range of high features south of the Imjin River. In turn, the three forward battalions maintained a brigade screen which was mobile and covered the DMZ [demilitarized zone]. In addition, there was a string of observations posts (OPs) manned during daylight and replaced by patrols during the hours of darkness.

The Black Watch was now fully operational and prepared for the possibility that the armistice might fail and the Brigade would be in action. It was a no-nonsense role; every aspect of soldiering had to be treated with the caution and respect it deserved. This graphic account by Ian explains how things were done:

Shortly after we arrived I was tasked with the command of the 2 RHC screen which was an augmentation of 4 Platoon, B Company. The manning of OPs by day and patrolling by night was rotated through the rifle companies. This task was coordinated and controlled by a forward Regulating Centre which communicated by line and radio. The OPs were well equipped with maps, air photos and high-powered observation equipment. After last light, the OPs were vacated and foot patrols covered the frontage along the DMZ with dogs and their handlers which

KATComs with the Black Watch, 1953.

were provided by a special British divisional unit. Our platoons which performed these duties did not include their KATComs (Korean Augmentation Troops Commonwealth), since the patrol dogs hunted by scent and not political orientation. The screen, on the other hand, was a mobile alert force of eighty soldiers maintained on thirty-minute notice to move to tactical positions which were supported by armour and artillery. These positions were separate and apart from OPs and were sited on the basis of likely approaches and forming up places. A lot of detail went into the plan for this operation. The fire plan was refined over a period of weeks and included direct and indirect tasks for both night and day operations. Second only to the fire plan was the movement plan, particularly routes in and out, with and without transportation.

An operation order dated 11 December 53 gives the details Ian had to follow. The pertinent data for the screen included

That it would observe and harass the enemy approaching the battalion position by:
- observing and reporting
- denying observations by the enemy

- interfering with enemy patrols discovered in the battalion position
- forcing the enemy to deploy [so that fire could be brought down on them].

This no-nonsense approach would have resulted in a rapid response had the Chinese violated the rules of the armistice. The deployment was exercised time and time again until the soldiers could do it in their sleep.

Ian has these words about some special people, his NCOs:

> My platoon sergeant was Bill Denne, who had previously served in Korea with 2 PPCLI. Similarly, R.A. Post, one of my section commanders, had served with 2 RCR. The other corporals were Spelay and Creor. As a platoon, we had remained together since the early days of Aldershot. I have always believed that for the infantry at least, real leadership originates with and is maintained by NCOs. The old infantry adage that an experienced sergeant and three good corporals can carry anything is probably true to some extent but it is certain that it never works in reverse.

Ian regarded his tour of duty in 1 Commonwealth Division as a valuable experience. The opportunity to function within a large formation does "not occur very often, at least for Canadians. Operational control as it applied in Germany was not the same thing, whether it was The Rhine Army or II German Corps."

After returning from Korea, Ian Firstbrook served on regimental duty and in staff positions. He retired in 1977 from the Canadian Forces and began a fourteen-year career with the National Research Council. He is now retired and lives in Nepean, Ontario, with his wife Nancy.

An Oral History From Those Who Were There

Some of the D Squadron NCOs (l-r): Randy Holman, Ken MacDonald, Bob Slaney, Murray Price, Ken Meeker, Lloyd Perkins and Frank Ainsworth, May 1954.

THE DRAGOONS ARRIVE AFTER THE ARMISTICE

The Royal Canadian Dragoons (RCD) played a small part in Korea, arriving after the armistice had been signed in July 1953. When the initial squadron was raised in Camp Borden (see the Jim Quinn story), almost half of the personnel were from the RCD and Lord Strathcona's Horse (Royal Canadians). The Strathconas continued with the Korea rotation until such time as they had to supply a squadron for NATO service in Germany. In *The Spur and the Sprocket*, Larry Worthington explains that after Lieutenant Colonel Amy assumed command of the RCD, his "immediate task was to fit "D" Squadron for special service in Korea. ... The Squadron, under Major A.L. MacDonald with Squadron Sergeant-Major E.W. Douglas, trained throughout the winter months at Petawawa and Meaford Tank Range then in April [1954] sailed from Seattle ... arriving in Pusan in May."

Bob Slaney was a twenty-one-year-old sergeant in D Squadron. He tells the story of the Dragoon Squadron that served in Korea from May 24 to November 14, 1954. The squadron had been formed from the Militia intake originally recruited for service in the NATO Brigade in Germany. The units that supplied the soldiers were the Regiment de Hull, the Three Rivers Regiment, the 8th New

Brunswick Hussars (Princess Louise's), the Halifax Rifles and the Prince Edward Island Regiment.

On a cool April evening in 1954, D Squadron formed up on the parade square in front of Bessborough Hall to be given their farewell speech. Everyone was startled when the inspecting General said "how much he hoped they would enjoy their service in Germany–he had been given the wrong speech." Regardless of the farewell words, the squadron left by train that night. As Bob Slaney recalls,

> For many of the soldiers it was their first view of the Rocky Mountains — the magnificent scenery was an impressive sight. The CNR train staff were most considerate and the meals were the finest the soldiers were to have until their trip back East upon completion of their Korean service. The troopship experience was memorable — except for the World War II veterans who were comparing it with their previous trips.
>
> Our Squadron Sergeant Major, WOII E.W. Douglas, MM, held regular morning parades on the port side main deck. Daily dress was coveralls and the US soldiers were great onlookers as the SSM bellowed, "Tain-Show [Attention]!" We docked at Sasebo, Japan, after a voyage of twenty-one days and we finally sat at anchor in Inchon Harbour off the West coast of the Republic of Korea. Our advance party had arrived earlier and I believe had already docked in Pusan.

There was to be no handover from the LdSH (RC) for they sailed in the same troopship that had brought in the RCD. The Squadron arrived in the Brigade area and started to take over the Sherman tanks recently vacated by the Strathcona's. There were four tank troops of four tanks each, plus the Squadron HQ in four tanks. Each troop had an officer, two sergeants and a corporal.

> I was second sergeant in 3 Troop — Lieutenant Laird Gordon was troop officer and Mel Favreau was troop sergeant. We were pleased with the condition of the tanks — the Sherman had a gasoline engine and was more powerful than our Canadian powered diesel tanks. Each tank had a full complement of 76 mm and .50-calibre and .30-calibre ammunition as well as signal flares and personal weapon ammunition. Each tank troop had a fifth tank that was fully bombed up [full ammunition] but all tools were removed — it was expected that these would be removed from the tank it was replacing (not very practical if it was a casualty caused by enemy fire). My own crew was in the nineteen- to twenty-two-year-old

range — at the time I was twenty-one. Trooper Harris was my wireless operator and loader, a Toronto lad who was a first-rate worker and good at fixing radio problems. Willie Veringa, a young Dutch immigrant, was the gunner, Archibald was driver and the youngest crew member was Johnny MacDonald from Cape Breton. [There were two drivers in the crew of five.]

Once the tanks were placed into the infantry positions, the steep hills caused a few close calls. Because 3 Troop was in reserve, it had to cover a position on the main supply route. Bob recalls,

Major A.L. MacDonald said he wanted my tank on top of the highest hill in the area. The only problem was that without digging, it was impossible to site the tank properly. Acting upon his orders I directed the tank to the top and teetered on a knife edge with no place to go. I ordered the operator, gunner and co-driver out of the tank as I was sure we had a great possibility of rolling the tank. Looking back it was a long way down. By orders over the intercom I directed Archibald back and forth to get us off the precarious perch and back down to a logical fire position, however when we tried to get up a slope to go on the main supply route the tank slid sideways and threw the track. We couldn't fix the track so we radioed for the armoured recovery vehicle. Sergeant J.J. Davis arrived with his crew, made a few unflattering remarks, blew the track with dynamite and we all worked to put the track back on. Unfortunately when Sergeant Davis went to follow us out, they threw a track. No comments.

Korea holds many memories for the former sergeant. On a Divisional exercise in the rain and mud, Sergeant Slaney's tank went down a slippery slope, slid off the road into the undergrowth and required some good ground guiding by Trooper Harris. As Bob says,

It made for an interesting time, and in later years when much was made of stress I looked back on that occasion. One morning the alarm went in the squadron area — we were quickly told it might be the real thing — MiGs were spotted heading for the DMZ. We were ordered to mount tanks and prepare the .50-calibre for action. Lieutenant Rosa put on his helmet and stood in the turret ready for action. Harris was behind our .50-calibre and I was doing a quick check of our troop. I looked up at all the serious faces and thought, "I wonder who will not be alive tonight," never considering myself. Fortunately the MiGs turned away and the all clear sounded.

In *The Spur and the Sprocket*, Larry Worthington wrote of an event that took place when the Dragoons were using Nightmare Range. Some of the Dragoons fired rounds that were outside of the safety zone and landed in the Brigade Headquarters area. Brigadier F.A. Clift, the Brigade Commander, sent the following message to Major MacDonald: "Dear Laird: Please come up and discuss things quietly before going on the offensive."

Bob Slaney speaks of his Squadron officers and senior NCOs with pride. Captain Alec Matheson, the Second in Command, SSM Douglas and the Squadron Quartermaster Sergeant Major Merve Lamb were all solid individuals. All of the officers looked after their men and there were "very few people problems". Bob does, however, remember one incident when justice was "seen to be done", but in fact was a miscarriage:

> On July 1st around ten a.m., I was in my tent when one of the sergeants yelled to me that the Sergeant Major wanted me at the Orderly Room at once, properly dressed. I went down the hill and immediately the Sergeant Major took me to the CO's tent and told me to take my beret and belt off. I was puzzled as I couldn't imagine what this was about. I was marched before the CO and charged with ammunition negligence. Shortly before the CO had walked through the tank park and found a full load of ammunition (76 mm, .50, .30, flares ,etc.) under a tarp behind a tank. The end of the tarp was flapping and he looked under and saw a partially full box of .50 ammo with water and mud in it. He told the Sergeant Major to charge the crew commander. I stated that I had unloaded all the ammo from my tank as it had to go to workshop for repairs, and that I did not have any part boxes, and I could tell him how much ammo each tank had as it was all written down in my field message book. I was not believed and was found guilty, fined $25 and given a reprimand. Disgusted would not be the term that would fit my mood after this frame-up, but I had no recourse.
>
> It took eight years to get to the bottom of that mystery when a friend confessed that his tank driver had put the part box of ammunition under my tank tarpaulin. The friend said that he didn't know about the charge until it was over and then felt it too late to do anything.

Entertainers of all sorts came to Korea. Bob remembers,

> A well-endowed singer wanted a soldier to join her on stage — a young private was pushed on stage by his buddies and, much to his red-faced embarrassment, she patted his cheeks, mussed his hair and proceeded to rip the epaulettes and pockets from his shirt in a display of passion.

Everyone could tell that the young soldier was not enjoying this act when another soldier jumped on the stage, grabbed the singer and bent her backward in a classic embrace, thoroughly kissed her then straightened up. He smiled at the audience and, to the delight of all the soldiers present, gave a bow and jumped off the stage. In today's world maybe he would have been disciplined, however all in attendance thought it fair play.

Though Bob saw no action against the Chinese, accidents did happen. Bob recalls how the excellent medical services prevented a disaster on one occasion:

We were on one of the tank ranges doing semi-indirect fire. It was a mark of good shooting to have several rounds in the air from the 76 mm, and this needed a fast loader. One gunner was popping rounds off quickly when, due to the speed of his loader, an accident happened. In his haste to load the nose of the round in, his hand hit the breech block. On recoil, the palm of his right hand was crushed against the back of the turret wall by the base of the round. His palm had a deep circular cut, and, holding his wrist to stop the flow of blood, his only comment was "Sure messed that up, didn't I?" A helicopter airlifted him and later he returned to the Squadron with full use of his hand.

When the Squadron's tour came to an end, the tanks were cleaned and returned to the Americans. The trip home to Petawawa was without incident.

Bob Slaney went on to a remarkable career. He rebadged to the Fort Garry Horse and became the Regimental Sergeant Major. He filled that position in Ottawa and again at the Canadian Forces Officer Candidate School, the Royal Military College, Canadian Forces Europe and finally at the Canadian Forces Leadership Academy in Base Borden, where he retired in 1987. He and his wife Ann live in the Okanagan Valley in British Columbia.

RSM Bob Slaney as Canadian Forces Europe Chief Warrant Officer

John Hayter, age nineteen.

GUARDSMAN ON HILL 355

John Hayter joined the Army in 1952 at the age of seventeen. The following year, when commissioned in the Canadian Infantry, he was (in his words) "the youngest officer in the Canadian Army". Originally he was slated to go to Europe with the Second Canadian Infantry Battalion from Camp Valcartier in Quebec. On October 16, 1953, the unit was renamed Fourth Battalion Canadian Guards. The Guards were in Korea from April 15 to November 16, 1954.

John joined the Unit in Korea as Number 6 Platoon Commander in Number 2 Company. The Platoon Sergeant was W. White, who "was almost as inexperienced" as John. John's platoon officer's notebook of the day notes the following:

> In addition to the Canadian soldiers, each Rifle Platoon was augmented by Koreans attached to the Commonwealth (KATComs). In my Platoon, there were five KATComs (actually the number was six, as will become apparent). Their names were the source of considerable amusement, particularly during roll call! A nominal roll of the teenagers/would-be soldiers was: Pak Kwan Sik, Lee Won Sik, Woo in Sool, Pak Tae Young, Choi Mjung Sik.

An Oral History From Those Who Were There

> The sixth KATCom materialized out of a conversation between Second Lieutenant G.L. (George) Harper, the Battalion Assistant Adjutant, and some of the practical jokers in the Mess. George arrived at my Platoon Headquarters' defensive position on the Wyoming Line. It was pay day, and George was required to pay the troops whether they were in our permanent base positions or in one of the successive defensive line positions in rear. After he paid the troops, it was my turn. George cried out, "Yu Yung Pup," and beckoned me forward to make a mark opposite this name on the roll with an inked little finger. Much to the delight of all the troops within hearing distance, in particular the KATComs, I dutifully rolled my little pinky in the ink pad, then did the same on the roll, and George ceremoniously paid me my Wan (scrip money). The platoon had recruited another KATCom and I had acquired yet another nickname, which some of my friends continue to take advantage of.

Even though the truce was in force and there was no direct contact between United Nations and North Korean soldiers, no one let down their guard. John recalls an event in which he almost shot his batman, Guardsman Simeon:

> I was lying on my bed surrounded by sandbags, with the canvas covering overhead, when the field telephone rang. The Duty NCO informed me that a North Korean had crossed over the demilitarized zone (DMZ) into South Korea and was headed in our direction. The NCO of course did not know the intentions of the "enemy" soldier, and whether or not he was armed. We went on full alert, but were told to remain in our present locations in order to more easily spot someone moving. When in my bunk, I slept with my 9 mm pistol under my pillow. I remained on the bed, took out the pistol, and waited to see what might happen. Within just a few minutes, I heard the unmistakeable sound of running feet headed in my direction. My "pucker" factor was at an all-time high as I lay there, pistol cupped in both hands and aimed at the entrance. Suddenly the makeshift door burst open, and standing there staring down the barrel of my 9 mm was Simeon. He quickly took stock of the situation and repeatedly shouted, "Don't shoot!" Needless to say I was [almost] as scared as he was, but he was looking sure death in the face. After we had time to recover our composure, the North Korean soldier must have heard my subsequent "conversation" with Simeon, because he surrendered to troops several hills away. To give him his due, Simeon was only trying to warn me of the North Korean deserter situation.

KOREA VOLUNTEER

Korea will be remembered by those who were there for the very hot summers, the dust, the rain, the mud and, of course, the bitter cold in winter. John certainly remembers the dust:

> I actually took a ruler out to measure the thickness on a particularly hot and dusty day. The depth measured seven inches! In our area the dust was a beautiful grey colour and had a consistency of very fine graphite. When the rains came, the dust was transformed into a grease-like substance. Our position was adjacent to a rice paddy which was tiered between two hills. Another of our rifle companies occupied the opposite hill. The mud moved down the rice paddy like a glacier moves, and captured everything in its path, including antitank and antipersonnel mines! It was not uncommon to find several of these mines lying in the middle of the road after a downpour. It made driving an exciting adventure!

The Korean War had been ongoing for three years when 4 Canadian Guards took over their duties. Routine in and out of the defensive positions was smoothly executed. Leadership, as always, was paramount. John recalls two of his superiors:

> Two of our company commanders had won the Military Cross in World War Two, one of whom was my company commander, Major Owen Kevin Hugh Kierans. He was a capable and confident officer whom I respected and learned a great deal from. He was ably supported by the company Second in Command, Captain C.V. (Chuck) Carlson, who was a Brigade-level track and field champion. Chuck was always there for the subalterns, and here again I received much support and advice. These two officers were well trained and capable of any task which we might be asked to perform.

John Hayter's unit did not have too much scope for original thought for when they replaced 3 R22ᵉR commanded by Lieutenant Colonel J. Poulin; the contingency plan had already been prepared and it was the basis for all training and deployment within 4 Guards. John explains: "We were ready for any eventuality. The handover had, of course, already taken place, however, the legacy left by Poulin was most useful. In any event, we did not think that the truce would be broken, and looked upon the posting as a dangerous mission short of war."

In a military situation where the routine becomes commonplace and is done by rote it soon becomes boring. Bored soldiers are not happy soldiers, and the task of keeping interest high was the main job of the platoon commander. Patrols into the DMZ were one of the main tasks for platoons in the line:

> One of our responsibilities was to man Hill 355 and to observe the enemy at work and play. I remember my first such mission, out on a spur in an OP. We could observe the entire enemy front for a considerable distance, over a number of their hill positions. The realization that those little figures over there were in fact the mysterious enemy was both exciting and very interesting. On my first watch I must have held that telescope to my eye for an hour straight. I also remember trying to figure out just what they were doing, for they were as active as ants. One could see the Chinese bosses, who wore a different style of padded uniform than the North Korean soldier, directing, pointing, waving, moving around. Patrols in the DMZ were common. On occasion, we would have an Alsatian dog with a British handler to accompany us on patrol. A barbed-wire fence had been erected in our sector of the DMZ, which was the line. Occasionally we would pass an enemy patrol within five feet on either side of the fence. My first encounter of this nature can best be described as "intense pucker factor". Even as a nineteen-year-old patrol leader, I was required to set an example for others; that is, I was required to be cool, stand tall, be alert, be cautious, go about my business and let others do the same, and do all of the good things we had been taught about being professional.

A well-established rest and recreation (R and R) program had been established in both South Korea and in Japan. The soldiers were provided with free transportation and low-cost accommodation. To a nineteen-year-old from Vegreville, Alberta, R and R was something to remember. Even today, forty years later, John recalls,

> R and R in Korea was not only pleasant, but educational. Two locations which come to mind are Inchon and Pusan. Inchon was a seaside resort which was comparable to some of the best. Pusan was more austere and closer to the indigenous Koreans. I was in Pusan as the representative of Canada at the United Nations Day ceremonies at the military cemetery. I actually sat in a chair marked "Canada". The Flag Party was from my platoon, and for the first time in my life I was representing something bigger than a platoon — heady stuff for a nineteen-year-old.
>
> R and R to Japan was almost a disaster. I had been saving my Wan for months. The day before departure I went to the Paymaster to get paid and was informed that there had been an error in my paybook; the

bottom line was that I was entitled to no more than $14! The doctor loaned me the amount required to survive in Japan for a week on R and R: Tokyo, the Ginza, the clubs, the food, Asahi beer, Saki wine, gift shops, bright lights and, yes, the ballet! I saw my first ballet, "Swan Lake", performed by Japanese dancers, except for the female and male leads who were British.

Hiroshima was overwhelming! I walked to Ground Zero, saw the shadows of people standing in a doorway and on the bridge burned into the concrete, and met the man on whom Life magazine had done an article. When he extended his hand, it resembled the skin of a tanned alligator and was quite distorted.

As with many other people whose stories are told in this book, John Hayter had just one truly operational tour in his more than thirty-year career. The lessons learned along the DMZ were never to be forgotten:

There were so many lessons learned both consciously and unconsciously. Care of my troops and of myself was always of greater concern than most other matters. I suppose this was because of the closeness one feels with others when away from home, in a remote place, with a somewhat unknown future, and where serious medical treatment was a long and bumpy ride away. I truly felt a stronger sense of responsibility than that which I had felt in Canada. I also found that if you take care of your troops, they reciprocate in spades.

That sense of responsibility was felt in other areas, too. I had the feeling that my training was thorough but not enough to cater to any and all situations. I did not feel confident in some situations and strove to be better to reach that confidence level. With each additional level of responsibility that I was given, that energy to be better seemed to appear. I do believe that it set a personal pattern for the remainder of my career. Our live-firing exercises were conducted on Nightmare Range. This was an opportunity to do an "advance to contact" using live ammunition. At first I thought that I was engaged in a cops-and-robbers fun time, but soon appreciated that I had one job and one job only: control of sections advancing through the woods, weapons pointed straight ahead, a round up the spout, firing on order. Occasionally, I would see a rifle barrel pointed in my direction as a soldier advanced around a tree. Later as a Company and Battalion Commander on similar exercises in Canada, I would caution subordinates about control or lack thereof.

John Hayter's Army service covered the next thirty-four years, with tours in Germany, Cyprus, England and Belgium. His last position was as Commander Northern Region as a Brigadier General. Since retirement he has been active in the academic field and the St John Ambulance. He and his wife Frances reside in Barrie, Ontario.

Second Lieutenant John Saunders, wearing the badge of the Royal Winnipeg Rifles, just prior to leaving for Korea.

QUEEN'S OWN
— THE LAST TO LEAVE

The 2nd Battalion The Queen's Own Rifles of Canada, under the command of Lieutenant Colonel W.H.V. Matthews, served in Korea from 26 March 1954 to 6 April 1955. They were the final Canadian infantry battalion to serve in Korea. They witnessed the 25th Brigade shrink in size, the RCAF cease flying to the Far East and the Royal Canadian Navy in the Far East reduce to just one ship. This story is of Lieutenant John Saunders and several other officers who served together through good times and bad.

Powder Horn magazine, 1969 to 1970, is full of recollections from this group of soldiers during their year in Korea. The editor, Lieutenant Colonel T.M.C. Marsaw, was a lieutenant in Korea at that time. The following excerpt from a *Powder Horn* article was written by "Boom" Marsaw:

> In the early days of the Regiment's return to active duty and for some time thereafter, the prerequisite for survival in the world of the infantry officer was in some indefinable way, directly or indirectly, related to his

strength of character. This phenomenon was communicated in part by the acquisition of nicknames.

- "Awful" Werry is one of the first to come to mind. Ron, as he is sometimes called, has the capacity to tell some of the most fantastic tales with such perfection that there are not many in his acquaintance who have not fallen victim.
- Then there was "Salty" Saunders. Prior to accepting a commission in the Regular Force, John had spent some time in the Navy. When he joined the Rifles at the ripe old age of 23 he was far from being an "Old Salt", but he had had a taste of the high seas and it was a natural tag.
- "Boom" Marsaw arrived with his handle, which had been acquired at Officer Candidate School. At the School, a young officer's social acceptability was measured in part by his participation in the Mess life. During an evening of Mess entertainment, he sang the part of the bass drum in "McNamara's Band" and came away as "Boom-Boom".
- Bill McAndrew was dubbed "Lumpy". The inspiration for this tag was a character by the name of "Lump-Lump", a loveable old tippler featured on the Red Skelton show. Bill demonstrated his ability to mimic the character and found himself saddled with the name.
- W.H.V. (Bill) Matthews (alias, the "Mad Shepherd" from his shepherd's-crook-carrying days) (alias, "Wild Bill") arrived at the Rifles with his tags. It can truthfully be said that he didn't disappoint us. His brand of leadership might have bothered many a Senior Officer, but endeared him to those privileged to follow him.

Deuce Horn – mascot of the 2nd Queens Own Rifles of Canada in Korea.

Another vital member of the unit was Deuce Horn, a massive Great Dane who had been given to the Queen's Own before the unit left for Korea. He was with the Queen's Own for years; where they went, he went. He died in Germany while still "serving" with 2 QOR of C.

John Saunders, Howie Traynor and Boom Marsaw commenced their Officer

Cadet training at the Officer Candidate School in Camp Borden, Ontario, in October 1951. From there, John's training continued at the Royal Canadian School of Infantry. He finally joined his first unit, the 2nd Canadian Rifles (later 2nd Queen's Own Rifles of Canada), based in Ipperwash, Ontario. John's story begins: "In early October 1953 we were warned we were going to Korea. We were to replace 3 RCR, who were almost at the end of their year in the Far East."

Ted Shuter, the Second in Command, wrote in the *Powder Horn*,

> On our way to the forward area by train we stopped as we met the departing 3rd Battalion, Royal Canadian Regiment. I met several old friends then, but they refused to get out of their train in case they missed it. It was not until a year later that I appreciated this peculiar attitude! Eventually leaving our train, we proceeded by road transport to the Battalion area — to look upon a way of life that we did not at first believe possible.

When the companies deployed in their assigned areas, C Company was given the South Korean KATComs who had been assigned to them, so many to each company. Lieutenant Colonel Matthews eventually decided to put all the South Koreans into one company. The officers of the company were chosen by their height, which meant that Ron Werry went to D Company, John to A Company and Derek Bamford to D Company.

About a month after deployment, a day arrived when the KATComs were not to be found; they had gone to a local village south of the Imjin River. When questioned, they said, "Queen's Own Number 10 [the worst] always hubba hubba [run run]." The marching pace of 140 paces to the minute was not to their liking! They did not return to serve under the Canadians.

John returned to C Company, with Boom Marsaw and Vip Vipond as the other two platoon officers. The company was in a holding position north of the Imjin River, close to the main supply route. The plan was to stop any North Korean or Chinese attack toward Seoul. Behind each position were defended positions from which the Queen's Own would fight. The companys' sent patrols forward to the demilitarized zone. It was a time of watching and waiting from positions from which the enemy could be observed. As the Commonwealth Division reduced, the Queen's Own became the only Canadian battalion left. Their last move took place just before Christmas 1954 when they moved into Maple Leaf Park. They were to remain there until their return to Canada.

Recreation, training and leave became very important to the soldiers when they were not in the front lines. One of John's many memories was of "Alec Matheson, Second in Command of D Squadron RCD, playing his bagpipes at many of our parties."

After the Queen's Own were chosen to remain in Korea, the soldiers began to place critical importance on the day planned to go home, which was supposed to be in March 1955. John recalls,

> One night there was a bit of a riot in the men's canteen as the soldiers were upset with not knowing when they were going home. Ron Werry was the Orderly Officer, and he went to see Lieutenant Colonel Matthews and said, "We have to do something." Bill Matthews grabbed empty sandbags and filled them with beer from the officer's mess and went to the canteen. He sat down with the men and said, "Have a beer and let's talk." This settled things down. Later on, the return date was changed again. This time the commanding officer got the entire battalion into the theatre and said, "I want you to bear with me. We have one more change!" For a few days some soldiers nicknamed him "Bear with me Matthews".

When asked if morale was a problem at the section and platoon level, John said not from his personal memory, as the other activities kept the soldiers busy. In the back of everyone's mind was the real threat that the cease-fire could break. Leadership at all levels was critical, but the Queen's Own came through this experience in a positive way.

One big problem they all faced was that of tent fires. John recalls a tragic event that took place within one month of going home:

> At the time we were living in Maple Leaf Park in quonset huts – steel sheds with wooden floors and partitions with small plexiglass windows and a door at each end of the hut.
>
> "Vip" Vipond lived in one along with Ron Werry, Charlie Belzile, Bill McAndrew, Ed Bobinski, Robbie "R.E." Robinson and I think Paul Zmean and a signals officer from Brigade, Lieutenant Fellows, I believe.
>
> This particular night, Vip Vipond had returned to his quarters earlier in the evening before the others. Vip was always cold and had the habit of turning his Aladdin oil (kerosene) heater up too high.
>
> Later the others came back, went to bed or stayed up talking in Robbie R.E.'s room. Charlie Belzile went outside, and it was he who noticed that the walls were hot and that a fire had started somewhere in the hut. Charlie banged on the walls, shouting, "Fire! Fire! Fire!" Ron Werry woke up and immediately started to dash out — but went back into his room to put on his trousers. By this time the smoke was so thick and hot that he

passed out at the door, and it was Charlie who pulled him out of the burning building — Ron Werry credits Charlie for saving his life.

Robbie R.E. pushed Bill McAndrew out through the window. The place was an inferno. Boom Marsaw and I lived in the building next door and the heat was so great that our windows started to melt, but we were able to hose it down and keep it from burning by using the mobile hose and water trailer.

The survivors did a count and realized that Vip Vipond was still in the building. The general feeling is that he suffocated.

The next day we were able to locate Vip's remains and were able to identify him only by his identification disks.

I took the funeral party to the UN cemetery in Pusan and laid him to rest. What a tragic loss.

On return to Canada, Bill Crew and I, along with my wife Audrey and Bill's fiance Joan, went to see Vip's widow, Helen. I had never experienced something like this before. It was a tragedy and we were lucky that no one else lost their life in that fire.

The battalion sailed home in April 1955, taking up residence at Gordon Head Army Camp in Victoria, British Columbia (current site of the University of Victoria).

John Saunders remained on regimental duty in Canada and overseas. In 1966 he was posted to Tanzania where he served for fourteen months as part of the Canadian Armed Forces Advisory and Training Team. He also served in Vietnam as a peacekeeper in 1973. John retired from the Armed Forces in 1977. At present, John is the Deputy Executive Secretary at the Canadian Corps of Commissionaires National Headquarters in Ottawa, Ontario. John and Audrey live in Nepean, Ontario.

Chapter Four

THE ROYAL CANADIAN AIR FORCE

The Royal Canadian Air Force was able to respond to the requirement for United Nations support in Korea in a most able fashion. The Air Force that survived the downsizing after the Second World War had retained a large number of Bomber Command crews with multi-engine experience. The ground crews were well-trained and more than able to maintain the North Star aircraft of 426 Thunderbird Squadron.

Pat Giesler confirms the air readiness of the UN Forces in her book, *Valour Remembered — Canadians in Korea*: "From the early stages of the war, the United Nations forces enjoyed complete supremacy in the air over the battlefield. ... The Canadians were credited with 20 enemy jet fighters destroyed or damaged."

Twenty-one Canadian fighter pilots served in Korea. They are listed below with the rank they held in Korea plus any decorations earned in Korea:

        F/L J.A. Omer Levesque;
        F/O J. Bruce Fleming, DFC (US);
        F/O G.W. Nixon;
        F/L L.E. "Larry" Spurr, DFC (US);
        G/C F.B. Hale, DFC (US);
        W/C R.T.P. "Bob" Davidson;
        F/L Ernie A. Glover, DFC (US), DFC (Commonwealth);
        S/L Andy R. MacKenzie;
        F/L F.W. Evans;
        F/O J.C.A. Claude La France, DFC (US);
        F/L R.E. Lowry;
        S/L J. Doug Lindsay;
        S/L E.G. Eric Smith;

F/O Andy Lambros;
F/L G.H. Nichols;
F/O R.D. Carew [bailed out at 43,000 feet and landed in friendly territory];
S/L John MacKay;
S/L Bill Bliss;
S/L W.W. Fox;
F/O J.B. Mullins and
S/L Duke Warren [after the armistice].

The Royal Canadian Air Force operated under strict Canadian political controls so the fighter pilot stories are of an individual nature. 426 Squadron's enviable record is covered in other books that recount the overall history of the RCAF.

Andy MacKenzie just before being shot down.

PRISONER FOR TWO YEARS

The story of Squadron Leader A.R. "Andy" MacKenzie, DFC, CD, tells a remarkable story of a long imprisonment by the Chinese. The excellent video produced in 1992 by Lieutenant Commander (retired) Ron MacDonald told parts of the story. Ron's assistance and a copy of the December 1978 *Airforce Magazine*, for which Andy wrote "Korea Re-visited", plus four issues of *Weekend Magazine* and a final interview with Andy resulted in this account.

Andy MacKenzie joined the RCAF in 1940. As a Spitfire pilot during the Second World War, Andy was credited with eight and a half victories. He remained in the RCAF after the war, and in 1951 he reformed and commanded 441 Silver Fox Squadron in North Luffenham, England. He flew the Sabre in one of the first squadrons of the Air Division, and it was here that he learned that his offer to go to Korea had been granted — he was to fly with the U.S. Air Force in Korea as a volunteer. Says Andy, "We had wanted to go to Korea as a squadron, but Canadian political policy did not allow this. Instead, selected senior pilots were sent to serve with the US Air Force to fill spots. I was the thirteenth to be sent. The tour was for six months or fifty missions, whichever came first."

KOREA VOLUNTEER

Mac, as the Americans called him, was assigned to 139 Squadron, 51 Wing, US 5th Air Force. Shortly after his tour began his entire flight was designated to go to Japan for two weeks' R and R. On 4 December 1952, Andy was about to board the C47 for Japan when he told Major Jackson Saunders, acting Squadron Commander and the Executive Officer, that "he preferred to stay and fly, for he had been in Japan just two weeks before and wanted to get his missions completed." Jackson said, "You can fly with me in the morning." Andy realized later that his decision to stay and fly was to change his entire life.

At noon the next day, Andy flew one of the sixteen aircraft taking off from K 13. Saunders was to Andy's left. The Squadron climbed to 42,000 feet heading north toward the mouth of the Yalu River. Andy was delighted when Jackson said, "If you see something you take the lead and I'll cover you." This pleased the RCAF pilot, as he wanted to get a MiG.

The following section is from the book *The Andy MacKenzie Story*, which was published by the RCAF in Metz, France, in the 1950s:

> With Saunders on my left and ahead, we quickly climbed to about 42,000 feet, following the west coast of Korea over the Yellow Sea toward the mouth of the Yalu River. The visibility was excellent. It was a clear, cold day, and the sun was high overhead and slightly to the south. ... We finally re-formed and started eastward on our patrol which had been laid down as parallel to and about 20 miles south of the Yalu River. Mine was the top flight and we were to patrol at 42,000, the others operating at slightly lower levels, ranging from 40,000 down to 30,000. There were three squadrons on this mission, with four flights each. We had patrolled once and were half-way along on our second milk run when the pilot flying No. 3 reported: "Cobra One, this is Cobra Three, there are some trails at 10 o'clock and slightly above." This indicated to Major Saunders and to others in the flight that there were some MiGs about. Saunders quickly snapped back: "Roger, I see them. Keep your eye on them."
>
> By now, it was about 12:55. Though my aircraft was moving along fairly well, I had reported to Saunders just a few seconds earlier that my main hydraulic control system had failed and that I was now operating on my auxiliary system. Under normal conditions I should have returned immediately, but because of the arrival of the MiGs and my eagerness to tangle with them for the first time, Saunders agreed that we would have quick go and return to our base as soon as possible.
>
> I could now make out about 20 MiGs flying west over the Yalu River in a sort of string formation in twos. Their tactics were to peel off in twos,

dive through our formation at high speed, curve back to the right and dive back into China again, figuring we would not pursue them, much like a baseball runner trying to steal second who can rush back and be safe on first. Most of our pilots were height conscious. That is, they always looked for enemy planes from above, due to the superiority of the MiG at high altitudes. The MiGs could operate more efficiently than we could over 40,000 feet. ...

As I watched the MiGs streaming along, I saw two peel off, cross the Yalu and make for us in a roaring dive. I cocked my wing to the left as I saw them approaching and they passed underneath me, with their guns blazing away. I was in a perfect position for a bounce–that is, an attack from above. I reported this over the radio, saying:

"Cobra Lead, this is Cobra Two. Two MiGs below going to three o'clock. Cover me!"

This indicated that I was going to lead an attack on these planes and that Cobra One should protect me against enemy attacks while I was firing. As I started into a dive for the attack, I suddenly realized that I had received no reply from Saunders. I dropped a wing for an instant to see if he was coming with me and to my astonishment found he was turning the opposite way. This meant we would be split up and that I would be going into the attack alone. Normally, we fight in pairs. When I saw what had happened, I decided to reverse my turn and join Saunders. He was now on my left wing, and from that direction I could see more MiGs coming in, which Saunders apparently had decided to go after. I still did not know whether he had received my communication, but because he was leader of the flight I had to take it for granted then that he wanted me to remain as No. 2 and to cover him in his attack.

At high altitudes and high speeds, ranging from 500 to 600 mph, turning quickly without loss of speed is difficult. Saunders had turned 180 degrees and was now flying west, and in order to stay with him I had to turn sharply, and as a result, lost speed, which left me way behind him. I found myself alone, but still had Saunders in sight at one o'clock high. I had full power on and the only way I could catch Saunders was to go into a shallow dive and regain the speed I had lost in the turn. As I started to dive, Saunders called me:

"Cobra Two, where are you? Am I clear behind?"

"I am at seven o'clock below," I replied, "and you're clear."

At that moment, Saunders started to fire, engaging not the two planes which had dived under me, but two others which had come in during this interval. Just as he started to fire, I noticed fighter fire [tracer bullets, which leave a trail of light] over my canopy. Before I could take any evasive action, my coop top [canopy] was blown off. Simultaneously, there were two strikes [explosions] on my right aileron, followed by three more in rapid succession on the fuselage. I tried to break to the left to evade more fire, but found that my aircraft had gone out of control and I was starting to roll to the left. I couldn't stop the roll. Since there was no point in staying in the aircraft, as I had no control any longer, I pulled the handles of the ejection seat and bailed out.

Many years later it was determined that Andy had in fact been shot down by a US fighter pilot, not a MiG. Needless to say, no fuss was made; mistakes do occur in war.

To return to the Andy MacKenzie story:

It was wonderful to feel the jerk of the straps and see that beautiful white expanse of silk blossoming out in the sky above. Everything seemed strangely quiet. Gone were the noises of battle, the exploding shells, and the din of radio chatter in my ears. In their place was the soft swishing sound of the air spilling out of my chute as I slowly swung back and forth in the sky. It was cold as hell. Except for this I found the drop not unpleasant. It was a bit difficult to breathe at that height but apart from a little choking up, I did not lose consciousness. It was pretty much like sitting in the top seat of a ferris wheel. The feeling of dropping was absent, and even though I was going down at a fair rate, it seemed so slow that I wondered if I was going to hang up in the sky all day.

Underneath I could see the Yalu River, part of northeast China and the big power station on the Yalu and the mountainous terrain of North Korea. My descent had actually slowed down as I neared the earth but I reversely got the sensation of dropping faster. I was beginning to wonder where I would land and what my chances of evading capture would be. The line of battle was far south in the area of the 38th parallel and I was over North Korea. As I got down to about 12,000 feet I could plainly made out houses, roads and moving vehicles. The drop from then on appeared very rapid indeed. As I neared the ground, I could see two trucks coming around a bend in the road and obviously heading in my direction. The thought passed through my mind that I should try to slip my chute so I could slip sideways and thus present a smaller target if they opened fire on me. It would also enable me to put more distance between us. I tried this but I found that I was too weak from lack of oxygen and had too little strength in my arms to work this successfully. So I gave up the idea and continued to drop as before. Below, the trucks were still coming along the road and following my descent. The lower I got, the more clearly could I make out that there were soldiers in the trucks.

I finally hit ground, landing on the side of a mountain, about 10 feet away from an old woman gathering sticks and grass for fuel. I'll never forget the surprised look on her face when I alighted at her feet. But after glancing up curiously, she went

Andy arrives in North Korea by parachute. (Drawing by Ed McNally)

right ahead with her work and paid no further attention to me. The trucks had now arrived at the bottom of the hill and I was busy removing my parachute, and dropping every piece of gear I could to make it easier for me to run for it. I thought that if I could get over the mountain it would put me out of sight of the soldiers, and with luck I might hide and wait for nightfall. But as I scrambled on all fours up the side of the mountain I glanced over my shoulder and saw the two trucks screech to a halt, the soldiers jump out and come running after me, shouting as they ran. Some were armed with Tommy guns, others with rifles. There were about 15 men in each truck and all 30 were hard at my heels. They were shouting and waving to me to come back, firing a warning volley of fire. I could hear the bullets bouncing off the rocks around me.

I realized that in my weakened condition I would never be able to reach the top of the mountain. So I stopped, got to my feet, turned around to face my pursuers and waited. They continued to beckon to me as they advanced, but the firing stopped. I then began to walk down the mountain to meet them. Half-way down I was surrounded. No attempt was made to strike me, but they kept me covered with their weapons. One man, who appeared to be the leader, motioned to me to raise my hands. I did so. Then he and several of his companions started to strip me of my .45 Colt revolver, which was in my armpit holster and of some of my clothing, such as my G-suit and Mae West.

Andy MacKenzie was about to enter the most trying time of his life. Before he was released he would spend 750 days in prison, 465 of them in solitary confinement under first the North Koreans, for three months, then the Chinese.

The events on that 5th day of December in 1952 will remain etched in Andy's memory. The truckload of soldiers he had seen from 12,000 feet now had him captive. He was blindfolded and driven to a building near the Yalu River where he was to face his first of many interrogations. The first questions he was asked were "how many children I had (four: two boys, two girls); how long I had been in the air force and so on. When I held up four fingers for the number of children they seemed impressed!"

The next truck, full of live pigs, took Andy over the Yalu and into China. Some time later he was returned to North Korea, where he was held in custody in a house for three months. The small room above the kitchen was full of lice and almost drove Andy to distraction. Andy's one major, fearful question was, "Did my government and my family know where I was and that I was a prisoner? Asking my captors did not do any good. I managed to get a note to an American flyer and when he got home he told my wife Joyce that he had seen me through a crack in the wall and I had blue eyes and reddish beard."

Andy's cell was so small he could not stand up. Covered in lice, he was driven to desperate measures. He tried to escape:

> This was a mistake, as I did not plan anything. I just ran out in the night. The guard at the entrance stopped me and I was told, "Something very bad will happen to you." I thought this might be the firing squad. I was so frustrated I tried to escape again. I was told, "You were warned." The next day a jeep arrived and I was sure I was going to die. (The Americans had told me that they didn't know what happened to downed aircrew for no one had returned.) I was handcuffed and put under a tarpaulin but

> two hours later I was taken out of the jeep and put into a solitary cell in a prison in China, and this is where I remained for the rest of my incarceration, a year and nine months.

The Chinese now started their psychological games on Andy. They treated him as if he had just been shot down over China. Pressure was brought to bear to get him to write a confession that he was miles north of the Yalu over China when he was shot down. Three American flyers in adjacent cells "wall-tapped" a message to Andy that the war was over.

Andy was treated differently from the US prisoners. He explains:

> I had to write a statement to say that I was shot down over China. I had to make my case clear or, I was told, "You'll be in China for the rest of your life because you have penetrated the sacred skies of China!" It took me many months to get my statement just the way they wanted it. At one time I got so angry I tore the paper into small pieces. I was told this would cost me. Later I came to understand that this one act did delay my release for one and a half years.
>
> I was not allowed to write to my wife Joyce until April 28th, 1954. My Dad's telegram arrived on July 14th and at the end of July I got Joyce's first letter.

Back home, Joyce and the four children were living a life of frustration and worry. When Andy went missing, the family was flown from England back to Montreal by the RCAF. Joyce went to the storage company in Montreal to get the family furniture. She was told, "Squadron Leader MacKenzie signed in the furniture and only he can sign it out." No amount of persuasion would change the storage company's attitude, so a desperate young mother was given "a bogus death certificate in her husband's name" by an RCAF officer who was willing to bend the rules. Joyce then set up the family home and waited in agonizing fear for news of her husband.

The long road home for Andy started when the Canadian diplomat Chester Ronning spoke to Chou En-lai, the Chinese Communist premier in Geneva, Switzerland. When asked about a Canadian flyer named MacKenzie, Chou said, "We'll take that under advisement and I'll let you know." Within a day Ronning was told, "Yes, we have MacKenzie and he will be released when the time is right." That was to be six months later.

When the news reached Andy that he was to be released he was filled with emotion. The day had been one of tension between the Canadian and the three US flyers. One of the USAF pilots wanted to hide a razor blade in case he needed a weapon. The ensuing argument resulted in a fight, and the Chinese guards came in to break it up. The prisoners said they were not fighting but exercising. Nonetheless, Andy, as the senior and the eldest, had to go before the senior Chinese officer. For all four men, the big concern was that they might be put back into solitary confinement.

> I stood in front of the Chinese officer and was spoken to in Chinese for half an hour. Then the interpreter took over. He repeated all the charges about invading China's sacred skies and then dropped a bombshell! He said that because of the generosity of the Chinese people I was being returned home! What a surprise, a fantastic experience! I broke down right there. I said, "How about my friends?" [meaning the three U.S. pilots]. I was told that they would tell me when I went back to the quarters. What awaited me was a farewell meal with fish and even a glass of wine. I couldn't eat anything I was so excited. At that point I weighed 125 pounds, down from the 204 I weighed before bailing out, but still food did not interest me. After dinner I was taken to the train and went from Mukden to Canton accompanied by Mr Chong and interpreters. [I spent over two days on the train.] We arrived in Canton but they wouldn't tell me when I was going home. I was allowed to shop for gifts to take home and Mr Chong paid the bill. Some days later on looking at the calendar in my room I discovered that December 5th was a Chinese holiday and was coloured red. Mr Chong said, "Does that day mean anything to you?" I said, "It sure does — two years to the day, that fateful event of being shot down."

It became obvious that 5 December 1952 was to be freedom day. Andy's story continues:

> I didn't realize I was to be released at exactly one p.m. so we had three hours to kill. They took me to a restaurant and tried to feed me. Of course I couldn't eat; I was too nervous and excited. At last it was one p.m., the time I had been shot down two years before. The scene at the bridge was really something. Five soldiers with automatic weapons were on the Communist side aiming their weapons at the five members of the Hong Kong police at the other end of a bridge. The bridge must have been two hundred yards long. Mr Chong had asked me to wave to him as I crossed the bridge. This was for the Chinese camera crews who were recording the event. I agreed and as soon as I got the waving over with I went in a dead run. I had seen Don Skene, my brother-in-law, and Mr Fraser [Canadian Trade Commissioner] waiting for me. I fell into their arms, so happy to be free again.

December 1952. Home at last with his family. Joyce and Andy with their children.

On looking back on his captivity, Andy says:

> I was never sentenced, never went before a court. The Chinese never treated me roughly, but I never trusted them for they told so many lies, but their truth was different from ours. Theirs was what they wanted to hear, not what in fact happened. Of course, when their questions produced answers they did not want to hear they changed the questions the next time to see if they could get the story they really wanted.

The RCAF flew Joyce MacKenzie to Vancouver, and Andy flew commercial air from Japan to meet her. The ordeal was over at last. He was home.

The American fliers who had been Andy's cell mates were released six months after him. When they arrived home, "we had a great reunion in Des Moines, Iowa. I'll never forget those fellows!"

Once the debriefings were over, Lester B. Pearson, the Minister of External Affairs took Andy under his wing. He arranged for a thirty-minute private interview with Prime Minister St Laurent:

> We sat in his office in two captain chairs placed in front of his large desk facing each other. He said how proud he was of me and my wife. He praised my actions and complimented me on how I had withstood the treatment in prison. He talked to me like a father to a son. He said I was a great symbol of Canada and freedom. I was so grateful to the government for getting me home. I had no scars on my body, but the scars on my mind will never fade.

Andy MacKenzie served in the RCAF in both flying and administrative duties. He also served in the North American Air Defence Command in the United States. Andy retired from CFB Rockcliffe, Ontario, in 1968. He is a past president of the Fighter Pilots Association and is the founding president of the National Capital Unit of the Korea Veterans Association. Andy is an active member in the RCAF Prisoner-of-War Association. Andy and Joyce live in Oxford Station, Ontario, where they raise Newfoundland dogs.

Ernie Glover, Canada's air ace, earned two DFCs.

TWO DFCS IN FOUR MONTHS

The late Ernie Glover was described by John Melady in *Korea: Canada's Forgotten War*:

> The most effective Canadian flyer in Korea, on the basis of combat kills, was a shy, handsome, slim, 29-year-old Flight Lieutenant named Ernie Glover. When the Korean War started, he gave Leaside, a Toronto suburb, as his home.

Ernie had flown Hurricanes with Number 1 Squadron Royal Air Force in the Second World War. He became a prisoner-of-war after being shot down while flying a Typhoon over France on May 19, 1943. He was imprisoned in Stalag Luft III along with Wally Floody (see "The Great Escape" in *Ordinary Heroes*). At the end of the War he was released from Stalag Luft III, returned to Canada and was released from the RCAF. In 1948 he rejoined the RCAF as a Flying Officer in a non-flying role until he converted first to the Vampire and then to the Sabre fighter. He was serving at RCAF Uplands, Ottawa, flying Mustangs when he volunteered to go to Korea.

By June 1952 Ernie was at Kimpo Airfield, Korea, as a fighter pilot with the

334th Fighter Squadron USAF, 4th Fighter Interceptor Wing. He had gone to Korea under the "six months or fifty missions, whichever came first" rule — the rule gave the RCAF pilots a ticket home out of the war.

Ron MacDonald's February 1989 videotaping of RCAF members provided a lengthy record of Ernie's service in Korea. Without that source, this story could not have been written. On the tape, Ernie explains that "The Sabre Es produced by Canadair were excellent aircraft. The Americans liked the Canadian version, for the workmanship was excellent."

In Korea, the Canadian pilots were integrated right into the USAF units. On the tape, Ernie explains that they "flew in two sections of two or a four-plane group". The rules were firm on one aspect: "You never flew alone; two was the smallest section." This was important, because a lone aircraft could be jumped by two or more Chinese MiG 15s, which were stationed north of the Yalu River in "MiG Alley". The UN aircraft were supposed to stay south of the Yalu, but strategic bombing of the Chinese airfields meant that there were missions north of the river.

In August, Ernie went on R and R to Japan. He returned to Kimpo in a rush when the air war heated up. On August 30, on his first mission back, Ernie was credited with two damaged MiGs. According to the videotape, in the short four months that F/O Glover flew in Korean skies he shot down three enemy fighter planes and damaged three others, with two of the three kills coming on successive days.

The enemy pilots were of various skill levels — some were "hopeless", others were quite good, and if you came up against a blue-painted MiG it was obvious that the superb flying must have come from an instructor pilot.

The Korean flights were far shorter than the flights Ernie had come to expect in the Second World War. The flying time from Kimpo to the Yalu River was just thirty minutes; after fifteen to twenty minutes over the target area, Ernie would be on his way back to base. Nonetheless, Ernie almost did not make it back to base on one occasion. John Melady quotes Ernie in *Korea: Canada's Forgotten War*:

> I almost ran out of fuel. I headed for Kimpo, along the coast. I'd go so far, then shut the motor off and glide. Then I'd relight it, climb a bit, and glide some more. ... Finally when I flamed out [engine stopped] for the last time, I didn't have time to go around [the airfield]. I had to come straight in. There was a problem ahead of me though. Another plane had crash-landed on the runway. So here I was. Out of gas and nowhere to go but down, except there was no place to land.

The tower delayed Ernie while they cleared the crash, and within seconds F/O Glover came flying in.

Ernie Glover was awarded two Distinguished Flying Crosses (DFCs): one from the USAF and one from the Commonwealth. His Commonwealth DFC was the first awarded to a Canadian since the end of the Second World War. In the videotape, Ernie explains the rules for gaining credits for downed or damaged enemy aircraft.

- [The claimed action] had to be seen by another pilot [who agreed] that the Chinese plane was damaged or had probable strikes on the aircraft,
- [The plane] had to be on fire [with the pilot] either parachuting from or going in with the aircraft destroyed.
- [The pilot] had to have the entire action on film from either the cine camera from the nose or from a gun camera.

Ernie's third damaged aircraft was not confirmed; he doubted that it ever would be.

Melady records this twenty-nine-year-old fighter pilot's view on shooting down a MiG:

> The adrenalin flows ... heart pumping a mile a minute ... head is on a swivel as you try to keep track of your own guys, as well as trying to watch the plane you're after — or you are trying to get the hell out of the way if somebody is shooting at you. ... You feel like walking on water. You get back and want to talk, talk, talk. You are laughing, joking, really high. It takes some time to unwind.

One common thread in all wartime fighter pilots' stories is how it feels to shoot down another aircraft. In Ernie's words, "You are after another machine. It is airplane against an airplane. ... Of course, if the guy you have just hit bails out, you see the parachute and then you remember that there was a man in that plane. ... You are just too busy to have too many second thoughts."

Ernie Glover remained in Korea for just four months. His 58 missions and his victories entitled him to return to Canada. He flew home on a 426 RCAF Squadron North Star. He remained in the RCAF, flying Sabres in Europe. He retired after twenty-nine years of service. Ernie died on September 9, 1992, in Belleville, his wife Ruth having died some time before him. Ernie left a large family of brothers and sisters and many nephews and nieces.

KOREA VOLUNTEER

Squadron Leader Allan Simpson at a Brigade observation post, December 1951.

AIR PHOTOS IN KOREA

Allan Simpson had a long and varied career as an RAF and RCAF pilot in the Second World War (see *Ordinary Heroes*). In 1949 and 1950 Allan took six months' training at the Canadian Joint Air Training Centre, Rivers, Manitoba. After the course in Photo Interpretation (PI) Skills, Squadron Leader Simpson was posted to Ottawa, Ontario:

> I worked in the Directorate of Air Intelligence at Air Force Headquarters in Ottawa. Apart from the school at Rivers, we were losing the PI skills. I managed to get approval to form a PI unit as a Flight in 408 (Photo) Squadron at RCAF Station Rockcliffe near Ottawa, in 1951.
>
> One of the first things I did was to arrange to go to Korea to get some wartime field experience in PI. Group Captain "Buck" McNair, DSO, DFC, CD, was our Air Attaché in Tokyo. He took me to a briefing at the USAF Far East Air Force Command Headquarters and arranged for me to get on a flight to Kimpo, near Seoul, Korea, where I was attached to the 67th Reconnaissance Technical Squadron. There I worked with American and British photo interpreters. Buck McNair gave me permission to fly on

operations over North Korea. On the night of 13/14 November, 1951, I flew with an American night photo recce crew.

The details of the flight are recorded here in their entirety, for editing would do an injustice to a fine story:

On the night in question I flew with a crew of the 13th Tactical Reconnaissance Squadron on their final mission of a tour of operations. The pilot was Lieutenant Erwin A. Thomassen. The D/R Navigator was Lieutenant Denis E. Verner and the Loran Navigator Jere E. Poole. The groundcrew were under the direction of Technical/Sergeant Alfred S. Klesitz. We flew in a Reconnaissance RB-26C, a type which I think was called The Invader. The trip took five hours and thirty-five minutes. We followed the railway line near the East Coast. Our route was Kimpo — Chunchon — Kojo — Wonsan — Kowon — Yonghung — Hamhung (twenty miles southwest of Chongjin) — Hungnam — Songjin — Chuuron Jan — return to Kimpo. At the most northerly point we were about 175 miles from Vladivostock in Siberia.

We made visual observations and took photographs. At points, the railway was damaged by American naval bombardment. Supply trains coming from the north would have to offload on one side of the break in the line. Then it would be manhandled and reloaded onto another train south of the break and sent on its way.

We carried no bombs but the North Korean railway crews didn't know that. One engineer pulled into a tunnel with the caboose partly exposed at one end and the locomotive just peeking out at the other. We encountered light flak near Kowon. There were both light and heavy flak batteries operating at or near Hamhung. We sustained no damage. It was the first and only time I had flown against the enemy with a USAF crew. Their efficiency and morale impressed me most favourably. A few days later, I received a message from Buck McNair. Air Force HQ in Ottawa had cancelled his authorization for me to fly on ops. So for the remainder of my stay there, I was grounded.

One of the main advantages of air photographs is that the user, a front-line soldier, can talk to the PI officer and, in a few instances, the pilot who flew the mission. This close three-way co-operation in Korea produced excellent results (see Ned Amy's story).

Allan spent three days visiting the headquarters of Brigidier General Rockingham:

"Rocky" and his staff were surprised to see an Air Force visitor. Majors Don George and Vic Jewkes were there. They were very considerate, hospitable and informative. I visited the Command Observation Post overlooking the Chinese positions. The field glasses I had bought in Tokyo came in handy.

The Chinese occasionally lobbed a mortar shell into our area. There was not much that could be done about it except to be thankful it had missed you. The Army lads didn't even flinch, but I would become airborne, which amused them. Lieutenant Colonel Geoff Brookes, RCHA, and Captain Clem Bouffard, R22ᵉR, were witnesses to my indoctrination. After that, I went back to Kimpo. Then I flew back to Japan and spent two weeks with the Strategic Recce Wing at Yokoda Air Force Base, and got back to Ottawa for Christmas.

Allan recalls a concert given by Danny Kaye just before Christmas 1951. Danny sang a Korean song with a Korean orphan.

Squadron Leader Allan Simpson retired from the RCAF in 1964. He is a Personal Financial Planner in Ottawa where he and his wife Connie now reside.

Danny Kaye learned a song in the Korean language and in December 1951 he called this orphan forward to sing it with him. The entertainer was performing at Kimpo US Air Force Base.

George Kightley after flying with 426 Squadron.

THUNDERBIRDS IN THE FAR EAST

In April 1939, George Kightley enlisted in the RCAF as an administrative clerk (AC 2) at Camp Borden, Ontario. He would have preferred aircrew training, but he did not have sufficient formal education. By the time the Second World War broke out in September 1939, George had been transferred to Air Force Headquarters in Ottawa. Promotion was rapid, from Corporal to WOII between June of 1940 and July of 1941, and George was commissioned from the ranks in the Administrative Branch in August 1941.

> All the while, my ambition was to become a member of the aircrew branch. The summer of 1942, I realized my dream when I was selected for aircrew training. I was transferred from my position as Executive Officer to the Deputy Air Member for Personnel at Ottawa to Toronto to update my educational qualifications to aircrew standards. This venture was successful and aircrew training followed, graduating as a pilot at Camp Borden in September of 1943. I was twenty-seven years old at this point, and as I was considered too old for operational flying duties, I was posted to Trenton for an instructors' course. I instructed on Harvards at

KOREA VOLUNTEER

RCAF Station Camp Borden for approximately one year, and then became station adjutant at Borden when the training programme began to fold in 1944.

Like so many who had not served overseas, George Kightley wanted to be selected for posting to the newly formed Tiger Force (war against Japan). Before this could happen, Japan capitulated. The war was over.

George was kept in the post-war RCAF and was transferred to the Communications and Rescue Squadron at Trenton, Ontario. In addition to the Harvard Aircraft, he became qualified on the Expeditor, Dakota and Norseman (floats, skis and wheels) and was one of the earlier pilots to become proficient on the Sikorski S51 helicopter. He was at the controls of the S51 during its first use — fighting forest fires at Sudbury, Ontario in May 1950. In December 1950, he was transferred to 426 (Thunderbird) Transport Squadron, which was then engaged in flying the Pacific in support of the UN activities in Korea. George recalls,

> I immediately volunteered and started training on North Star aircraft at Dorval in February of 1951. I successfully completed my conversion to North Stars in March of 1951 and was transferred to McCord Air Force Base at Tacoma, Washington where 426 Squadron was co-located with the US Air Force Squadron also working on the Korean Air lift. I was accompanied on this move by my wife Evelyn and four-year-old son Rob.

As mentioned in *Valour Remembered*, "The Thunderbirds flew six hundred round trips from North America to Japan, counting more than 13,000 passengers and three million kilograms of freight and mail without a loss." Says George,

> I completed thirteen round trips to Japan, the first two of which had the return trip via Wake Island and Honolulu carrying wounded from Korea to the hospital in Honolulu. The stops in Honolulu were a pleasant interlude which were all too short. On the other trips, outbound and return, we operated through Shemya, and Elmendorf Air Force base at Anchorage, Alaska. The "Legs", which produced the worst flying conditions, were actually portions of each Leg. Leg 1 was from Tacoma to Elmendorf, Leg 2 was from Elmendorf to Shemya, and Leg 3 was from Shemya to Tokyo. Each Leg provided its own peculiar brand of weather at some point along the way, although the Elmendorf to Shemya Leg usually provided the unexpected and the unwelcome. Our normal cruising altitudes ranged between 8,000 and 15,000 feet as the North Stars were not pressurized and oxygen was available only on an emergency basis.

An Oral History From Those Who Were There

> Shemya provided its own problems. As the story goes, it has some type of precipitation 365 days a year, and the only place you could expect fog with a sixty-mile-an-hour wind (explainable as very low cloud). Instrument approaches were the rule rather than the exception. The only instrument landing aid was the ground controlled approach. The controllers were exceptional and in the worst of conditions they provided guidance right past the point of touch-down.
>
> The captain of the aircraft was always responsible for the safety and flight of the aircraft. The captain was always designated by the operations officer or his staff. They operated as a crew with the captain detailing the duties; if two or more qualified pilots were aboard, they would share the take-offs and landings.

The unsung heroes were the ground crews. They were exceptionally good, always available and worked long hours to provide the best in serviceable aircraft. During thirteen trips across the Pacific, and during the period George was with 426 Squadron, he was fortunate not to have had a single engine failure.

George comments on his fellow officers in 426 Squadron:

> When the Korean airlift started, it would be safe to say that the pilots were mostly experienced four-engine pilots with wartime experience. As the airlift progressed, new blood (such as myself) was brought in and trained. Some were training command instructors and some were fairly recent graduates. All in all, a good cross-section of RCAF aircrew. Don't forget the navigators and radio operators. This happened in the days when we were still very dependent on hands-on navigation and dependent on the radio officer for en route and terminal weather, which was paramount. Computers and reliable radio communication was still a thing of the future! Our flight engineers were exceptional as well, experienced and dedicated; I never heard an engineer nor crewman complain about the hours he had to work nor the weather he had to face to complete his tasks.
>
> One trip that sticks out in my mind was early in my days with the Squadron. We were returning from Tokyo, and due to variable and strong headwinds forecast for our route to Shemya we decided to land at Misawa in northern Japan to top up with fuel. Having completed this refuelling, we once again took off for Shemya. It was a night trip and shortly after take-off flying at 11,000 feet over top and a thick undercast and in and out of the overcast, we were over the North Pacific. Our route was to take us well south (we hoped) of the Kuril Islands (part of the

KOREA VOLUNTEER

> Soviet Union). After a couple of hours, a break occurred in the undercast and much to our amazement there was a large number of lights below us. This indicated that either the Japanese fishing fleet was heading out to sea or we were over a city. Hasty deliberation amongst the crew decided that a heading of 180 degrees true (due south) was in order and, after a decent interval, a turn toward Shemya was again made. It is assumed that we were blown further north due to winds aloft higher than had been forecast. Despite this minor detour, we arrived safely at Shemya without having awakened the sleeping bear!

None of the crew members with whom George was associated ever received special recognition or a decoration for duties performed.

George's story concludes thus:

> Before checking out on the North Star, I had a total of 2200 hours flying on single- and twin-engine aircraft. As the North Star was my first four-engine aircraft, I have nothing with which to compare it. But excluding the noise, it was a real thrill to be in charge of an aircraft which, at that time, was extremely large and magnificent.
>
> Following my two-year stint with 426 Squadron, I was transferred as Commanding Officer of the RCAF unit at Fort Churchill, Manitoba and was there during the period that the US Air Force was flying materials from Churchill to the Dew Line early warning sites.

After Fort Churchill, George Kightley spent about five years in Moose Jaw, Saskatchewan, as a squadron commander and chief standards officer during the period when the RCAF was providing flying training for the NATO Forces. His final transfer before retirement was to Air Force Headquarters, Ottawa, Ontario. He retired in June 1963 with just over twenty-four years of service. George then joined the civil service and worked in personnel until he retired in 1976.

George and his wife Evelyn, who was a Women's Division Flight Officer during the Second World War, spend their retirement in Huntsville, Ontario, during the summers and Lake Wales, Florida, during the winters.

An Oral History From Those Who Were There

Epilogue

THOSE WHO SERVED IN THE LAND OF THE MORNING CALM

More than forty years ago, Canadian volunteers left their homes in peacetime to fight for freedom on the other side of the globe in Korea, the "Land of the Morning Calm".
    Commemoration. *Canadians in Korea*, Pat Giesler

When I first joined the Canadian Army (Reserve) in October 1947, the final demobilization after the Second World War was happening. There was an urgency in the political and military minds to get back to the pre-War status quo. I was about to go into my final year at Cobble Hill High School on Vancouver Island when the Korean War began. This event, more than any other, caused me to join the Active Force in January 1952. When I reported to the Royal Canadian Armoured Corps School there was an almost indecent haste to push the recruits through the eight-week basic training course to send us to the two regiments to be readied for Korea. I went to Lord Strathcona's Horse (Royal Canadians) in Calgary, the regiment supplying reinforcements and replacement squadrons for Korea. When I was accepted for officer training that summer and ultimate posting to The Royal Canadian Dragoons, my chances for a posting to the Far East vanished until 1954. By then the war was over, and I left the Army for a few months to think about my future. Six months later, I rejoined.

    The soldiers of the 1950s were at a disadvantage compared to the soldiers who invaded Sicily in 1943 or those who crossed the beaches of Normandy the next year. The 1950s' soldiers did not have the long period of training, and they were subjected to the "one year and then back home" syndrome. As ably told by so many in this book, there was a constant upheaval in Korea, with people leaving at the end of their obligations and lesser-trained replacements coming in.

The war was different in many ways from the 1943–45 years. The air superiority of the UN Forces and the lack of an aggressive naval enemy made things different for the RCAF and RCN. The war on land was against an enemy skilled in human wave attacks, in which the value placed on human life was perhaps less than in any army Canadians had faced before. As Harry Pope recounted, "One had to force the enemy to fight on our terms." Sixteen nations fought the Communists, which meant that the UN Forces also had to deal with the problems of differing languages. The Canadian Infantry Brigade was indeed fortunate to have operated within the Commonwealth Division for, in many ways, it was a repeat of Second World War procedures.

During the many interviews for this book I saw no sign of reluctance to tell me of experiences in Korea. Rather, the veterans offered great cooperation in helping me write their personal histories. The handful who said no had their personal reasons but, even then, they often gave me the name of a confrère who had a story. I suppose the one single element that made Korea veterans keen to speak was the Canadian Volunteer Service Medal — Korea. That one medal was the significant object that recognized every 1950–54 veteran from Canada who became a Korea volunteer.

Why the "Land of the Morning Calm"? In the *Korean War Almanac*, Harry G. Summers Jr. writes, "After a generation [1911 to 1948] of Japanese rule, Korea, the country was labelled *Chosen*, the ancient name preferred by the Japanese occupiers." I first heard about Chosen, Land of the Morning Calm, in my officer cadet days in a lecture by Captain Norm Buckingham, a former liaison officer at Brigade. In *Korea: Canada's Forgotten War*, John Melady explains that the country was "so named because of the softness of the Korean mornings, which is due in part to the mists that cover its mountains at that time of day."

I doubt that the softness of the mornings is remembered by many of the Korean War veterans. The heat and dust in summer, the bitter winters, the glutinous mud and the ever-present possibility of death from enemy action or accident are the memories of the people who served there.

Acknowledgements

It took sixteen months to research this book. I had very few reference books in my own library, but many people loaned me books that had a direct connection with their own story. Each of the quotations I used from published sources is credited, but not footnoted. Instead, I have listed bibliographical information in these acknowledgements. Personal quotations have been reproduced as written or as I taped them. I have resisted condensing or editing personal accounts, for to do so might have taken away something that was important to the individual whose story was being recorded. However, where there was a variance between memory and a published historical record, I used the latter.

As an amateur historian, I sought the help of the professionals in the Directorate of History, Department of National Defence. Nonetheless, the final book is my responsibility; any errors rest entirely with me.

Some of the books I used deserve special mention. They are listed below.

Chapter One: Why Korea? and **Chapter Three: The Canadian Army**

John Melady, *Korea: Canada's Forgotten War* (Macmillan of Canada, 1988). This book was inspirational and of great value in my research; Melady's book was also the source of Pat O'Connor's poem Korea. Lieutenant-Colonel Herbert Fairlie Wood, *Strange Battleground: The Operations in Korea and Their Effects on the Defence Policy of Canada* (Queen's Printer, 1966). Herbert Wood taught me how to study military history for my Army promotional examinations. His book is still the Bible, for no other official history has been written. The copy I used was on long-term loan from the Army Officers' Mess library in Ottawa. George Bell, a long-time friend, gave me his personal insight into the Army Headquarters planning of 1950. Edmund Griffiths also gave me his recollections. Douglas McArthur, Reminisences (McGraw-Hill, 1964). Harry G. Summers Jr, *Korean War Almanac* (Facts on File, 1990). James L. Stokesbury, *A Short History of the Korean War* (Quill, William Morrow, 1988). Max Hastings, *The Korean War* (Michael Joseph, 1987). Joseph C. Goulden, *Korea: The Untold Story of the War* (Times Books, 1982).

KOREA VOLUNTEER

Chapter Two: The Royal Canadian Navy

Thor Thorgrimsson and E.C. Russell, *Korean Waters 1950–1955* (The Naval Historical Section, Canadian Forces Headquarters, Department of National Defence, 1965).

Chapter Three: The Canadian Army

C.N. Barclay, *First Commonwealth Division* (Gale and Polden, 1954). Jeffery Williams, *Princess Patricia's Canadian Light Infantry* (Leo Cooper–Secker & Warburg, 1972). *Infantry Journal*, Autumn 1992. Major G.D. Mitchell, RCHA, *Right of the Line* (RCHA History Committee, 1986). G.W.L. Nicholson, *The Gunners of Canada* (McClelland & Stewart, 1972). *The War Diary of 2 PPCLI* (obtained for me by Colonel John Bremner).

Chapter Four: The Royal Canadian Air Force

Airforce Magazine, 2(4) (Dec 1978). Allan Simpson, *We Few* (Hoot Owl Press, 1983). John Marteinson, *We Stand on Guard* (Ovale Publications, 1992). Pat Giesler, *Valour Remembered — Canadians in Korea* (Veterans Affairs Canada, 1982). I must mention the great assistance I received from Lieutenant Commander (Retired) Ron MacDonald of Belleville, Ontario. His extensive video recordings of so many RCAF members provided me with a wealth of information on Korean War veterans.

... and thanks to ...

My final acknowledgements go to Desmond Morton, who kindly agreed to write the forword in my book; Les Peate, Korea Veterans Association, for his advice and help; all the staff at Throop Photo, Nepean, Ontario, for the great job they did on some of the photo reproductions; Heather Ebbs, my editor and a former president of the Freelance Editors' Association of Canada; Tim Gordon, Leanne Enright and the staff of General Store Publishing House, Burnstown, Ontario; and Robert Hoselton of EarthLore for the layout of this book. Last but certainly not least, I thank and acknowledge all those veterans of the Korean War who shared their stories with me.

I could not have produced this book without the patience, skill and understanding of my wife Elaine, who suffered through my handwriting and countless rewrites of this, my seventh book.

Index

Note: Regiments of Canadian Army are mentioned so frequently throughout the text, that they have not been included here.

Acheson, Dean, 1
Addy, Paul, 199
Ainsworth, Frank, 210
Alexander, Viscount, 76
Allan, Jim, 35
Allan, Liz, 91
Allan, Russ, 87-91
Allard, Jean V., 125, 132, 156-7, 172-173, 198-9
Allen, Rick, 121-23
Amgak, 15, 20
Amy, Jean, 93, 99
Amy, Ned, 92-99, 198, 210
Anderson, "Dogface", 145
Archibald (driver), 212
Armer, E.J. "Squint", 101, 158
HMCS *Assiniboine*, 11
Atchison, A.J., 59
HMCS *Athabaskan*, 5-8, 10-13, 15, 22
Australian Army, 97-98
 3 Royal Australian Regiment, 39-40, 172, 207

Bailey, Tony J.B., 49, 58
Baker, Jeff, 35
Banton, Doug, 118
Baptist, Flora, 151-4
Barkhouse, W.E., 59
Barnett, Barney, 162, 182
Barr (Sgt), 84
Batsch, J., 164
HMS *Belfast*, 20
Bell, George, 23-26
Bell, John, 145
Belzile, Charlie, 224-5
Bergeron, Bruno, 131
Berry, Peter, 123
Besley, Keith, 42-45
Besley, Shirley, 45
Bingham, Peter, 145-46
Bliss, Bill, 227
Boates, H.B., vi
Bobinski, Ed, 224
Bogert, M. Pat, 35, 78, 144
Boss, Bill, 72, 156, 163, 180
Bouffard, Clem, 243

HMCS *Bras d'Or*, 11
Brennan, Mike, 50
British Army, 98
    27th Brigade, 33
    29th Brigade, 38-9, 198
    Black Watch Regiment, 194
    First Middlesex Regiment, 39
    8th Hussars, 82, 84-5
    King's Own Scottish Borderers, 123
    Royal Artillery, 59
    Royal Norfolks, 161
    Royal Tank Regiment, 123
British Commonwealth Communications Zone Medical Unit, 153
British Commonwealth Hospital, 153
Brock, J.V., 7, 10-11
Brookes, Geoff, 243
Brown, Clifford, 104, 110
Brumwell, E.C. "Skinner", 158
Buckingham, Norm, 249
Buxton (WO II), 90

C

Cameron, J.R., 164
Campbell, Bill, 171-3
Campbell, D., 20
Campbell, Gisele, 173
Campbell, K.L., 120, 148, 198
Campney, Ralph, 34
Camponi, Len, 104
Canadian Armoured Squadron, 32
Canadian Army, 23-225
    4th Field Squadron, 191
    23rd Field Squadron, 192, 194
    59th Field Squadron, 191

Canadian Army Special Force, 24
Canadian Provost Corps, 25 Field Detention Barracks, 140-1
Canadian Red Cross Society, 151-4
Canadian Reinforcement Group, 43, 169
Carew, Dianne, 159
Carew, Pat, 155-59
Carew, R.D., 227
Carlson, C.V., 217
Carrier, J.L.R., 48
Carroll, N.W., 59
Carter, Chuck, 193-4
Cassels, Jim, 33, 85, 94-5
HMCS *Cayuga*, 5-7, 10, 17-21
HMCS *Cedarwood*, 12
Chail-li, vi, 68-9, 72, 200
Changgo-ri, 74
Chinnampo Harbour, 10
Choi Mjung Sik, 215
Chongyang-do, 20
Choppeki Peninsula, 15
Chou En-lai, 234
Chubb, Gerry, 82
Chun Chon, 123
Claeys, John, 152
Clancy, John, 95
Claxton, Brooke, 23-26, 34, 47, 76, 80
Clift, F.A., 213
HMS *Cockade*, 21
Coghill, G., 20
Collier, Andy, 10
HMS *Collingwood*, 17
Commonwealth
    Base Ordnance Depot, No. 1 Sub-Depot (Mechanical Transport Stores), 201
    Commonwealth Division, 33, 55, 59-60, 93-95, 97-8, 130, 138, 185, 196-8, 209, 223, 249
    Battle School, 138

Junior NCO School, 156, 161
Provost Company, 140
1st Telecommunications Workshop, 189
Connelly (PPCLI section commander), 162
USHS *Consolation*, 153
Conway, F.W., 59
Corbiere (Lt), 80, 83-4
Cornish, Vic K., 60
Cowan, Clint, 125
Craig, R.A., 59
Creor (Cpl), 209
Crew, Bill, 225
Crew, Joan, 225
Crowder, Douglas, 203
Crowder, Norm, 200-4
Crowder, Patricia, 201
Crowder, Ruth, 201, 203
HMCS *Crusader*, 5, 11
Cyr, J.C., 19
Cyundo, Pack, 20

Dalton, Betty, 15-6
Dalton, Edward, 12-16
Danby, Dick, 93
Dare, Mike, 98, 198
Davenport (US Col), 19
Davidson, Bob T.P., 226
Davis, J.J., 212
de Hart, John "Jack", 111-116
Debert (Lt), 80
Demara, Ferdinand Waldo, 19
Denne, Bill, 209

Deuce Horn (mascot, Queen's Own Rifles), 222
Dextraze, Frances, 47-8, 51
Dextraze, Jacques A. "Jim", 45-51, 54, 65, 71-2, 81, 85, 126-128
Dixon, "Tiny", 107
Donahue, Jerry, 116
Douglas, E.W., 210-1, 213
Dubé, J.L.Y., 84

Edwards, Claire, 11
Edwards, Gordon, 6-11
Eisenhower, Dwight D., 130
Elizabeth II, Queen of Great Britain and Ireland, 147
Ellis, Bill, 125, 156-158
Elvidge, R.E., 15
Enos, Ray, 89
HMCS *Esquimalt*, 15
Evans, F.W., 226
Evans, Lewis, 193
Eveleigh, Doug, 80, 85
Evoy (Sgt), 183

Favreau, Mel, 211
Fellows (Lt), 224
Fernets, J.M., 189
Finney (Capt), 31

Firstbrook, Ian, 205-09
Firstbrook, Nancy, 209
Fleming, J. Bruce, 226
Fleurey, Ray, 135
Floody, Wally, 238
Flynn, Roger, 63
Forbes, Charlie, 49
Foulkes, Charles, 38
Fournier, Jean, 135
Fox, W.W., 227
Francis, Alice, 110
Francis, Ron, 100-10
HMCS *Fraser*, 17
Fraser
   (Canadian Trade Commissioner), 235
Freeman, Dean, 121
Frewen (Capt), 20
Fuller (CSM), 68

Gardner, Russ, 121, 145
Gauvreau, Guy, 47
USNS *General E.T. Collins*, 171
USNS *General H.B. Freeman*, 177
USNS *General Hugh Gaffey*, 109
USNS *General Patrick*, 32
George, A.E., 59
George, Don, 31, 35, 88, 243
Girard (PPCLI section commander), 162
Glendinning (Lt), 80, 83
Gloucester Valley, 136
Glover, Ernie A., 226, 238-40
Glover, Ruth, 240
Gordon, Laird, 211
Gosselin, J.P.L. "Goose", 31, 56

Graham, Dominick, 23
Grant (PPCLI section commander), 162
Griffiths, Edmund "Tojo", 27
HMCS *Griffon*, 16
Guerin, Louise, 154

Haeju, 21
HMCS *Haida*, 5
Hale, F.B., 226
Hamilton, Anna, 36
Hamilton, Charlie, 29-36, 65
Handspiker, E.J., 88
Haramura, Japan, 138, 177
Harkess, Harry, 161
Harper, George L., 216
Harris (Trooper), 212
Hawkins, Tony, 101
Hayter, Frances, 220
Hayter, John, 215-20
Herman, Art, 139
Hill 129, 122
Hill 159, 136
Hill 162, vi
Hill 166, 85
Hill 169, 136
Hill 210, 50, 107, 136
Hill 227, 145
Hill 269, vi
Hill 329, 48, 74
Hill 346, 197
Hill 355, 88, 108-09, 136, 138, 145-148,
   161, 185, 197, 218
Hill 407, 68
Hill 677, 39

255

Hiro, Japan, 103, 140
Hiroshima, Japan, 169, 218
Hodge, John, 2
Holland, Hannelore, 142
Holland, Jim, 140-42
Holman, Randy, 210
Holmes, Don, 145-46
Hong Kong, 9, 21
Hotchin, Robert, 19
Hurl, David W., 13-4
HMCS *Huron*, 5
Hutchinson (Pte), 183
Hutton, Dorothy, 71-72
Hutton, Hugh, 71-2

Imjin River, 207, 223
Inchon, 8, 88, 153, 207
Indian Army, 98
HMCS *Iroquois*, 5, 15, 154
Iwakuni, Japan, 135

Jaffee, Major, 146
James, Jack, 124
James (Lt), 85
USNS *James O'Hare*, 111
Jenkins, Roy, 19
Jewkes, Vic, 79-81, 83-85, 104-06, 122-23, 243
Johnson, Doug, 63, 65

Johnson, Vic, 121
Joint Organization for Clandestine Organizations (JOCK), 18

Kakhul-bong, vi, 68-9
Kamavarr, Ber, 114
Kapyong, 37-8, 40-1, 178
KATComs *see* Korean Augmentation Troops Commonwealth (KATComs)
Kaye, Danny, 243
Keane, Bob A., 54, 68, 71
Keir, Billie, 78
Keir, Ken, 76-78
Kemsley, Arthur, 178
Kennedy, Jake, 80
Kennedy, Ken, 80-1, 83, 85
Kidd, Dave, 14
Kierans, Owen Kevin Hugh, 217
Kightly, Evelyn, 245, 247
Kightly, George, 244-47
Kightly, Rob, 245
Kim Hen Gun, 5
Kim Il Sung, 2
Kimpo, 238-9, 241, 243
King, Andy, 135
King, Dudley, 15
Klenavik, Klink, 145
Klesitz, Alfred S., 242
Korean Army, 39
    1st Division, 185
Korean Augmentation Troops Commonwealth (KATComs), 98, 178-81, 208, 215-6, 223
Korean Marines, 8, 19

Korean Navy, 5, 20
Korean Service Corps, 182
Kowang San, 147
Kowloon, China, 9
Koyoto, Japan, 153
Kure, Japan, 21, 34, 84, 169, 172, 177, 201

La France, J.C.A. Claude, 226
Lajombre (Pte), 104
Lamb, Merve, 213
Lambros, Andy, 226
Lamothe, Gilles, 48
Landymore, W.M., 15, 154
Laughton, Bob C.D., 33, 62-4
Lee Won Sik, 215
Leslie, Teddy *see* McNaughton, Teddy
Levesque, J.A. Omer, 226
Levesque, U.J., 59
Lewis (CSM), 145
Lindsay, J. Doug, 226
Little (Sgt), 175
Logan (Maj), 207
Loomis, Dan, 143-50
Lowry, R.E., 226

McAndrew, Bill, 222, 224-5
MacArthur, Douglas, 2-4
McCarthy, Bill, 67-70
McClelland (Lt Col), 128-29
MacDonald, A. Laird, 210, 212-3
MacDonald, Gordon, 200, 204
MacDonald, Johnny, 212
MacDonald, Ken, 210
Macdonald, Strath (Lt), 80, 83, 122
Macdonald, R.B., 163
MacDonald, Ron, 228, 239
MacDonald, Terry, 204
McDougall, Duncan, 187-90
McDougall, Jean, 190
McDougall, Pamela, 199
MacDuff (Lt), 49
McIndoe, "Red", 158
MacKay, John, 227
MacKenzie, Andy R., 226, 228-37
MacKenzie, Joyce, 233-4, 236
Mackenzie (Lt), 40
McKeown, B.P., 59
Macklin, W.H.S., 24-25, 47-8, 128
MacLachlan, Tony, 161, 186
McLellan, Harold A. "Mac", 57-61
McLellan, Monica, 61
McNair, Buck, 241-42
McNaughton, Teddy, 77, 111, 113-14, 135
McNeil, Charlie, 161
McPhail, "Oop", 177
Mahar, Bob, 145
Manley, R.W., 59
Mann, Peter, 162
Maple Leaf Club, Tokyo, Japan, 153
USNS *Marine Adder*, 32, 76, 88
MSTS *Marine Lynx*, 206-7
Marsaw, T.M.C. "Boom", 221-3, 225
Matheson, Alec, 213, 224
Matthews, W.H.V., 221, 224
Mayer, Pamela, 199
Mayer, Paul, 196-199

Medland, R.D., 68
Meeker, Ken, 210
Megill (Brig), 92
Meynell, Jerry, 118
Mills, Wally, 40
USS *Missouri*, 9
Momberquette, Joe, 162
Moogk (Col), 144
Mulholland, Moe, 70
Mullin, F.A., 164
Mullins, J.B., 227
Murray (Maj Gen), 198
Murray (Sgt), 84

Naechon River valley, 179
USS *Nautilus*, 22
Neelin, Bob, (Lt), 80, 83, 122
New Zealand Army, 98
    Field Regiment, 39-41
    Royal New Zealand Artillery, 59
HMS *Newcastle*, 17
Nichols, G.H., 227
HMCS *Nipigon*, 22
Nixon, G.W., 226
HMCS *Nootka*, 5
North Korea Air Force, 4

O'Connor, Pat "Paddy", v-vii
Operation Cheerful, 20-1
Operation Initiate, 48
Orr, A.W., 59
Owen, Fabiole, 120
Owen, Gordon, 117-20
Owens, D., 59

Pak Kwan Sik, 215
Pak Tae Young, 215
Panmunjon, 119-20
Paradis, J.J., 50
Parun-ni, 188
Patterson, Don, 147
Peacock, Bob, 144
Peacock, Dorothy, 170
Peacock, Gordon, 168-70
Pearson, Lester B., 3, 237
Pengyang-do, 19, 21
Penney, Dick, 192
Penney (Pte), 104
Perkins, Lloyd, 210
Pero (Cpl), 118
Perry, L.V., 77
Petersen, J., 20
Peterson (Pte), 104
Pierson, D., 20
Pike, Les, 44
Pilcher, Geoff, 176, 181
Pinkerton, Sam M., 58
Pitts, Herb, 160-7, 182
Pitts, Marianne, 167

Plomer, J., 17
Plouffe, Phil, 50
Poole, Jere E., 242
Pope, Sheila Kathleen, 133
Pope, William Henry "Harry", 126-33, 249
Poulin, J., 217
Powers, Gary, 66
Prentice, "Rocky" Rhodes, 163
Price, Murray, 210
HMCS *Prince David*, 17
USNS *Private Joe Martinez*, 38
Pruner, Don, 121, 135
Purvis, Bob, 79
Pusan, 31-2, 34-35, 57, 76, 103, 121-122, 177, 204, 210-11, 225
Pusan United Nations Memorial Cemetery, 4

Quinn, Edna, 86
Quinn, Jim, 32, 49, 65, 72, 79-86

Rapley, Gordon, 193
Reid (Sgt Maj), 201
Republic of Korea Army
   see Korean Army
Rhee, Syngman, 2
Rhodes, Neil, 163-4

Richardson (Maj), 144
Ringma, Bob, 202
Rivers, A.M., 189
Roberts, Jack, 193
Robinson, Robbie "R.E.", 224-5
Rochester, Don, 52-56
Rockingham, John "Rocky", 29-35, 37, 48-49, 52, 66, 72, 76-78, 81-2, 86, 123, 128, 242-3
Rodenbush, Lorne, 62-66
Rodenbush, Vivian, 66
ROK (Republic of Korea) Army
   see Korean Army
Ronning, Chester, 234
Rosa (Lt), 212
Ross, R.M., 205
Routledge, Ron, 134
Rowsell, Eric, 161
Roxborough, J.S., 155
Royal Canadian Air Force, 11, 25, 42, 77-8, 226-247
   426 Thunderbird Transport Squadron, 226-7, 245-7
Royal Canadian Armoured Corps, 100, 155-6
Royal Canadian Engineers
   57 Independent Field Squadron, 54-55
Royal Canadian Army Medical Corps, 42-5
   25th Field Ambulance, 43
   25th Field Dressing Station, 153
   38th Field Ambulance, 153
   38th Field Dressing Station, 154
Royal Canadian Army Ordnance Corps, 200, 204
   Mobile Laundry and Bath Unit, 54, 200-3
Royal Canadian Army Pay Corps, 168

Royal Canadian Artillery,
    2nd Regiment RCHA, 59-61
Royal Canadian Army Service Corps, 33, 44, 72
    54 Canadian Transport Company, 62-65
Royal Canadian Electrical and Mechanical Engineers, 85, 187, 189
    191 Infantry Workshop, 188
Royal Canadian Navy, 5-22, 25
Royal Canadian Corps of Signals, 76
Royal Navy, 4, 11
Royal Netherlands Battalion, 112, 114-5
Rutherford, Bruce, 123, 126

HMCS *Saguenay*, 17
St Laurent, Louis, 3, 23, 76, 237
HMCS *St Laurent*, 17
Sami-ch'on River valley, 106, 116-17, 126, 155
Sargent, J.A., 68
Sasebo, Japan, 5, 9, 12, 18, 21, 206, 211
Saunders, Audrey, 225
Saunders, Jackson, 229-30
Saunders, John, 221-225
Sauvé, Paul, 47
Saxon, Don, 17-22
Saxon, Renee, 22
S.B. Buckner, 121
Schlapback, Jack, 77
Schmidlin, Laurie, 191-2
Scott-Moncrieff, A.K., 21
Seoul, 3, 147, 153, 177
Sequin, Kathe, 75

Sequin, Lawrence "Lou", 73-5
Sevigny, Georges, 138
Shaw, "Smokey", 85
Shields, Tom, 14
Shuter, Ted, 223
Simeon (Guardsman), 216
Simonds, Guy, 32, 47, 76, 81
Simpson, Allan, 241-43
Simpson, Connie, 243
HMCS *Sioux*, 5-7, 10, 22
Skavberg, R.J., 15
HMCS *Skeena*, 17
Skene, Don, 235
Slaney, Ann, 214
Slaney, Bob, 210-4
Smale, Bill, 135, 138
Smith, Eric, 226
Snider, Chris, 174-86
Snider, Ethel, 195
Snider, Karl, 191-5
Snider, Maurine, 186
Snow, L.A., 59
Sok-to, 20
Soulier, Ron, 14-5
Spelay (Cpl), 209
Spurr, Larry E., 226
Steven, Ron, 123
Stickland, Don, vi
Stirling, Bill, 88-89
Stone, Esther, 41
Stone, James "Big Jim" Riley, 37-41, 65, 86
Stroud, A.G., 59
Suwon, 38

Taegu, 123
Taewha, 15, 19
Tait, R. Hammish, 138
Taylor, Pete, 69
Thant, U, 199
Therrien, J.P.A., 49
Thistle, J., 59
Thivierge, "Pop", 108
Thomas, Bob, 93
Thomassen, Erwin A., 242
Thwaites (Sgt), 86
Tighe, Pat, 39
Todd, H., 15
Tok Chok To, 8
Tokyo, Japan, 153, 218
Traynor, Howie, 222
Tremblay, Bob, 137
HMS *Triumph*, 7
Trudeau, L.F., 48, 135-36
Trudeau, Pierre Elliott, 51, 139

Uijongbu, 69, 154, 156, 161, 200
United States Air Force, 4, 96
    67 Reconnaissance Technical
        Squadron, 241
    139 Squadron, 229
    334 Fighter Squadron, 239
    6147 Tactical Control Group, 123
    Mosquito Group, 123-4
United States Army, 10, 38, 77, 118
    1st Marine Division, 185

3rd Infantry Division, 95
7th Infantry Regiment, 50
7th US Infantry Regiment, 50
United States Marines, 19, 21, 106
United States Navy, 3-4
Uri-do, 20

Veringa, Willie, 212
Verner, Denis E., 242
HMS *Vernon*, 17
Vickers (Lt Col), 33
Vipond, Helen, 225
Vipond, Vip, 223-5
Vokes, Chris, 93

Walker, W.H., 38
Ward, Bill, 121-25
Ward, Eleanor, 125
Warren, Duke, 227
RFA Wave Knight, 11
Welland, Bob P., 7, 11, 15
Wellsman
    (PPCLI section commander), 162
Wenkert, J.M., 59
Werry, Ron, 222, 224-5
West, Mike, 92, 95, 111, 148, 198
White, J., 59
White, W., 215
Whiticar (Capt and Maj), 31-32, 65

Wilson, J., 60
Wilson, Tug, 63
Wilson-Smith, Norm, 88, 93-94
Winslow (Sgt Maj), 166
Withers, Alison, 139
Withers, Ramsey, 121, 134-39
Wolsari, 20
Woo in Sool, 215
Wood, F., 20
Wood, Herb, 30, 161, 166, 176
Woods, J.R., vi
Worthington, Peter, 123, 179
Wosan, 119
Wright, F.M. "Marsh", 158
Wright, W.D., 59
Wyant, Hal, 80, 83-4, 122
Wyatt, Henry, 108

Yokahama, Japan, 88, 121, 172
Yon Dong Po, Japan, 90, 153

Zmean, Paul, 224

About the Author

John Gardam was born in England in 1931 and at age fifteen immigrated to British Columbia. He attended high school on Vancouver Island, where in 1947 he joined the Reserve Army and in 1951 the Active Force. He is a graduate of the University of Manitoba in History.

In 1984, after retiring from the Regular Force, John became the Assistant Secretary General for the Canadian Agency, Commonwealth War Graves Commission, in Ottawa. From 1989 to 1992 he was responsible for overseeing the Department of National Defence's part in the production of Canada's Peacekeeping Monument in Ottawa. In 1980 he was made an officer of the Order of Military Merit.

John retired from the Canadian Forces in December 1992 after forty-five years of Regular and Reserve service. Currently, he is the Project Director for the Department of National Defence program Canada Remembers — a commemoration of the fiftieth anniversary of the end of the Second World War.

John and Elaine Gardam live in Nepean, Ontario. They have four married sons and seven grandchildren. Korea Volunteer is John's seventh book.

For more copies of

KOREA VOLUNTEER

send $17.95 plus $3.00 for GST, shipping and handling to:
GENERAL STORE PUBLISHING HOUSE
1 Main Street, Burnstown, Ontario
Canada, K0J 1G0

Choco to A.I.F.	$14.95
Valour On Juno Beach	$14.95
Black Crosses Off My Wingtip	$14.95
The Ridge	$14.95
Trepid Aviator	$14.95
The Wing And The Arrow	$14.95
In The Line Of Duty	$39.95
Mud and Blood	$14.95
Ordinary Heroes	$14.95
One Of The Many	$14.95
Fifty Years After	$14.95
The Canadian Peacekeeper	$12.95
The Surly Bonds Of Earth	$12.95
The Memory Of All That	$14.95
No Time Off For Good Behaviour	$14.95
To The Green Fields Beyond	$14.95
Time Remembered	$14.95

For each copy include $3.00 to cover GST, shipping and handling.
Make cheque or money order payable to:

GENERAL STORE PUBLISHING HOUSE
1 Main Street, Burnstown, Ontario
Canada, K0J 1G0